SPORTS COACHING

The application of the theoretical underpinnings of coaching to practice is a central concern in sport. How should academic research seek to inform applied practice, and how should practising coaches integrate research into their professional activities? *Sports Coaching: A Theoretical and Practical Guide* is the first book to truly integrate academic research on sports coaching with an assessment of and recommendations for applied practice.

With every chapter written by a coaching researcher and a practising coach, the book clearly and concisely introduces the academic evidence base and discusses how and why theory should be integrated into practice. Made up of sections on coaching practice, coach education and development, the use of sport science support and coaching special populations, the book constitutes a comprehensive guide to the theory and practice of sports coaching.

Chapters are clearly and consistently structured, allowing students and coaches opportunity to gain a firm understanding of the core theoretical principles of sports coaching and the ways in which they can guide practice. The book is a vital resource for any sports coaching student, researcher or practitioner to develop their evidence-informed practice.

Ed Cope is a Lecturer in Sports Coaching at Loughborough University, UK. Ed teaches on modules related to the disciplinary area of coaching pedagogy, and has published widely in the areas of coach behaviour, coach education and children's attitudes towards and experiences of sport.

Mark Partington is a Senior Lecturer in Sports Coaching at Edge Hill University, UK, where he coordinates and teaches a number of modules that integrate pedagogy and practical knowledge in coaching practice. Mark has used a number of qualitative methods in his research with professional coaches and coach developers including field note observations, interviews and focus groups and the quantitative method of systematic observation. As well as being a researcher, Mark has experience as a coach in performance and development environments.

SPORTS COACHING

A Theoretical and Practical Guide

Edited by Ed Cope and Mark Partington

Routledge
Taylor & Francis Group

LONDON AND NEW YORK

First published 2020
by Routledge
2 Park Square, Milton Park, Abingdon, Oxon OX14 4RN

and by Routledge
52 Vanderbilt Avenue, New York, NY 10017

Routledge is an imprint of the Taylor & Francis Group, an informa business

British Library Cataloguing-in-Publication Data
A catalogue record for this book is available from the British Library

Library of Congress Cataloging-in-Publication Data
A catalog record has been requested for this book

ISBN: 978-0-8153-9208-8 (hbk)
ISBN: 978-0-8153-9209-5 (pbk)
ISBN: 978-1-351-20003-5 (ebk)

Typeset in Bembo
by Swales & Willis, Exeter, Devon, UK

CONTENTS

ILLUSTRATIONS

Figures

Tables

CONTRIBUTORS

Zoe Avner
Department of Sport, Exercise and Rehabilitation
Northumbria University, UK

John Bell
Bowdon Hockey Club, UK

Philip Boardman
Portsmouth Football Club, UK

Jake Campbell
Wigan Athletic Football Club, UK

Ed Cope
School of Sport, Exercise and Health Sciences
Loughborough University, UK

Christopher Cushion
School of Sport, Exercise and Health Sciences
Loughborough University, UK

Greg Doncaster
Department of Sport and Physical Activity
Edge Hill University, UK

Lois Fidler
The English Football Association, UK

Ryan Groom
Department of Life Sciences
Manchester Metropolitan University, UK

Edward Thomas Hall
Department of Sport, Exercise and Rehabilitation
Northumbria University, UK

Luke Jones
Department of Sport, Health and Exercise Science
University of Hull, UK

Mark Laycock
Newcastle Falcons Rugby Football Union Team, UK

Áine Macnamara
School of Sport and Health Sciences
University of Central Lancashire, UK

Aiden McNulty
Newcastle Falcons Rugby Football Union Team, UK

Joseph Mills
St. Mary's University, Canada

Ian Minto
Cambridge University Women's Rugby Football Club

Derek Morgan
The English Cricket Board, UK

Mark Partington
Department of Sport and Physical Activity
Edge Hill University, UK

Neil Plimmer
Brighton Junior Golf and Junior Golf Alliance, UK

James Ponton
Newcastle Falcons Rugby Football Union Team, UK

Craig Richards
The Rugby Football League, UK

Rebecca Sawiuk
Department of Psychology and Sport Science
University of Hertfordshire, UK

Iain Simpson
Oakham School, UK

Benjamin Stanway
Department of Sport
University of South Wales, UK

Anna Stodter
Cambridge Centre of Sport and Exercise Sciences
Anglia Ruskin University, UK

Chris Towlson
Department of Sport, Health and Exercise Science
University of Hull, UK

Robert Townsend
Te Huataki Waiora Faculty of Health, Sport and Human Performance
University of Waikato, New Zealand

Don Vinson
School of Sport and Exercise Science
The University of Worcester, UK

Jack Walton
The English Football Association, UK

Amy Whitehead
School of Sport and Exercise Sciences
Liverpool John Moores University, UK

SECTION I
Introduction

INTRODUCTION

Ed Cope and Mark Partington

Background and purpose

We have collectively been teaching in higher education and supporting coach development for over ten years. In this time a recurring theme has presented itself: students and inexperienced coaches who are embarking on a coaching or related career have significant difficulty understanding and making sense of theoretical concepts. This is not surprising. Why would it be? We reflected back on the early stages of our coaching careers and engagement in academic study and remember feeling completely lost and confused by some of the academic theory presented. It was only when we started coaching on a regular and consistent basis that we could make sense of these concepts. We felt this was because we could see the theory manifest itself through our practices. Once this started to happen, we, like many others used these as thinking tools to help us understand why things were happening in the way they were. The use of theory also helped us to think, rationalise and then implement certain types of coaching that we felt was best for our learners and specific context. And so, some time ago we started talking about how we could help our students and coach learners better understand the importance and relevance of theory despite having limited practical and/or academic experience. It was from these discussions that the idea for this book was born.

We wanted to develop a resource that student coaches, as well as the broader coaching population, could refer to that enabled them to understand the place of theory and how this related to practical experiences. We wanted to take what at times can appear as relatively abstract concepts, and enable readers to make more concrete links to their practice. To achieve this aspiration, we considered the need to create a text that reported the practical application of specific coaching topics in combination with theoretical explanation. While we appreciate there is no replacement for experience, through providing coaches with insights from practitioners in particular domains and disciplines of coaching, we could assist them in starting to consider information and how this relates to their existing knowledge and practice.

In the midst of stating what we consider as the benefits of this book, we must not lose sight of what it is not able to do. We are wholly aware that no resource is the panacea, and this book is no different. For those engaging with this book, to find its contents valuable and useful in making sense of different topic areas, there is a requirement for them to connect what they are reading with their own practices. Rarely are findings directly transferable given that research is undertaken in often very specific contexts. So, for this to happen often requires the person or people engaging with the research to make connections between this and their own practice. This is what we are asking readers to do when engaging with this book: to consider the discussions presented and what this means for their practice.

Book structure

The decision to include the individual chapters that form this book was based on the belief that these are core areas in relation to the practice of sports coaching. Of course, these are not the only areas, but (a) we had to exercise an element of pragmatism in terms of what was, and was not, included, and (b) we wanted to be led by the practitioner's insight and the areas they believed they had knowledge, understanding and experience of in practice.

Once we had the chapters agreed, we categorised these into a series of sections. Section II, immediately following the introduction, is focused on coaching practice and first deals with developing a coaching philosophy and provides a process by which this can occur. Often the development of a philosophy of coaching is discussed as a straightforward one, rather than delving into the way in which this happens through experience. In Chapter 1, a discussion ensues on what a coaching philosophy is, and how one was arrived at, with a key message being how this was not simple or straightforward to develop. In Chapter 2, a guide to analysing coaching behaviour, a coach developer's insight was drawn upon to articulate how they undertook the analysis of coach behaviour, and by doing so, the valuable insight it was able to give them when supporting coaches' development. In Chapter 3, guidance is given regarding how coaches can think about structuring their coaching practice. This is achieved by the authors drawing upon a framework promoted by the National Governing Body (NGB) in rugby union, and how this is applied in practice. The final chapter of this section explores the concept of athlete-centred coaching, by clearly establishing the characteristics of this approach, and how these are then applied in practice. What the authors of this chapter do when discussing athlete-centred coaching is consider the numerous contextual challenges coaches face. In this way, they move beyond a discussion that positions athlete-centred coaching as something which is 'easily done'.

Section III of this book is focused on coach education and development. It starts with discussing the significant role mentoring plays in a coach's development through drawing upon the mentor/mentee experiences of an elite female football coach. Staying consistent with the theme of other chapters, recommendations are provided for the principles that constitute an effective mentor/mentee relationship. Chapter 6 focuses on reflection and reflective practice. Reflective practice is one of the most prominent topics in sports coaching, and so helping coaches understand how to reflect is important. In this chapter, reflective strategies are provided from the perspective of a practitioner, which are made sense of through theoretical insight. Chapter 7 follows on from Chapter 6 in continuing discussions around reflective practice; however, this chapter places a focus on a specific reflective practice strategy called 'think aloud'. The benefits of using a think aloud approach are discussed, and then followed by practical guidance for how coaches can embed a protocol within their practices.

Section IV is made up of three chapters concerned with the process of undertaking performance analysis, considerations for growth and maturation and furthering coaches' knowledge of developing their athletes' psychological skills for excellence. Understanding how to work in a multidisciplinary manner and/or understanding multidisciplinary demands has become an important part of a coach's role. These chapters have been written with the intention of supporting coaches when working with performance analysts and sport scientists.

Section V is the final section of this book and deals with the subtleties of coaching different population groups. The section starts with discussions concerning the coaching of female athletes, and how coaches need to think, and subsequently act, when working with this group. Following this is a chapter dedicated to the coaching of disabled athletes. The authors take a critical stance here by asking readers to challenge their understandings of disability, before presenting a practitioner's perspective of working with disabled athletes in cricket. The final section of this chapter, and book, centres on the coaching of children and young people, highlighting the importance of adapting coaching approaches and practices for this population, and providing a reflective account from an experienced children's golf coach.

Chapter structure

A criticism we hear more and more levelled at academic work is one of accessibility. While we do not necessarily share this position, we do appreciate some of the arguments made, and so the 'issue' of accessibility was a central factor in our decision to structure chapters as we have. Foremost in our thinking was that readers could relate to the content of the book and understand what was discussed. We believed that a way of achieving this was to draw upon insights from practitioners who, over many years of experience in the field, had developed a number of different strategies. We wanted these insights communicating via reflective commentaries or narratives. The power of stories as a form of communication that people can relate to has been widely accepted both in coaching and other educational disciplines. However, these are not intended as universal truths and therefore should not be taken as facts. We present the stories with the intention that they serve as thinking tools that better enable coaches to make sense of their own experiences.

Each reflective insight was supported by an academic who had worked with or was working with the practitioner who had contributed to the chapter. This explains why practitioners' examples were across a range of sports. The role of the academic was to use research evidence and theoretical principles to help the reader understand where these appeared within the practitioner's reflections. A commonly used term to express a desire in coaching is the 'bridging of the theory/practice gap'. We wanted to eliminate such a dichotomy by presenting the theory and practice together. How readers engage with this book is of course up to them, but to get the most from it, we feel it serves an iterative purpose whereby coaches engage with the content, consider what it means for them in their practice, try out the proposed ideas, before re-engaging in the book to use the practitioners' insights, as a reference to their own experiences.

Following the practitioner/academic sections, each chapter is concluded with a list of recommendations for practice. These are not intended as prescriptions for practice, but rather some reflections to consider, and/or tangible ideas to think about applying in practice. However, a real strength, we feel, of this text is that the recommendations have derived from a combination of practitioner and theoretical discussion.

Who is the book for?

We have stated where the idea for this book evolved from, and have made reference already to the audience who we feel this text is predominantly aimed at. However, we also feel this book has something for coaches with different types of experiences and levels of expertise. The practitioner content comes from practitioners who have spent many years 'honing their craft'. Therefore, from this perspective, we hope this book will serve useful for all coaches when thinking and relating to the shared reflective commentaries.

SECTION II

A guide to coaching practice

1

A GUIDE TO UNDERSTANDING COACHING PHILOSOPHY

Moving to a philosophy of coaching

Mark Partington and Jake Campbell

Introduction

Coaching philosophy is one of the core topic areas and focus for discussion in sports coaching (Jenkins, 2010). It forms a central component somewhere along the coaching pathway of nearly all National Governing Body (NGB) coaching courses and on most University coaching degree programmes. Often the focus of discussion and introduction to the concept of coaching philosophy resides around the development of one. The justification for this, it has been claimed, is that coaches cannot operate without a coaching philosophy (Cassidy, Jones & Potrac, 2016). Therefore, spending time articulating a philosophy would seem a prerequisite for coaching practice.

Recently, Cushion and Partington (2014) wrote a critical analysis of how coaching philosophy had been conceptualised by academic scholars, NGBs, coach educators and coaches. Cushion and Partington (2014) questioned the extent to which much of the coaching literature pertaining to coaching philosophy actually represented ideas that informed coaches' practice. Instead the term coaching philosophy is positioned, similarly to Green (2002) in teaching, as an ideology. An ideology is a set of myths and explanations that appear self-evidently true to a group of people (Brookfield, 2009). Therefore, Cushion and Partington (2014) argued current use of the term 'coaching philosophy' confuses coaches' values and beliefs or similarly related terms with ideological statements of intent and/or technical and tactical knowledge of the sport. Therefore, while the research attention in this area, on first impression, seems dense, when studied in greater detail, conceptual clarity concerning a coaching philosophy is lacking, and is thus underdeveloped.

While the purpose of this chapter is not to discuss the issues with the coaching philosophy literature (see Cushion & Partington, 2014), it is important that these are considered if attempts are to be made to develop a philosophy of coaching that can guide decisions made in practice, and not simply an ideological coaching statement. Therefore, the ideas presented by Cushion and Partington (2014) will be used as a basis on which this chapter is built. As discussed, there is confusion concerning what a coaching philosophy consists of, with different descriptors provided in the coaching literature and coach education. Therefore, for clarity we define a coaching philosophy as a set of personal values and beliefs (Hardman & Jones, 2013). A value is something (e.g. fun) viewed as important by a coach, and a belief is a the notion that a particular proposition (e.g. creating a fun practice helps motivate players) is true.

The purpose of this chapter is to offer guidance to those wishing to develop a philosophy of coaching. However, unlike past literature this chapter will attempt to provide a more realistic account of how to do this by drawing upon and learning from the reflections of Jake Campbell, a football coach, who has developed his values and beliefs over an eleven-year coaching career. This process involved Jake writing an initial commentary about coaching philosophy and answering questions such as: what is a coaching philosophy? What have been your experiences of coaching philosophy? How does it operate in your environment? How have you found developing and implementing a philosophy of coaching? From here, more detail was acquired through discussions with Jake about what he had written. As authors we hope this will highlight the challenges of developing individual values and beliefs that are representative of coaching practice, while at the same time serving as a framework for practice and a starting point for reflective learning.

An English youth football coach's commentary by Jake Campbell: understanding of coaching philosophy and moving to a philosophy of coaching

My name is Jake Campbell and I am currently the Assistant Academy Manager and Head of the Youth Development Phase at Wigan Athletic Football Club. I have been coaching at Wigan Athletic Football Club Academy for ten years. My highest qualifications include a BSc (hons) degree in Science and Football and a UEFA A License and Advanced Youth Award. The aim of this section is to give my reflections on coaching philosophy and how through an education process I developed and articulated a philosophy of coaching. I hear coaching philosophy all the time in football: in the academy, the media and even the parents of the academy players. I first came across coaching philosophy on my National Governing Body Level 1 football coaching course. I remember the very first day walking into the classroom sitting down, and after an introduction about the course by the coach developers, being told to write down in the pack provided my coaching philosophy. No framework or specific questions were given to help this process. I actually remember writing down how I thought the sport should be played both technically (i.e. comfortable during a 1v1) and tactically (i.e. playing out from the back). I did not really write anything specific about my coaching (e.g. how, when and why) and did not see the value in the process as I felt that I knew it, so why write it? I was not challenged on what I wrote down nor did I refer to it again when coaching.

After discussions with the lead author one thing that has become clear about coaching philosophy is that most people associate it with technical and tactical knowledge of the sport. Obviously for academy coaches this knowledge is important but, in the past, we have spent little time discussing our coaching or what we feel is important when coaching in this environment. A welcome change by the National Governing Body on recent coach education has been the separation of playing philosophy (i.e. knowledge of the sport) and coaching philosophy (i.e. how and why related to coaching). However, coaches still focus on the knowledge of the sport and when asked about their coaching philosophy generally discuss how they feel their sport should be played tactically. As well as coaching philosophy being associated with technical and tactical knowledge, it also seems to be a buzzword used to explain any type of coaching practice. For example, when asked about why we have done something in a particular way in a coaching session, in the past, I used to say it was because of my coaching philosophy with little detail or thought given. It is not until I went through the process of observing my coaching that I developed an understanding of why I coached in a particular way.

Alongside reviewing visual and audio recordings of my coaching sessions, I have been through a reflective process with a mentor that has helped me think about and articulate my values and beliefs. With a mentor, I have spent time thinking about and discussing my axiology and moral values, and ontological and epistemological beliefs. Although this language was new to me, once I started to answer questions related to these philosophical concepts it got me to really think about myself, coaching and the practice I wanted to create for my players. During this development process I made sure my articulated values and beliefs were clearly defined and I could see how these would look in a coaching session. When I struggled to define or clearly link to practice, I drew upon new knowledge (e.g. academic sources, discussions with coaches and coach developers). Having a framework (similar to the one provided in this chapter) with a focus, but also the flexibility, has helped me understand what is important to me as a person and a coach. Now my philosophy of coaching has been clearly articulated, I think about it during my coaching and therefore my interventions are thought out before they are implemented based on my values, beliefs and then, importantly, the player's needs. This at first was a tricky process, but the more I implemented a carefully thought-through intervention the more I have got used to it. I take time now during my coaching to think about who I am implementing an intervention with, what to say, when to say it and how to say it. The time taken to make these decisions I see as valuable, and although I probably now have fewer interventions during a coaching session, I feel they are more appropriate for the players. By developing a philosophy of coaching I have also become more aware of how I want to coach and how I actually coach. I have been able to make informed adjustments to my coaching. Additionally, I use my articulated values and beliefs to engage in discussions with other coaches about coaching. I still refine my philosophy of coaching, it is not static, through new knowledge and experiences.

What is (and equally what is not) a coaching philosophy?

Despite a coaching philosophy being positioned as underpinning coaches' practice, coaches, as Lyle and Cushion (2017) suggest, get on with the business of coaching focussing on more tangible aspects of coaching practice, such as session content and organisation. Coaches, therefore, appear to prefer to ground coaching in a common-sense view of experience and practice (Cushion, 2013, 2016), developing greater, but unreflective knowledge and understanding (Cushion, Armour & Jones, 2003). Hence, one does not need to be a philosopher of coaching in order to be a coach (Lyle & Cushion, 2017). As Jake initially suggested in the above commentary, coaches do not see value in spending time developing a coaching philosophy, but researchers continue to push the agenda that 'a coach's philosophy is [...] of particularly great importance' (Camire, Trudel & Forneris, 2012, p.244). An issue here may be because coaches are currently left to define their own coaching philosophy. It would seem that there is a limited understanding of what is meant by a philosophy, what it should include, how it is structured and how it impacts practice (Cushion & Partington, 2014; Lyle & Cushion, 2017). Indeed, the current body of coaching philosophy literature does little to help this matter, with a range of different definitions described as a set of goals, actions and values (Bennie & O'Connor, 2010); beliefs, values, principles and priorities (Kidman & Hanrahan, 2011); or personal assumptions of axiology, ontology and ethics (Hardman & Jones, 2008, 2013). These understandings often being definitions for, rather than empirically supported definitions of, coaching philosophy (e.g. Burton & Raedeke, 2008; Cassidy et al., 2009; Jenkins, 2010, 2017; Kidman & Hanrahan, 2011; Vealey, 2005). This, alongside philosophy not being linked to coaches' practice, represents a significant gap in our understanding and confusion for coaches wanting to develop values and beliefs that support their practice.

To help with our understanding, firstly, coaching philosophy should be separated from the technical and tactical articulations of a sport that has nothing to do with coaching or philosophy. The splitting of philosophy (i.e. values and beliefs) from a technical and tactical model (i.e. knowledge of the sport) could give coaches more opportunity to think about how, when and why they implement certain coaching methods instead of mainly focusing on 'how to play football'. This separation could help coaches to identify a philosophy of coaching (Cushion & Partington, 2014; Hardman & Jones, 2013; Lyle & Cushion, 2017) that would help guide their actions and interactions. Instead of a focus on how to play the sport, when thinking about an individual philosophy of coaching, discussions on the characteristics and qualities of pedagogy, learning, context and individual player needs would be beneficial. An opportunity for coaches to develop a philosophy of coaching that includes an understanding of coaching and learning may result in an ability to intellectualise the coaching process. This knowledge and understanding could inform coaches' actions to counter the effects of ideology to then help make more informed decisions about practice based on the player's needs. If coaches had a clear separation between a technical and tactical model and their philosophy of coaching, including an awareness of their practice, it could allow them to make informed situational coaching decisions based on their individual environment and player needs.

Philosophy has a part to play in structuring a coach's practice, so understanding philosophical enquiry in sports coaching is worthy of attention. A philosophical understanding of coaching philosophy has been advocated by Hardman and Jones (2008, 2013), who proposed a philosophy of coaching that consists of two factors relating to values and one relating to beliefs: axiology, which include values of importance (i.e. winning); ethics, which include moral values (i.e. time wasting) and ontology, which includes beliefs about the nature of existence, including a core set of features that provide personal significance and a central source of meaning – self-understanding, social expression and self-esteem. Epistemological assumptions that include beliefs about learning are also important to consider (e.g. Cushion & Partington, 2014; Light, 2008; Light & Evans, 2013; Lyle & Cushion, 2017). For example, Grecic and Collins (2013) suggest that 'epistemology is important because it is fundamental to how we think and without the ability to understand how we acquire and develop knowledge, we have no coherent path on which to base our thinking' (p.152).

As highlighted by Jake, one of the main problems is that coaches are often asked to develop a philosophy before they have gained any real amount of coaching experience. Coaches will be asked questions along the lines of 'what type of coach do you want to be?' or 'what are your coaching values and beliefs?'. We discussed, in the introduction to this chapter, what the issues are with asking such questions (e.g. ideological statements instead of values and beliefs that actually link to the coaches' practice), but this aside, this process usually results in coaches spending periods of time writing down a list of statements that they believe provide answers to these types of questions: there is little value in doing this. The first problem with this is that a list of statements in itself does not represent a coach's values and beliefs which link to their practice. Clearly, coaches need a framework when developing a coaching philosophy or when being asked to articulate one (Burton & Raedeke, 2008).

It is apparent that whilst philosophy has been suggested as a central feature in the coaching process, instead of underpinning practice it is more attuned with the ideology of an organisation that is influenced by social factors (Cushion & Partington, 2014). There is a danger, then, that while coaches believe they have a clearly articulated philosophy, in reality, this is not the case due to the impact of social context. A coach is not simply an isolated cognitive being, but instead a socially embedded individual within a context (e.g. Carless & Douglas, 2011; Cushion, 2013; Cushion & Jones, 2014). Instead of developing a philosophy of coaching without understanding the possible impact of a coach's organisation, it is important to illuminate the relationship between coaching philosophy and practice, and how this is shaped by context. Indeed, Carless and Douglas (2011) suggest that currently:

little account is taken of contextual pressures and constrains when writing philosophies. Consequently, when produced they lack flexibility and creditability to be truly functional.

(p.58)

The gaps in understanding between *what* (practice), *why* (articulation of practice) and social context need to be taken into consideration when developing and articulating a philosophy of coaching. Philosophical questions, by nature, cannot be answered quickly or easily. This is because they demand coaches to think in a critically reflexive[1] manner about their coaching in order that taken for granted assumptions, generated over time and through personal experiences and the environment become acknowledged (Cushion & Partington, 2014). What makes reflexive thinking particularly challenging is that coaches' values and beliefs are not easily accessible due to coaches' poor self-awareness and impact of the social context, and therefore are not automatically identifiable. However, if coaches are given a framework to support them, and time, they can identify clear values and beliefs that link and support their coaching practice.

How to develop a philosophy of coaching

In the previous section, we clarified our position on what does and does not constitute a coaching philosophy. What we now aim to do is offer guidance on how to develop a philosophy of coaching (i.e. values and beliefs) that can link and underpin practice. Firstly, however, it is important for coaching organisations, coaches and education providers to understand and provide a clear separation between a technical and tactical model of the sport and philosophy of coaching. As highlighted in Jake's commentary, currently there is a confusion with coaching philosophy being linked to how to play the sport instead of being associated with coaching or philosophy. How to play the sport is still very important, as is coaches' knowledge of technical and tactical aspects in their sport, but in our opinion, this should be equal to a coach's understanding of coaching (how to coach and why to coach in that way). Having a clear philosophy of coaching, that includes values and beliefs, will support coaches when making decisions on how and why to coach in a particular way based on the individual player's needs.

To develop a philosophy of coaching there is a requirement that coaches immerse themselves within philosophical inquiry, which means asking themselves questions related to values and beliefs about 'who you are and why we are here' (ontology), 'how you have come to know what you know' (epistemology) and 'what do you value' (axiology). To help the process of developing a philosophy of coaching, understanding one's axiological and ethical values and ontological and epistemological beliefs can provide a core set of features to coaching that provide personal significance and a central source of meaning, self-understanding, social expression and self-esteem (Hardman & Jones, 2013).

```
┌─────────────────────────────────────────────────────────────┐
│ Philosophy of coaching                                        │
│ Awareness of...                                               │
│ ... values (definition: a view of importance)                │
│        – Axiology – what is important.                        │
│        – Ethics – what is moral.                              │
│ ... beliefs (definition: a proposition or premise to be true) │
│        – Ontology – nature of reality.                        │
│        – Epistemology – nature of knowledge.                  │
│ ... how your values and beliefs look in practice              │
│                                                               │
└─────────────────────────────────────────────────────────────┘
```

FIGURE 1.1   Philosophy of coaching

A clearly articulated view of the world and themselves that links to actual practice would inform the decisions coaches make in relation to their actions.

Figure 1.1 is a philosophy of coaching framework that could be utilised with coaches to help them become aware of their values and beliefs. To help achieve this awareness, the use of video feedback and reflective conversation could be utilised (see Chapter 2 and Chapter 6).

Recommendations for developing a philosophy of coaching

1) Separate your technical and tactical model (i e. knowledge of the sport) when developing a philosophy of coaching. Put these technical and tactical views to one side and focus on your values and beliefs related to coaching.

2) Identify values that are important. Some of the following questions might help this process:

   - Axiology – what is important:
     What motivates you to be a coach? What values are the most important to you and why? How do they look in practice?
   - Ethics – what is moral:
     How do you expect players to behave in your coaching sessions?
     How do you want to behave with the players? What actions do you want to encourage and discourage?

3) Identify your beliefs associated with sport coaching. Some of the following questions might help this process:

   - Ontology – nature of reality:
     How can your coaching contribute to the pursuit of a meaningful life? What are your roles as a coach?
   - Epistemology – nature of knowledge:
     How do you believe players learn? What do these beliefs look like in practice? What can you do to facilitate this in practice? What practice activities would you implement and why? What kind of coach behaviours would you use and why?

4) Link what you articulate as your values and beliefs to your practice. Be aware of the ideological statements in your sport and organisation that have nothing to do with your practice. If you cannot clearly define and explain how something looks in practice remove it from your philosophy of coaching.

5) Continue to refine and be aware of your philosophy of coaching in relation to your actual practice, environment and players.

Note

1 We use the word 'reflexive' rather than 'reflective' here due to the iterative interplay between ideological statements and actual values and beliefs that inform coaches' practice.

References

Bennie, A., & O'Connor, D. (2010). Coaching philosophies: Perceptions from professional cricket, rugby league and rugby union players and coaches in Australia. *International Journal of Sports Science and Coaching*, *5*, 309–320.

Brookfield, S. (2009). The concept of critical reflection: Promises and contradictions. *European Journal of Social Work*, *12*(3), 293–304.

Burton, D., & Raedeke, T. D. (2008). *Sport psychology for coaches*. Ilinois: Human Kinetics.

Camire, M., Trudel, P., & Forneris, T. (2012). Coaching and transferring life skills: Philosophies and strategies used by model high school coaches. *The Sport Psychologist*, *26*, 243–260.

Carless, D., & Douglas, K. (2011). Stories as personal coaching philosophy. *International Journal of Sport Science & Coaching*, *6*, 1–12.

Cassidy, T., Jones, R. L., & Potrac, P. (2009). *Understanding sports coaching: The social, cultural and pedagogical foundations of coaching practice* (2nd ed.). London: Routledge.

Cushion, C. J. (2013). Applying Game Centered Approaches in coaching: A critical analysis of the 'dilemmas of practice' impacting change. *Sports Coaching Review*, *2*(1), 61–76.

Cushion, C. J. (2016). Reflection and reflective practice discourses in coaching: A critical analysis. *Sport, Education and Society*, *23*(1), 82–94.

Cushion, C., Armour, K. M., & Jones, R. L. (2003). Coach education and continuing professional development: Experience and learning to coach. *Quest*, *55*, 215–230.

Cushion, C. J., & Jones, R. L. (2014). A Bourdieusian analysis of cultural reproduction: Socialisation and the 'hidden curriculum' in professional football. *Sport, Education and Society*, *19*(3), 276–298.

Cushion, C. J., & Partington, M. (2014). A critical analysis of the conceptualisation of 'coaching philosophy'. *Sport, Education and Society*, *21*(6), 851–867.

Grecic, D., & Collins, D. (2013). The epistemological chain: Practical applications in sports. *Quest*, *65*, 151–168.

Green, K. (2002). PE Teachers in their figurations: A sociological analysis of everyday 'philosophies'. *Education, Sport and Society*, *7*, 65–83.

Hardman, A. R., & Jones, C. R. (2008). Philosophy for coaches. In R. L. Jones, M. Hughes, & K. Kingston (Eds.), *An introduction for sports coaching: Connecting theory to practice* (pp. 64–72). London: Routledge.

Hardman, A. R., & Jones, C. R. (2013). Philosophy for coaches. In R. L. Jones, M. Hughes, & K. Kingston, *An introduction for sports coaching: Connecting theory to practice* (2nd ed., pp. 99–111). London: Routledge.

Jenkins, S. (2010). Coaching philosophy. In J. Lyle & C. Cushion, *Sports coaching: Professionalisation and practice* (pp. 233–242). London: Churchill Livingstone Elsevier.

Jenkins, S. (2017). Beyond 'crude pragmatism' in sports coaching: Insights from C.S. Peirce, William James and John Dewey. *International Journal of Sports Science and Coaching*, *12*(1), 8–19.

Kidman, L., & Hanrahan, S. J. (2011). *The coaching process* (3rd ed.). London: Routledge.

Light, R. (2008). Complex learning theory - Its epistemology and its assumptions about learning: Implications for physical education. *Journal of Teaching in Physical Education*, *27*, 21–37.

Light, R. L., & Evans, J. R. (2013). Dispositions of elite-level Australian rugby coaches towards game sense: Characteristics of their coaching habitus. *Sport, Education and Society*, *18*(3), 407–423.

Lyle, J., & Cushion, C. J. (2017). *Sport coaching concepts: A framework for coaching practice* (2nd ed.). London: Routledge.

Vealey, R. (2005). *Coaching for the inner edge*. Morgantown: Fitness information technology.

2

A GUIDE TO ANALYSING COACHING BEHAVIOURS

Mark Partington and Jack Walton

Introduction

Research focused on investigating coaches' behaviour has been, and continues to be, a popular area of research inquiry. The choice of behaviours a coach utilises impacts on athletes' psychological well-being, which includes their motivation and confidence (Mageau & Vallerand, 2003), their ability to engage in activities such as problem solving and decision making (Smith & Cushion, 2006) and their physical capabilities through skill acquisition (Ford et al., 2010). It is not surprising then that this area of study has received widespread attention and scrutiny in the coaching literature (Cope, Partington & Harvey, 2017). Coaching behaviours can be described as how coaches communicate and interact (e.g. instruction, questioning or feedback) or not (e.g. silence on-task and silence off-task) with their participants during training or competition. Although coaching is a social activity with a number of influences affecting practice (e.g. culture, tradition, power, organisation), the behaviours coaches use in training and competition, are one of the few controllable components of the coaching process (Cushion, Ford & Williams, 2012; Cushion & Partington, 2014). Because of this, the behaviours coaches' employ can be analysed and changes can be made if required (see Partington, Cushion, Cope & Harvey, 2015). This might explain why the behaviour of coaches, particularly in training settings, has received, and continues to receive such widespread attention in the coaching literature (see Cope, Partington & Harvey, 2017). Coaching behaviours identified in past studies have included many different types of interactions between coach and athlete, generally the most common being, instruction and silence.

The purposes of this chapter are: (1) to give examples of how a coach developer analyses coaches' behaviour; (2) to discuss why coaches might want to analyse their coach behaviour; (3) to discuss some thoughts from the authors on coach behaviour, and; (4) to offer practical guidance for how coaches and coach developers can analyse coaching behaviour and use this information during coach development.

A coach developer's commentary by Jack Walton: analysing coach behaviour to support coaches' development

In my role as a coach developer, I have the opportunity to support coaches within their own environment and whilst coaching their own players. The majority of coaches with whom I work are grassroots volunteers giving up their time to coach local youth football teams. As this role has evolved, I have sought to explore methods which allow me to hold a more objective lens to identify what coaches do in an attempt to empower them to increase awareness and then give them opportunity to rationalise and plan their behaviours depending on the individual players and environment they operate in.

As technology has developed, I have found more coaches starting to use creative methods in an attempt to develop their own practice – for example, visual and audio recording, then watching back their coaching session. From experience, technology can be a wonderful servant if used well but a terrible master if not. Sometimes simply a tally chart (i.e. frequency) on a notepad can be the most effective tool when systematically recording coaching behaviours. It really depends on the situation and what is being analysed. For example, when supporting the development of a coach who valued the importance of his players being able to think for themselves during competition, we decided to track the number of commands (see Table 2.1 for a definition) the coach made during a match and to which players, as a measure of alignment between a belief about learning and actual coaching interactions. I used a wireless radio microphone system that enabled me to hear what the coach was saying from a distance and keep a tally (i.e. frequency) of the players who received commands from the coach. This information served as a platform for discussion and helped the coach to understand the rationale for the choice of their behaviours.

I also recently worked with a coach who didn't feel his coaching sessions were very effective in their use of time. We decided to focus on session management as the coach behaviour to track. With a stopwatch during the hour-long session I timed the duration that the players were taken off task. This data was used during a reflective conversation with the coach to help identify the purpose of taking the players off task. Two reasons discussed with the coach were when they had to set up the next practice and when dealing with players' misbehaviour. Further conversation included why the players were off task and what specific strategies we (coach and coach developer) could put in place to try and decrease time and increase efficiency between practices, limit misbehaviour and therefore decrease the session management time in future training sessions. The coach then had one of the parents on the stopwatch in the following weeks to provide him with the data that would help him to reflect back on their session.

TABLE 2.1 Examples of coaching behaviours and definitions

Behaviour	Definition
Command	An instruction from the coach which tells the player(s) what to do, leaving little or no choice (e.g. 'Play forwards on your first touch')
Question (narrow)	Only a single or a few answers that the coach may be looking for the player(s) to recall (e.g. 'What should you do here?')
Question (broad)	A range or multiple answers, to engage a player(s) to think (e.g. 'How might you create space for your teammate here?')
Management	Organisation of practice or player(s). Not related to learning or technical/tactical content. (e.g. 'Stay inside this area' or 'Come in and listen')
Feedback/praise (general)	Positive statement not relating to learning or a specific technical or tactical attempt (e.g. 'Well done')
Feedback/praise (specific)	A positive verbal statement used to re-enforce or improve the next attempt of a player's performance (can be delivered concurrently or post) (e.g. 'Well done for keeping your head up')
Challenge	A suggestion to the player(s) which leaves choice of their actions (e.g. 'Try to play forwards on your first touch')
Encouragement	An attempt to stimulate effort (e.g. 'Keep going!')

Reflecting on the coaching behaviours literature

Literature in education (Gibbs, 1988; Schön, 1983, 1987) and more recently in sports coaching (Cassidy, Jones & Potrac, 2004) has highlighted the importance of reflecting on practice. Reflection is an essential tool to aid understanding and development that can be utilised by coaches to evaluate personal performance (Carson, 2008; Gilbert & Trudel, 2005; Partington et al., 2015). However, coaches have been found to mainly rely on emulation of other coaches, own intuition and traditions of the sport/club, rather than analysing their own coaching to support or make changes to their behaviours (Williams & Hodges, 2005). More recently some National Governing Bodies have included in their coach education curriculum opportunity for coaches to build an understanding of their own coaching practice by utilising reflective practice (Cropley, Miles & Peel, 2012; Stodter & Cushion, 2017).

Gilbert and Trudel (2001) demonstrated that coaches who utilise reflective practice during individual learning, develop their strengths and areas for improvement from experiences. By means of reflection coaches can therefore enhance the learning and attainment of their performers (Trudel, Gilbert & Tochon, 2001). Knowles, Borrie and Telfer (2005) suggest the inclusion of structured and monitored reflective practice opportunities to be made available in coach education, and coaches to be provided reflective tools. Within this kind of framework, reflection is deemed central to learning and requires theoretical underpinning, structured support and active development of reflective skills (Knowles et al., 2005). Fernandez (1997) states that if practitioners employ a consistent critical reflection on action there will be an improvement in professional knowledge and development of the actual behaviours performed. However, coaches have been identified as having a poor self-awareness of the actual behaviours they implement in practice (Partington & Cushion, 2013). Therefore, analysing a coach via visual and audio recording and making explicit the behaviours they use in training and/or competition is an important starting point in the reflective process (Carson, 2008; Partington et al., 2015).

Past findings and current understanding of coaching behaviours

Coaches occupy a position of centrality and influence in the athletic setting (Cushion, 2013). A coach's words and actions strongly influence the athletes' performance and development, in addition to their social and emotional well-being (Cushion, 2013; Horn, 2008). However, coaches have been found to only recall limited amounts of information (Mesquita, Rosado, Barroja & Januario, 2007). It is therefore important that a coach delivers the most appropriate coaching behaviours towards athletes in both competition and practice settings.[1] In addition, there is a need for coaches to provide clear and precise behaviours to their athletes, as the memory simply cannot process long and ambiguous messages into the long-term memory store (Craik & Lockhart, 1972). In addition, an overly prescriptive approach to instruction and feedback can result in poor retention and skill transfer from training to competition (Hodges & Franks, 2002; Shea & Wulf, 2005). The effect on the athletes' ability to process the coaches' information could be reduced due to the performance level at which the athletes were competing. At an elite level of competition, the negative effects of arousal and errors in attention focus will decrease the capability of the athlete successfully processing all the information (Maslovat, Chua, Lee & Franks, 2004). Therefore, it is important that a coach performs the most appropriate behaviours in both training and competition settings.

Research into the area of coaching behaviours began in the 1970s and attempts by investigators in the past have been to identify the personality traits (Kenow & Williams, 1999), characteristics (Bloom, Schinke & Salmela, 1997) and/or behaviours exhibited by successful coaches (Bloom, Crumpton & Anderson, 1999; Jones, Housner & Kornspan, 1997). These coach behaviour studies, however, do not fully account for the complexity or dynamic interactive nature of coaching (Cope et al., 2017; Cushion, 2010; Nash & Collins, 2006). The fundamental problem is that effectiveness means different things to different people, particularly at the elite or performance level (Lyle & Cushion, 2017). In addition, good coaching might not always be effective coaching and the omission of effective coaching guidelines in coaching literature, indicates 'a lack of appreciation of the effectiveness concept and a lack of appreciation of the coaching process mechanisms' (Cross & Lyle, 1999, p. 49). Lyle (2002) agrees that identifying coaching effectiveness is an important but seemingly intractable problem.

Coaching behaviours need to change to adapt to the interchangeable and individual situations that occur (Cushion, 2010). The specific context that a coach is directly engaged in will ultimately shape the coaches' behaviour and depending on that specific context will determine whether that behaviour performed is effective. Traditionally coaches in the past have performed behaviours that have been highly directive, instructional or prescriptive (Kidman, 2001). However, to develop athletes who can perform when not under direct control (i.e. in a competition) requires a coach to construct knowledge experientially through questioning, summarising, reflecting and listening (Downey, 2003). It is more influential on athlete's long-term learning to shape and guide practice opportunities for players to learn, rather than a coach dictating the learning process (Williams & Hodges, 2005).

The coaches' behaviour not only affects the athletes' performance but will also influence the athlete's attitudes, self-esteem and psychosocial development (Black & Weiss, 1992; Bortoli, Robazza & Giabardo, 1995; Liukkonen, Laasko & Telama, 1996). Although athletes receive health benefits from being directly engaged in participation sport, they can often experience negative feelings such as low-self esteem, aggressive behaviour and excessive anxiety. These feelings are influenced by the quantity and quality of the coaches' behaviour and have been negatively impacted upon in the past (Robazza & Bortoli, 1998). This predicament is happening in both training and competition that decreases the athletes' performance and learning (Rosado & Mesquita, 2009). Therefore, a coaches' choice of behaviours needs to promote inclusion, equality and fairness to create an environment where athletes feel comfortable to make mistakes that they can learn from in both a training and competition setting. The majority of athletes need a relaxed and comfortable environment to apply themselves to their full potential (Jones, Armour & Potrac, 2004; Lyle & Cushion, 2017). This type of environment will also increase self-esteem and reduce aggressive behaviour and excessive anxiety of the athletes (Rosado & Mesquita, 2009).

In a team setting it can be difficult to provide coaching behaviours that suit all the athletes in one team or group. Depending on the specific context, the athletes who usually need more extrinsic motivation often determine a command style of coaching due to the constant encouragement needed to sustain a high level of performance and self-esteem. However, it could be argued that for some athletes this is a less enjoyable and creative environment to perform in. Coaches should therefore base their behaviours on individual characteristics of athletes including their confidence, receptivity to coaching and willingness to learn (Solomon, 2002).

Past literature in coaching tends to focus on the technical aspects of coaching behaviour and does not identify why coaches perform certain behaviours in a specific situation (Cope et al., 2017). A more suitable view in present research is that effective coaching requires a match between the coach behaviour, practice and context as well as the athlete's development and specific needs (Cushion, 2010, 2013). Only more recently has coaching research accepted the importance of identifying coaching behaviours in an applied setting and understanding the rationale and situation that determines the coaches' behaviour. Therefore, when analysing coach behaviour, it is not about identifying effective coaching behaviours but is instead looking at 'how' and 'why' coaches perform certain behaviours within their context (Cope et al., 2017). For example, the professional football coach in Potrac, Jones and Armour (2002) study rationalised a high use of instruction as he felt he needed to be perceived as controlling the coaching environment to ensure job security. Furthermore, as this coach operated within a performance context, he believed that there was an expectation placed on him from the players to demonstrate his 'knowledge of the game'. Therefore, understanding why the coach implemented instructional behaviour helped to explain that individual agency and social structures impacted on the coach's behaviour (Jenkins, 2010), and more generally, have provided much needed insight into how coaches think about their coaching (Smith & Cushion, 2006). If we can firstly identify what behaviour a coach is using in their practice and then secondly the rationale, through conversations, coach developers can support and develop their understanding of coaches' practice.

It is clear that current research has identified that coaching does not occur in a contextual vacuum (Bowes & Jones, 2006; Gilbert & Trudel, 2005). A coach therefore has to implement a number of different behaviours to deal with the complex and diverse nature of coaching (Cushion, 2013; Saury & Durand, 1998). Practice is therefore not neutral as coaching behaviours take shape in a number of different ways depending on the individual situation. Coaching behaviours are therefore directly affected by social situations that are influenced by coaches' personal characteristics, the athletes' personal characteristics and any contextual factors (Cushion, 2013; Lyle, 2002; Potrac, Jones & Cushion, 2007).

Systematic observation of coaching behaviour [what] and reflective conversations [why]

To identify the behaviours of coaches to help support the reflective process, it is important to firstly identify a coach's behaviour in practice. Systematic observation has been suggested to be the most effective way to find out what it is coaches do (Brewer & Jones, 2002). Systematic observation is a technique adapted from physical education research of the 1970s that has been used to identify a coach's behaviour in past research and practice (Siedentop & Tannehill, 2000). Systematic observation provides a method to give an account of a coach's behaviour. Many different research studies have used systematic observation to record coaches' behaviour and practice activities in a number of different sports (Cope et al., 2017). These studies have revealed the value of observation instruments and recording what coaches do in both training and competition. Within these studies a number of observation systems (see Cope et al., 2017) have been developed and modified to analyse the coaching behaviours performed in a specific context.

The main systematic observation instrument that is typically used in past coach behaviour research is the Arizona State University Observation Instrument (ASUOI) (see Lacy & Darst, 1989). Although more recently the Coach Analysis and Intervention System (CAIS) developed by Cushion, Harvey, Muir, and Nelson (2012) has been utilised as it captures in more detail and at a number of different levels the behaviours a coach implements during training and competition. The multi-level aspect of the instrument means that primary behaviours (i.e. instruction, questioning and silence) have a series of secondary behaviours attached to them (i.e. recipient, timing, content).

There are many different ways to systematically observe coaching behaviour in research such as interval recording, time sampled recording and event recording (see Cope et al., 2017). For coach development, simply using a time recording method (e.g. stopwatch) and/or frequency method (e.g. tally) can record the information needed to make a coach aware of their behaviours. A time recording method can be achieved using a stopwatch, started when a behaviour begins and then stopped when it is completed in one episode. The use of frequency can highlight the number of times a behaviour is implemented during one full training session or competition (including pre, during, intervals and post). Percentage of time or frequency of behaviour can then be identified by simply calculating the time or number of behaviours divided by the total and multiplied by 100. Percentages have been used in research to clearly show the amount of certain behaviours that have been implemented.

The systematic observation of coaches' behaviours in training or competition identifies what coaches do, which is an important starting place for the reflective process. An athlete and coach are not simply isolated cognitive beings, but instead social individuals embedded within the context (Cushion & Jones, 2014). Consequently, there remains a need to know why coaches perform certain behaviours in specific situations, to determine what factors determine their coaching behaviour. As academics and practitioners, we recognise the social sphere of coaching and the importance of using this understanding to support coaches more effectively. Therefore, it is important to have reflective conversations on why a coach performs their identified behaviours in a specific situation. This link between systematic observation of coaching behaviour and reflective conversations provides opportunity to increase awareness and think about the underpinning knowledge informing coaches' actions to then, if needed, make changes. Partington et al. (2015) identified in a study, with five professional football coaches, that firstly identifying their coaching behaviours and then having conversations using the data supported their change in instruction, questioning, feedback and use of silence.

Recommendations for analysing coaching behaviour

Step 1: live or video recording of the coach in a practice session or competition

Ideally, we would recommend visual and audio recording of the coach in training or during competition and reviewing with a timecode (See link: www.you tube.com/watch?v=XZZa9cklNjM). This would allow the coach or coach developer the opportunity to watch the recording and hear the behaviours to then systematically record either time spent, frequency or both. If watching live, we would recommend reducing the number of coach behaviours systematically observed (e.g. no more than three); however, when using visual and audio recording you can pause and rewind to allow more behaviours to be systematically observed. A recording of a coach, using technology, can provide an accurate baseline from which to start analysing and tracking coach behaviours. Technological advancements have opened up the opportunity for a coach to record his or her own coaching using equipment such as a camera, tripod and microphone (or headphones with a microphone). The coach or coach developer can capture audio and visual recordings then edit footage based on their chosen behaviours using free software (See link: www.youtube.com/watch?v=KUME_rXL3rk).

Step 2: type of systematic recording and possible coach behaviours to identify

It is easy to get overwhelmed and end up focusing on nothing in an attempt to capture everything. Decide on what behaviour change could have the most positive impact on your practice. Then decide on how this behaviour is most appropriately systematically observed. For example, I may want to inform myself, as a coach, how many times I stop the players training to convey coaching points. I could track the number of times that I stop the players (frequency) and the length of time for which I stop them (time). In addition, as a coach you may want to identify the coaching behaviours you want to use in competition. You can choose and then define your own coaching behaviours to systematically observe and record in training or competition. In Table 2.1 we include some examples of coaching behaviours and definitions. At this point here, a coach can become more aware of the behaviours they want to implement and how they ideally operate in practice.

Step 3: reflective conversation and action plan

Depending on the learner, using the systematic observation data collected, alongside the visual and audio recordings of the coach in training and/or competition can be a useful starting point to then structure a reflective conversation between coach and coach developer. It is increasingly being found that a more capable other is important in this process to trigger change. We would recommend using the systematic observation data to increase awareness and then to discuss possible improvements or highlight strengths in behaviour related to what the coach wants to achieve, linked to the environment they are working in and their players.

Summary

The complex and dynamic nature of the coaching process requires a coach to have a vast array of interchangeable behaviours to primarily assist athletes in achieving peak performance and development (Cushion & Jones, 2014). Literature has suggested it is these different behaviours as performed by a coach that separates the excellent practitioner from the average one (Lyle & Cushion, 2017). Also, if coaching behaviours did not modify from one context to another, athletes' learning and motivation would decline (Weiss, Amorose & Wilko, 2009). Therefore, the level of knowledge and skill of a coach is insignificant if the transfer process is ineffective.

It is important to have a systematic observation process that is an appropriate education tool for you within your own context and equipment constraints. We recommend systematically observing behaviour to increase a coach's awareness of what they are doing in training and/or competition. This can be done live or post event using a frequency, time or both, to fit with what the learner wants to understand about their own behaviour.

To understand a coach's actions exploration of what guides an individual's practice is needed as this provides a framework for their coach behaviour delivery (Cushion & Partington, 2014). Therefore, after a coach's behaviour has been systematically observed it would be beneficial to use the data collected to have a reflective conversation (see Chapter 6). The reflective conversation can be a useful tool in exploring why certain behaviours have been implemented. This can increase awareness of not only what the coach implements in practice but also why they have chosen particular behaviours to implement. From here, if needed, changes can be made to the quantity and/or type of coach behaviours implemented.

Note

1 We argue that coaches should make a choice on the 'most appropriate coaching behaviours', that they critically choose to implement, based on their past experiences (e.g. educational, coaching), but also the athlete and environment (Cassidy et al., 2004; Cushion, 2016).

References

Black, J. S., & Weiss, M. R. (1992). The relationship among perceived coaching behaviors, perceptions of ability, and motivation in competitive age-group swimmers. *Journal of Sport & Exercise Psychology, 14*(3), 309–325.

Bloom, G. A., Crumpton, R., & Anderson, J. E. (1999). A systematic observation study of the teaching behaviors of an expert basketball coach. *Sport Psychologist, 13*(2), 157–170.

Bloom, G. A., Schinke, R. J., & Salmela, J. H. (1997). The development of communication skills by elite basketball coaches. *Coaching & Sport Science Journal, 2*(3), 3–10.

Bortoli, L., Robazza, C., & Giabardo, S. (1995). Young athletes' perception of coaches' behavior. *Perceptual & Motor Skills, 81*(3), 1217–1218.

Bowes, I., & Jones, R. L. (2006). Working at the edge of chaos: Understanding coaching as a complex, interpersonal system. *Sport Psychologist, 20*(2), 235–245.

Brewer, C. J., & Jones, R. L. (2002). A five-stage process for establishing contextually valid systematic observation instruments: The case of rugby union. *Sport Psychologist, 16*(2), 138–159.

Carson, F. (2008). Utilizing video to facilitate reflective practice: Developing sports coaches. *International Journal of Sports Science and Coaching, 3*(3), 381–390.

Cassidy, T., Jones, R. L., & Potrac, P. (2004). *Understanding sports coaching: The social, cultural and pedagogical foundations of coaching practice.* London: Routledge.

Cope, E., Partington, M., & Harvey, S. (2017). A review of the use of a systematic observation method in coaching research 1997–2016. *Journal of Sports Sciences, 35*(20), 2042–2050.

Craik, F., & Lockhart, R. (1972). Levels of processing: A framework for memory research. *Journal of Verbal Learning & Verbal Behavior, 11,* 671–684.

Cropley, B., Miles, A., & Peel, J. (2012). Reflective practice: Value, issues, and developments within sports coaching. Sports Coach UK original research. Leeds: SCUK.

Cross, N., & Lyle, J. (1999). *The coaching process.* Oxford: Butterworth Heinemann.

Cushion, C. J. (2010). Coach behaviour. In J. Lyle & C. Cushion (Eds.), *Sports coaching: Professionalisation and practice, churchill livingstone* pp. (43–62). London: Elsevier, 2010.

Cushion, C. J. (2013). Applying Game Centered Approaches in coaching: A critical analysis of the 'dilemmas of practice' impacting change. *Sports Coaching Review, 2*(1), 61–76.

Cushion, C. J. (2016). Reflection and reflective practice discourses in coaching: A critical analysis. *Sport, Education and Society, 23*(1), 82–94.

Cushion, C. J., Ford, P., & Williams, A. M. (2012). Coach behaviour and practice structures in youth soccer: Implications for talent development. *Journal of Sport Sciences, 30*(15), 1631–1641.

Cushion, C. J., Harvey, S., Muir, R., & Nelson, L. (2012). Developing the coach analysis and intervention system (CAIS): Establishing validity and reliability of a computerized systematic observation instrument. *Journal of Sport Sciences, 30*(1), 201–216.

Cushion, C. J., & Jones, R. L. (2014). A Bourdieusian analysis of cultural reproduction: Socialisation and the 'hidden curriculum' in professional football. *Sport, Education and Society, 19*(3), 276–298.

Cushion, C. J., & Partington, M. (2014). A critical analysis of the conceptualisation of 'coaching philosophy'. *Sport, Education and Society, 21*(6), 851–867.

Downey, M. (2003). *Effective coaching: Lessons from coach's coach.* London: Thomson.

Fernandez, E. (1997). Just doing the observations: Reflective practice in nursing. *British Journal of Nursing, 6,* 939–943.

Ford, P. R., Yates, I., & Williams, A. M. (2010). An analysis of practice activities and instructional behaviours used by youth soccer coaches during practice: Exploring the link between science and application. *Journal of Sports Sciences, 28,* 483–495.

Gibbs, G. (1988). *Learning by doing: A guide to teaching and learning methods.* Oxford: Further Education Unit.

Gilbert, W., & Trudel, P. (2001). Learning to coach through experience: Reflection in model youth sport coaches. *Journal of Teaching in Physical Education, 21,* 16–34.

Gilbert, W., & Trudel, P. (2005). Learning to coach through experience: Conditions that influence reflection. *Physical Educator, 62,* 32–44.

Hodges, N. J., & Franks, I. M. (2002). Modelling coaching practice: The role of instruction and coaching. *Journal of Sport Sciences, 21,* 793–811.

Horn, T. S. (2008). *Advances in sport psychology.* Champaign, IL: Human Kinetics.

Jenkins, S. (2010). Coaching philosophy. In J. Lyle & C. Cushion (Eds.), *Sports coaching: Professionalisation and practice* (pp. 233–242). London: Churchill Livingstone Elsevier.

Jones, D. F., Housner, L. D., & Kornspan, A. S. (1997). Interactive decision making and behavior of experienced and inexperienced basketball coaches during practice. *Journal of Teaching in Physical Education, 16*(4), 454–468.

Jones, R. L., Armour, K. M., & Potrac, P. (2004). *Sports coaching cultures: From practice to theory.* London: Routledge.

Kenow, L., & Williams, J. M. (1999). Coach-athlete compatibility and athlete's perception of coaching behaviors. *Journal of Sport Behavior, 22*(2), 251–259.

Kidman, L. (2001). What is empowerment as a coaching approach? *Rugby League Coaching Manuals, 23*, 27–30.

Knowles, Z., Borrie, A., & Telfer, H. (2005). Towards the reflective sports coach: Issues of context, education and application. *Ergonomics, 48*, 1711–1720.

Lacy, A. C., & Darst, P. W. (1989). The Arizona State University Observation Instrument (ASUOI). In P. W. Darst V. H. Mancini, & D. B. Zakrajsek (Eds.), *Analyzing physical education and sport instruction* (2nd ed., pp. 369–377). Champaign, IL: Human Kinetics Publishers, c1989.

Liukkonen, J., Laasko, L., & Telama, R. (1996). Educational perspectives of youth sport coaches: Analysis of observed coaching behaviors. *International Journal of Sport Psychology, 27*(4), 439–453.

Lyle, J. (2002). *Sports coaching concepts: A framework for coaches' behaviour.* London: Routledge.

Lyle, J., & Cushion, C. J. (2017). *Sport coaching concepts: A framework for coaching practice* (2nd ed.). London: Routledge.

Mageau, G. A., & Vallerand, R. J. (2003). The coach-athlete relationship A motivational model. *Journal of Sports Sciences, 21*, 883–904.

Maslovat, D., Chua, R., Lee, T. D., & Franks, I. M. (2004). Contextual interference: Single task versus multi-task learning. *Motor Control, 8*(2), 213–233.

Mesquita, I., Rosado, A., Barroja, E., & Januário, N. (2007). Athlete's retention of coach's instruction before a Judo competition. *Journal of Human Movement Studies, 7*(3), 402–407.

Nash, C., & Collins, D. (2006). Tacit knowledge in expert coaching: Science or art? *Quest, 58*(4), 465–477.

Partington, M., Cushion, C., Cope, E., & Harvey, S. (2015). The impact of video feedback on professional youth football coaches' reflection and practice behaviour: A longitudinal investigation of behaviour change. *Reflective Practice, 16*(5), 700–716.

Partington, M., & Cushion, C. J. (2013). An investigation of the practice activities and coaching behaviours of professional top-level youth soccer coaches. *Scandinavian Journal of Medicine and Science in Sports, 23*(3), 373–382.

Potrac, P., Jones, R., & Armour, K. (2002). "It's all about getting respect": The coaching behaviours of a top-level English football coach. *Sport, Education and Society, 7*(2), 183–202.

Potrac, P., Jones, R., & Cushion, C. (2007). Understanding power and the coach's role in professional english soccer: A preliminary investigation of coach behaviour. *Soccer & Society, 8*(1), 33–49.

Robazza, C., & Bortoli, L. (1998). Mental preparation strategies of Olympic archers during competition: An exploratory investigation. *High Ability Studies, 9*(2), 219–224.

Rosado, A., & Mesquita, I. (2009). Analysis of the coach's behavior in relation to effective and non effective players in basketball. *International Journal of Performance Analysis in Sport, 9*(2), 6–16.

Saury, J., & Durand, M. (1998). Practical knowledge in expert coaches: On-site study of coaching in sailing. *Research Quarterly for Exercise & Sport, 69*(3), 254–266.

Schön, D. (1983). *The reflective practitioner: How professionals think in action.* San Francisco: HarperCollins.

Schön, D. A. (1987). *Educating the reflective practitioner.* San Francisco: Jossey-Bass.

Shea, C. H., & Wulf, G. (2005). Schema theory: A critical appraisal and reevaluation. *Journal of Motor Behavior, 37*(2), 85–101.

Siedentop, C., & Tannehill, D. (2000). *Developing teaching skills in physical education.* (4th ed.). Mountain View, CA: Mayfield Pub. Co.

Smith, M., & Cushion, C. J. (2006). An investigation of the in-game behaviours of professional, top-level youth soccer coaches. *Journal of Sports Sciences, 24*(4), 355–366.

Solomon, G. B. (2002). Sources of expectancy information among assistant coaches: The influence of performance and psychological cues. *Journal of Sport Behavior, 25*(3), 279–286.

Stodter, A., & Cushion, C. J. (2017). What works in coach learning, how, and for whom? A grounded process of soccer coaches' professional learning. *Qualitative Research in Sport, Exercise and Health, 9*(3), 1–18.

Trudel, P., Gilbert, W., & Tochon, F. (2001). The use of video in the construction of knowledge and meaning in sport pedagogy research. *International Journal of Applied Semiotics, 1-2*(2), 89–112.

Weiss, M. R., Amorose, A. J., & Wilko, A. M. (2009). Coaching behaviors, motivational climate, and psychosocial outcomes among female adolescent athletes. *Pediatric Exercise Science, 21*(4), 475–492.

Williams, A. M., & Hodges, N. (2005). Practice, instruction and skill acquisition in soccer: Challenging tradition. *Journal of Sports Sciences, 23*(6), 637–650.

3

BUILDING A HOUSE OF C.A.R.D.S.

The practice structures of coaches in a professional rugby union academy

Edward Thomas Hall, Aiden McNulty, Mark Laycock and James Ponton

Introduction

Our aim in this chapter is to provide insights into the practice structures used by coaches of the Newcastle Falcons Rugby Union academy. We report how training session activities are organised and adapted to purpose-fully develop creativity, awareness, resilience, decision-making and self-organisation (C.A.R.D.S.) among players aspiring to compete professionally. This chapter is timely because the C.A.R.D.S. framework of priority outcomes, recently developed by England Rugby to help players explore the boundaries of their capabilities, is being widely promoted to coaches by the National Governing Body. In pursuit of our aim, we explore the integration of theory connected to the organisation of training activities through real-world examples from the academy setting, drawing on contemporary research evidence to illustrate their application in everyday coaching practice.

A glimpse at how we coach

Each season, we set out to create opportunities for every player in the Newcastle Falcons academy to explore the boundaries of their capabilities and adapt to the changing nature of the game of rugby union by developing creativity, awareness, resilience, decision-making and self-organisation (C.A.R.D.S.) skills (England Rugby, 2017). In this section, we provide real-world examples from the academy setting of how we structure training activities with the aim of developing C.A.R.D.S. Being constrained by space, we are unable to give exhaustive coverage to our practice structures, but the examples offer a glimpse into *how* we coach and to how the individual C.A.R.D.S. skills are strongly interrelated.

Creativity

England Rugby (2017) define creativity as 'the skill to achieve a specific outcome in different ways'. To promote creativity, as with each of the C.A.R.D.S. skills, we adapt the rewards (e.g. points) and constraints (e.g. rules) of activities used in training, whilst also recognising that purposeful practice will be needed to refine the effectiveness of any action after its initial attempt. Typically, we make amendments to field dimensions, scoring zones and prerequisites to score or regain the ball (e.g. 2v1 must be executed first; four passes maximum), alter team groupings or the laws connected to the tackle area and substitute other objects for the rugby ball. Players may also be awarded 'bonus points' for successfully attempting a novel solution to the challenge posed by these constraints.

As an illustration of these principles, 4v4 and 5v5 games of 'end ball' are used with forwards focussing on lineout strategies, with each team attempting to move the rugby ball from one end of a 30m x 15m pitch to the other using successful lineout throws and catches. Mirroring Fenoglio's (2003) findings from academy football, we see a more diverse range of solutions explored by players in their efforts to retain and intercept the ball in this activity, as well as more numerous lineout throws completed by hookers (over more varied distances and trajectories), when compared to larger or full-sided games of the same duration. In turn, this enables critical discussions with and among players related to the more and less successful strategies they attempted under different circumstances, which informs subsequent awareness, decision making and self-organised coordination of action. Similarly, it helps to inform the personal constraints and challenges we apply to players to promote further exploration of the boundaries of their capabilities. For instance, a hooker who is comfortable throwing to the nearest 'pod' might be constrained by only being able to use a front-pod option twice in the ensuing period of the game. Alternatively, they may only be able to gain one point for each successful front-pod throw but can gain five points each for throws completed to options behind the front pod. Bonus points are awarded for teams using deception (within the laws of rugby) to successfully win the ball in unconventional ways.

Awareness

Awareness is understood by England Rugby (2017) as 'the skill to recognise individual and collective opportunities to support decision making'. Passos, Cordovil, Fernandes and Barreiros (2012) confirm the importance to rugby players of perceiving opportunities in the environment, not only for themselves but also for others, because being aware of these can support effective decision making. We regularly add constraints to individual players during games using bibs and headbands as indicators of their 'superpowers'. The player wearing a headband on the blue team, for instance, might need to be grabbed by two defenders before a simulated tackle is achieved, whereas all other players can be tackled by one defender. At the same time, the player in a headband from the red team might gain an instant turnover of possession if they tackle the blue player with the headband. Thus, players are challenged to be aware of their own and others' strengths and weaknesses, and the opportunities for action these present, which we have found promotes the creative exploration of solutions through coordinated decision making and self-organisation.

Sometimes, constraints are applied without us drawing players' attention to them, such that they are required to be continually aware of their changing environment. For instance, the coned boundaries of a small-sided game might be quietly expanded to see if players recognise this additional space in which they can attack and defend. Similarly, on a standard rugby pitch, full-sided play is regularly restarted from different areas (e.g. Scenario A: lineout on defending team's five-metre line; Scenario B: attacking scrum on the middle of the halfway line). The effect is to constrain players' starting positions relative to the pitch boundaries, the ball and each other, which has been shown to influence emergent decision making and action in rugby union (Correia et al., 2012). We often add contextual information to these situations that challenges players to adapt and make decisions under pressure (resilience), such as the defending team in Scenario A being four points ahead in the final minute of a game, so that they need to prevent a try and the attacking team score a try within a given time in order to achieve their objective.

Resilience

England Rugby (2017) consider resilience to be 'the skill to adapt to pressure'. Therefore, some of our place kickers have completed competitive kicking sessions together in front of 8000 spectators during half time in the senior team's league matches. Time pressure is often imposed by us on skill execution (e.g. 'you've got 30 seconds to try and get the ball back through an interception') and self-organisation during training (e.g. 'you've got one minute to discuss a strategy to stop them winning the ball at the front of the lineout'). Competitive pressure, focussed on skill execution, is regularly added to how games are restarted (e.g. 'best body shape in a 1v1 scrum gets the ball to start the game'; 'if the red player can score a drop goal from here, they get the first attack' etc.). Moreover, speed and fatigue are used to challenge players. For example, a tennis ball can be passed more quickly between attackers than a rugby ball. Replacing the rugby ball with a tennis ball in small-sided games places additional pressure on defenders' decision-making skills and self-organisation.

Making frequent amendments to the constraints of training activities (as above) is itself a form of adversity, as players need to remain aware and quickly adapt to respond to the new challenges posed. We accentuate this by making controversial refereeing decisions during training (e.g. not calling a tackle even if a player is touched; ignoring a knock on). Similarly, we might call 'next try wins' but actually allow the activity to go on for another three tries, all of which is intended to challenge the players to positively adapt to the naturally variable interpretations of rugby's laws by real referees, remaining aware and self-organised in order to make good decisions even under fatigue and when frustrated or disappointed.

Decision making

Becoming an effective decision maker involves developing 'the skill to select an effective action in all situations' (England Rugby, 2017). Underpinning this, players must be aware of relevant opportunities (affordances) in the playing environment and correctly interpret these before they can act (Araujo, Davids, Chow, Passos & Raab, 2009). To achieve this, building on the scenario examples above, we include representative volumes of different origins of ball possession and durations of breaks in play. For example, there are on average 18 scrums per match (an origin of possession) at the level our athletes are aspiring to play (International Rugby Board, 2014). Accordingly, we try to include restarts from various 'scrum' situations in training sessions (perhaps in sub-units of 1v1, 3v3 or 5v5, as well as 8v8). We also try to base breaks in training activity (e.g. for coach whole-group instruction, feedback or questioning, player discussion and reflection, transitions between activities and water breaks) on the typical duration of breaks in match play. This helps to challenge players' resilience, for example, to efficiently discuss a strategy for the forthcoming passage of play under relevant time pressure. Decision making and awareness are also developed using video-based training. Here, players are tasked with reviewing themselves, their opponents and other players (e.g. the club's senior players and team). This is combined with notational analysis of performance, showing statistical profiles of patterns of play, which together support players' awareness and detection of action possibilities underpinning decision making (Passos, Araújo, Davids & Shuttleworth, 2008).

Self-organisation

Self-organised players will have 'the skill to use information to effectively coordinate themselves' (England Rugby, 2017). We use constraints to emphasise the importance of players organising themselves, because it is the players who make decisions during match play. For example, when amending constraints and challenges, as described above, we sometimes quietly pass this information to only one player on each team, allowing the broader training activity to continue. This allows us to observe how effectively players then share information to co-adapt as groups. We also try to disrupt the traditional structures of training sessions observed in many coaching contexts to further challenge players to coordinate their actions. For instance, rather than being kept in a group together, we have tried placing water bottles individually at intervals around the playing area. Players must, therefore, split up to retrieve a water bottle during rest periods, which accentuates their need to actively reassemble so that information and strategies for subsequent play can be explored.

Theory-informed practice structures

The term 'structure' seems unfashionable in coaching at the moment, perhaps because it conjures up images of rigidly traditional, heavily coach-led and strictly controlled training environments. Coaches we talk to often try to distance themselves from these ideas, making claims instead to a more 'contemporary philosophy' that is less structured. Alongside this, we regularly hear buzzwords such as 'game sense', 'player-centred' and 'empowerment' combined to describe coaches' intentions, as if these few words alone coherently capture, in its complex entirety, some kind of structureless 'right' way to coach rugby.[1] Our point here is not to say these particular ideas are wrong; indeed, there is growing evidence available, specific to rugby union, which enables critical appreciation of the benefits and challenges of their implementation (e.g. Hodge, Lonsdale & Ng, 2008; Light & Robert, 2013; Reid & Harvey, 2014). Instead, our concern rests on how frequently these and similarly simplistic descriptors of coaching are exposed as poorly understood, partly-formed or hollow rhetoric when we probe a little deeper and ask coaches to translate their claims into reality. All too regularly, we observe coaching practice that (unknowingly) ignores, deviates from or contradicts the concepts and research evidence associated with the terms used by coaches to describe it. Yet, the value of any claimed approach to coaching should be evident not only in the coach's ability to articulate its principles and justify its worth through logical argument, but in an embodied practical mastery of these things in practice.

As we hope to have illustrated through the examples given above, a degree of structure is integral to the coaching process. We take structure to mean the organisation and adaptation of the physical and socio-cultural learning environment including its spatial (space) and temporal (time) characteristics, which incorporate the arrangement of participants (e.g. players and coaches) and resources (e.g. cones, bibs and balls) together. Without at least some structure, coaching, as a series of purposeful interactions between coach(es) and athlete(s), simply could not occur. Consequently, absolutist claims that treat structure as being a bad thing and directly opposed to agency (freedom) as a good thing in coaching do not hold. Instead, we draw upon broader thinking about the causes of human social behaviour, notably from Pierre Bourdieu (1977), among others, who argued that structure does not exist without agency and vice versa.[2] Such thinking avoids positioning behaviour either as something entirely caused by external influences (deterministic) or as decided entirely by free will (voluntaristic). As Lemert (2012, p. 42) explained, what people think and do is 'simultaneously a result of social rules and of their own individual flourishes'. In other words, social organisation should be understood to create possibilities and constraints for action (also called *affordances*), the coach's skilful orchestration of which can help to direct the coaching process towards certain objectives by mediating learning.

In our own attempts to skilfully orchestrate the coaching process, we draw upon a range of concepts from dynamical systems theory, representative design, non-linear pedagogy, constraints-led coaching and games-based approaches. Importantly, each of these ways of thinking – including the C.A.R.D.S. framework itself – shares a common foundation: a constructivist learning theory. Constructivism views knowledge as something actively *constructed* by learners as they experience situations and interactions with others (Light & Wallian, 2008). This contrasts with outdated notions of knowledge as being inert and separate from the learner, which suggest knowledge can be passively transmitted from the coach – as an expert – to the player – as a novice recipient. Rather than being rooted in authority, dictating players' learning through excessive instruction and decontextualised repetition, we approach our coaching as interactive facilitators of the coaching process. Again, we emphasise that facilitation is not a totally 'hands off' approach; it is about stimulating players to become active thinkers, who share responsibility for their learning, make decisions, explore solutions and accommodate new experiences. Consequently, we believe our task as coaches is to support players to engage in interpretive sense-making and processes of adaptation as they participate in the learning environment together. It is for these reasons that we to pay close attention to how the learning environment is structured as we seek to develop C.A.R.D.S.

Building on these constructivist foundations, we hold a series of research-informed beliefs that are relevant to structuring the training environment: (1) rugby can be characterised as a highly complex system composed of numerous interacting components (e.g. individual players etc.), which create dynamic, non-linear and emergent conditions (Light, Evans, Harvey & Hassanin, 2015); (2) these conditions produce uncertainty as well as constraining and affording opportunities for action by players (Passos et al., 2008); (3) the effectiveness of players' tactics, strategies and decision-making is heavily dependent on their ability to notice and then act upon these affordances (Renshaw, Davids, Shuttleworth & Chow, 2009);[3] and (4) transfer of learning from training to performance will, therefore, be more effective if training environments are designed to be representative of match environments (Pinder, Davids, Renshaw & Araújo, 2011). It is worth stressing the point that actions are tied closely to perception, cognition and social interaction, so we try to organise training activities in ways that help players become attuned to key sources of information in their environment and to explore together skilful solutions to the affordances of these circumstances. Without this, players will lack sensitivity to or awareness of the most relevant stimuli for action. For instance, in a study of rugby coaching practice, Hall, Gray and Sproule (2016) noted that training activities were frequently restarted by coaches when a group lost possession of the ball, which prevented players from exploring transitions from defence to attack and attack to defence when a turnover occurred in open play. Given that 13 per cent of tries came from turnovers in a recent men's Junior Rugby World Cup (International Rugby Board, 2014), this suggests training should be structured in ways that enable academy players to perceive, decide and act in response to transitions in possession.

To ensure purposeful training, where players explore solutions to situations that are representative of match conditions, we draw upon principles from both constraints-led and games-based pedagogy research, as well as non-linear pedagogy research. Constraints, which we have referred to extensively in describing *how* we coach, are simply the demands we manipulate in any activity that serve to amplify certain information available to players within the learning environment in pursuit of particular goals (Carvalho, Correia & Araújo, 2013). These have been classified into individual or *organismic* (e.g. emotions, physical size, motivation), *environmental* (e.g. weather conditions, socio-cultural influences) and *task* constraints (e.g. rules, boundaries, equipment; Newell, 1986). By manipulating the constraints of the learning environment (e.g. by changing player groupings, pitch boundaries and scoring mechanisms) we try to prompt players to:

> search for alternative task solutions (improving their ability to cope with inherent performance variability) in dealing with unpredictability.
>
> *(Passos et al., 2008, p. 132)*

Newcastle Falcons academy players generally experience constraints in non-linear games, meaning their skills are developed in game-based activities that are more authentic to the complexities of rugby union match play; rather than developing skills in the less authentic, technically focussed, blocked practice of highly-repetitive drills. In line with constructivist learning theory and the C.A.R.D.S. skills, our careful and strategic manipulation of the structural boundaries (constraints) of training activities situates learning as problem-solving, the players as active learners and decision makers and positions us (the coaches) as orchestrators, steering and shaping a dynamic, interactive and engaging coaching process (Jones, Bailey & Thompson, 2013). Thus, we use and modify the constraints of games to promotes players' individual and collective awareness of affordances, their resilient adaptation to changing pressures over time and a coordinated self-organisation of behaviour as the boundaries of their capabilities are creatively explored in search of solutions to the problems posed by the learning environment.

Summary and recommendations

We have presented examples of how training session activities are organised to purposefully develop creativity, awareness, resilience, decision-making and self-organisation (C.A.R.D.S.) skills in Newcastle Falcons academy players. Our major focus has been on the use of constraints in non-linear games, which unnaturally ignores the importance of the coach's complementary behaviours to the effectiveness of these structures (and others), because coach behaviour is discussed in greater detail elsewhere. Still, we hope to have raised awareness of principles from representative design, non-linear pedagogy, constraints-led coaching, a games-based approach and constructivist learning theory, as well as an appreciation of what these can look and feel like in practice (Reid & Harvey, 2014).

We have introduced ideas about how to manipulate the learning environment to challenge academy rugby players to seek a range of effective solutions to performance-relevant cues. We recommend you explore and critically reflect on how the following can be implemented in your own coaching context:

1) Develop match-like training scenarios incorporating representative volumes of different origins of ball possession (e.g. scrums, lineouts, penalties, free-kicks and other restarts and turnovers) along with representative durations of breaks in play.[4]

2) Plan a range of constraints that can be adapted in each training activity to accentuate different (relevant) affordances that prompt players to search for varied performance solutions.

3) Ensure individuals and groups are supported to reflect upon how effective their tactics, strategies and decision-making are in different situations, and to plan how these could be developed, improved and adapted for other scenarios.

4) Identify in advance how you will notice players demonstrating each of the C.A.R.D.S. skills, and how you will then reward and challenge these, further taking account of players' learning needs.

We hope that those reading this chapter will consider critically the important role the coach plays in structuring the coaching process. Skilfully orchestrating affordances by manipulating the constraints of games used in training sessions can create opportunities for players to test the boundaries of their capabilities and direct the coaching process towards the purposeful development of C.A.R.D.S. skills. This is about challenging players as active thinkers and decision makers to be aware of their learning environment, and through co-ordinated self-organisation to creatively and resiliently explore solutions to the challenges and opportunities they face. To achieve this, we believe coaches also need C.A.R.D.S. skills: *creativity*, to generate and evaluate different constraints and coaching practice that challenges players appropriately; *awareness*, to consciously notice their own and others' contributions to the learning environment; *resilience*, to adapt well under pressure and in the face of challenges; *decision-making*, to make good choices about what to do (and not do), as well as knowing how to do this effectively and why; and *self-organisation*, to co-ordinate oneself and others to maximise the outcomes of the coaching process through planning, co-operation and shared critical reflection.

Notes

1 Such terminology has gained traction through its promotion in rugby coach education in the UK and further afield since the mid-1990s (Reid & Harvey, 2014).

2 We also recognise that socio-cultural relations (i.e. structure/agency) shape coach behaviour, but a broader, more holistic discussion is beyond the scope of this chapter.

3 Affordances are perceived opportunities for action (action possibilities) provided by the environment (Passos et al., 2008).
4 These should also ensure adequate recovery time for player wellbeing and desired training effects.

References

Araujo, D., Davids, K. W., Chow, J. Y., Passos, P., & Raab, M. (2009). The development of decision making skill in sport: An ecological dynamics perspective *Perspectives on cognition and action in sport* (pp. 157–169). Nova Science Publishers, Inc.
Bourdieu, P. (1977). *Outline of a theory of practice*. Cambridge: Cambridge University Press.
Carvalho, J., Correia, V., & Araújo, D. (2013). A constraints-led approach to skill enhancement in tennis. *ITF Coaching and Sport Science Review, 60*(21), 10–11.
Correia, V., Araújo, D., Duarte, R., Travassos, B., Passos, P., & Davids, K. (2012). Changes in practice task constraints shape decision-making behaviours of team games players. *Journal of Science and Medicine in Sport, 15*(3), 244–249.
England Rugby. (2017). How cards are shaping England's next generation. Retrieved from www.englandrugby.com/news/features/how-cards-are-shaping-england-next-generation/?sf104769049=1&webSyncID=5bc03163-59c5-01e2-89ab-91db87966b3a&sessionGUID=e4eaa0b5-d16c-eebc-0289-e12165082c59
Fenoglio, R. (2003). The Manchester United 4 v 4 pilot scheme for U-9's part II: The analysis. *Insight FA Coaches Association Journal, 6*(4), 21–24.
Hall, E. T., Gray, S., & Sproule, J. (2016). The microstructure of coaching practice: Behaviours and activities of an elite rugby union head coach during preparation and competition. *Journal of Sports Sciences, 34*(10), 896–905. doi:10.1080/02640414.2015.1076571
Hodge, K., Lonsdale, C., & Ng, J. Y. Y. (2008). Burnout in elite rugby: Relationships with basic psychological needs fulfilment. *Journal of Sports Sciences, 26*(8), 835–844.
International Rugby Board. (2014). *IRB Junior World Championship 2014: Statistical analysis and match review*. Retrieved from www.worldrugby.org/game-analysis?lang=en
Jones, R. L., Bailey, J., & Thompson, A. (2013). Ambiguity, noticing and orchestration: Further thoughts on managing the complex coaching context. In P. Potrac, W. Gilbert, & J. Denison (Eds.), *Routledge handbook of sports coaching* (pp. 271–283). Oxfordshire: Routledge.
Lemert, C. C. (2012). *Social things: An introduction to the sociological life* (5th ed.). Lanham, MD: Rowman & Littlefield Publishers.
Light, R. L., Evans, J. R., Harvey, S., & Hassanin, R. (Eds.). (2015). *Advances in rugby coaching: An holistic approach*. London: Routledge.
Light, R. L., & Robert, J. E. (2013). Dispositions of elite-level Australian rugby coaches towards game sense: Characteristics of their coaching habitus. *Sport, Education and Society, 18*(3), 407–423. doi:10.1080/13573322.2011.593506
Light, R. L., & Wallian, N. (2008). A constructivist-informed approach to teaching swimming. *Quest, 60*(3), 387–404. doi:10.1080/00336297.2008.10483588
Newell, K. M. (1986). Constraints on the development of coordination. *Motor Development in Children: Aspects of Coordination and Control, 34*, 341–360.
Passos, P., Araújo, D., Davids, K., & Shuttleworth, R. (2008). Manipulating constraints to train decision making in rugby union. *International Journal of Sports Science & Coaching, 3*(1), 125–140.
Passos, P., Cordovil, R., Fernandes, O., & Barreiros, J. (2012). Perceiving affordances in rugby union. *Journal of Sports Sciences, 30*(11), 1175–1182.

Pinder, R. A., Davids, K., Renshaw, I., & Araújo, D. (2011). Representative learning design and functionality of research and practice in sport. *Journal of Sport and Exercise Psychology, 33*(1), 146–155.

Reid, P., & Harvey, S. (2014). We're delivering game sense … aren't we? *Sports Coaching Review, 3*(1), 80–92. doi:10.1080/21640629.2014.967519

Renshaw, I., Davids, K. W., Shuttleworth, R., & Chow, J. Y. (2009). Insights from ecological psychology and dynamical systems theory can underpin a philosophy of coaching. *International Journal of Sport Psychology, 40*(4), 580–602.

4

ATHLETE-CENTRED COACHING

An applied example from junior international field hockey

Don Vinson and John Bell

Introduction

The extent to which the concept of athlete-centred coaching (Kidman, 2001, 2005; Kidman & Lombardo, 2010) has resonated with the international community has exceeded almost all other coaching discourse over the past decade (Nelson, Cushion, Potrac & Groom, 2014). As well as featuring prominently in numerous academic coaching texts (e.g. Cassidy, Jones & Potrac, 2009; Gilbert, 2017; Light, 2017; Pill, 2018), athlete-centred coaching has also been embraced by a large number of National Governing Bodies (NGBs) both in the UK (e.g. England Hockey (Great Britain Hockey, 2015), England Rugby (Rugby Football Union, 2017), England Netball (England Netball, 2007) and the Football Association (The Football Association, 2015) as well as in numerous other countries around the world including Canada, Finland and New Zealand – to name but a few (Romar, Sarén & Hastie, 2016). Furthermore, athlete-centred coaching has also been espoused by some highly successful field hockey coaches (e.g. Ric Charlesworth (Light, 2013), Danny Kerry (Richardson, 2015) and Beth Anders (Gilbert, 2017)).

The appeal of athlete-centred coaching is easy to understand; at its simplest level, the term means putting the needs of the athlete at the forefront of the coaching process. Such an altruistic perspective has resonated strongly with coaches and few would argue with the noble intentions of practitioners espousing an athlete-centred approach (Denison, Mills & Konoval, 2017). Yet the application of an athlete-centred approach is far from straightforward. The purpose of this chapter is to explore some practical and theoretical challenges with applying an athlete-centred approach. To begin, we offer some reflections related to our attempts to be athlete-centred coaches emanating from our experience of coaching within the England Hockey U16s girls National Age

Group (NAGs) programme. Our reflective narrative includes some practical examples of relatively simple and problematic applications of athlete-centred principles, some minor tensions which currently exist and will also outline some potentially more subtle challenges. We will then turn to the core theoretical principles underpinning an athlete-centred approach drawn from the literature, how these conceptions have evolved (or not) over the past decade and how the theoretical considerations might help explain some of our applied reflections. Finally, we will offer some suggestions and recommendations to those attempting to be athlete-centred coaches.

Athlete-centred coaching: coach reflections

It is important to start by outlining the context of the NAGs environment as there are a number of factors we need to describe which inform our reflections below. The NAGs programme for U16s runs from September to July each year and features around 30 squad members who have been selected through the England Hockey Player Pathway (talent identification and development) activities. There are approximately 35 'contact' days per year, comprising around 12 training days with the remainder dedicated to competition. The majority of the contact occurs after March/April each year with training days restricted to just one or two per month prior to that. Training activity usually features two to three day residential camps. The competitive matches are usually framed over a three-day series against one opposing team. Staffing for the programme comprises a Head Coach (John), Assistant Coach (Don), Goalkeeper Coach/Performance Analyst, Manager and Physiotherapist. The staff are employed on daily rates and so for all us, whilst these roles are incredibly important, they only represent a small part of our working lives. The programme is coordinated and administered by the full-time professional workforce of England Hockey. The budget to support the NAGs programme is tight and painstakingly balanced. If they are able, the girls are asked to make a partial contribution to the camps in order to sustain the maximum number of contact days possible across the year. For all the staff, it is an utter privilege to be involved with the NAGs programme and we are incredibly passionate about facilitating the best possible environment for the girls to develop. For the past two years we have used the strapline 'development and detail' as the overarching concept through which we hope to contribute to the ultimate goals of the NAGs programme which are to:

- Develop an oversupply of players for the U21 and Elite Development Programme (mainly U23) who have the potential to be world-leading senior internationals;
- Provide frequent, exceptionally high-quality, contact time;
- Provide exposure to junior international competition with a view to supporting and accelerating player development;
- Provide high quality education that effectively prepares young players for performance environments.

In addition to understanding the context of the NAGs environment, it is important to make the connections to the current broader focus of Great Britain Hockey. In 2015, Great Britain Hockey published the Golden Thread – a system to guide the delivery of all hockey coaching sessions in Great Britain from absolute beginners to the full-time centralised programme for elite international athletes (the Golden Thread system therefore also applies to our NAGs environment). The five points of the Golden Thread suggest that all hockey coaching sessions should feature: (i) fun, (ii) loads of touches of the ball, (iii) (physical and mental) stretch, (iv) looks something like the game and (v) constant decision making. To accompany the Golden Thread, Great Britain Hockey (2015) proposed that a games-centred (GCA) and question-led approach was the desirable model of coaching practice for hockey; England Hockey has been a strong proponent of these ideas with more recent emphasis on contextual and constraints-led approaches (see Renshaw, Davids, Shuttleworth & Chow, 2009).

To illustrate a practical application of these ideas, we offer the following practice as a typical activity which we have frequently used within the NAGs environment:

The overload/underload game:

- The purpose of the game is facilitate players' exploration of situations when they have a numerical advantage or disadvantage. We want them to explore how they might alter their collective attacking/defensive shape and priorities whilst adhering to the broader principles of play we have discussed throughout the programme (for example, to play 'forward, first, fast').

How the game works:

- The game is played across the width of half a hockey pitch complete with two full-sized scoring circles (16 yards) and a goal at each end.
- 7v7 plus a goalkeeper for each team (with at least one rolling substitute)
- Normal hockey rules are applied with the following modification:
  - If a team has a shot on target, wins a penalty corner or scores a goal, that team is allowed to deploy an eighth outfield player (to make 8v7)

    - 1 point is awarded for an action which gains an extra player
    - 3 points awarded for scoring a goal when 8v7 (scoring team has overload)
    - 5 points awarded for scoring a goal when 7v8 (scoring team has underload)

The game continues for the duration set by the coach – frequently in 3–4 periods of 6–8 minutes. We think this game comfortably meets the five elements of the Golden Thread. The intensity of the activity can be adjusted by altering the base number of players on the pitch (e.g. reducing to 6v6) and by the length of time of each period to ensure there is appropriate 'stretch' to the activity. The gaps between the periods of activities present opportunities for the coaches to ask questions. Often this questioning will involve a degree of collaborative strategising to challenge each team to solve the problem of how they could be more successful as an attacking or defensive unit. This could also be a time for more individually focused questions or some group Q&A – whatever best suits the purpose of the activity at that time for the particular athletes competing in the game. Our experience is that when games like this meet the five elements of the Golden Thread, the athletes are almost always keen to exchange ideas and offer potential solutions to the problem posed by the activity. To this point then, such GCA and questioning-based practices can comfortably be considered to be athlete-centred because they are commensurate with the approach originally outlined by Kidman (2001) discussed in detail within the theory section below. However, whether the athletes are then able to apply the ideas they have generated in the next period of play is less certain. Nonetheless, we are confident that through a GCA approach and appropriate questioning we have been able to generate a degree of athlete involvement in the learning process and this is what makes such coaching, at least to some degree, athlete-centred.

One of the most important mechanisms through which we seek to be athlete-centred coaches in the NAGs environment is through Individual Development Plans (IDPs); an online goal-setting document. The key principles underpinning the IDP are that the athletes take the responsibility for the completion of these documents and that each player is encouraged to consider as broad a range of developmental factors as they can (not just about technical and tactical aspects). We see this as a democratic educational device in that it represents a mechanism through which we can help the players develop in areas that they identify and, therefore, think are most important. Our job is to help them refine their initial drafts so that their goals are relevant, realistic and measurable. We do this through a series of one-to-one meetings at training camps and by comments that we will post through our online learning platform. The content of the IDP then shapes our individual discussions that we will have with each athlete before and after each competitive game. Table 4.1 shows a simplified model example of what a player's IDP might look like.

Whilst many of the principles surrounding the formation and refinement of the IDP documents represent an ideal fit as a democratic, educationally focused, holistic tool, there are a number of challenges to their implementation that will challenge us practically. For example, we have found real challenges with athlete readiness to participate in this process. U16s represent the youngest age group of international competition in field hockey in the UK. Therefore, the athletes we work with are mostly absolute novice junior international athletes. Whilst many of the athletes are ready to engage and have some experience of democratic educational approaches at school, there are always a small number who lack the necessary skills, especially early in the programme. Therefore, for a small number of athletes we end up providing many of the areas of focus and ideas

TABLE 4.1 A simplified model example of an Individual Development Plan

Discipline	Development area	Progress measure	What help do I need and who can help me?
Hockey-specific	Helping the team get forward, first, fast.	Increase the percentages of my passes I play forwards	Video analysis with school and NAGs coaches
Set-piece	Be a more consistent penalty corner stopper	Increase the percentage of successful traps I make	Friends and team mates to practise with
Physical	Improve my acceleration	Improve by 5m and 10m sprint time	Working through NAGs S&C programme with school coach
Psychological	Being better at putting mistakes behind me	Not feeling like mistakes are negatively impacting my game	Encouragement from team mates
School work and examinations	Be better organised in terms of revision	Create, and stick to, a year-planner for revision	Help and advice from parents and teachers
Other	Continue to improve my Cello playing	Pass my Cello Level 5 and devote at least four hours per week to practice	Accountability from parents and Cello teacher

about progress and so the document has much more of our 'voice' than we would ideally like. This kind of document will be a core feature of their international hockey experience all the way through to senior level. Despite these concerns, it is important to acknowledge that the IDP has been refined over a number of years to be the most practically useful document it can be with the athlete as the predominant focus. Therefore, whilst the IDP might not be perfect and has its limits, we believe it has an important part to play in the long-term development of the athletes.

Whilst we do everything we can to promote the most athlete-centred and developmental environment, it is unavoidable that the NAGs programmes are heavily influenced by selection. There is an inevitable, and incredibly strong, desire on behalf of the athletes to be selected, be part of the team and to represent their country as a junior international athlete. Furthermore, because of the budgetary constraints, there are actually very few contact days before we have to start selecting – which means we have not had as long as we would have liked to really get to know the athletes well. This is further inhibited by our very part-time roles which mean we can only devote a very limited time to phone calls and contact via our online portal which otherwise might help us to deepen the coach–athlete relationship away from training camps. This frequent lack of depth in the coach–athlete relationship yields a number of concerns of us as coaches that might prevent us from being as authentically athlete-centred as we would like to be.

Another aspect which challenges us is the extent to which the selection-focus of the NAGs programme negatively influences our ability to be authentically athlete-centred in terms of the promotion of individuality and creativity; this applies to both our on-field and off-field practice. For example, we strongly promote on-field innovation and creativity in decision-making. Yet, it is clear through our one-on-one discussions, that the girls often perceive such 'risky' behaviour – which may result in a loss of possession or missed opportunity, as potentially damaging to their selection prospects. Furthermore, off the field, there are a number of rules and behaviours to which we introduce the girls because they will be apparent at every stage of their development through the system. These rules are set with good intent and, at one level, may seem relatively incidental – such as always carrying your water bottle, always bringing a notebook and pen to meetings, what time to go to bed on camp. We have carefully considered the balance between the 'rules' we put in place and the degree of freedom we allow and we're fairly comfortable that we've pitched this as best as we can given the resources we have and that the girls have enough 'room' to be themselves. Nevertheless, it is possible that such common-sense rules, sitting under the broader shadow of selection, contribute to quite a high degree of conformity within the group. Clearly there will always be rules and behaviours to which international athletes have to conform if they want to be a part of the system: we are comfortable with that, but it doesn't mean we are not challenged by it. It is a constant challenge to us to help them find ways to balance between conforming to the behaviours we would expect of an international athlete and encouraging their individuality and creativity – which we consider to be a fundamental part of an athlete-centred environment. It is important to stress that our approach changes each year as we make decisions on how to best facilitate an athlete-centred environment given the constraints of the system, our own beliefs and the particular needs of the athletes. Every coaching context is unique and so what athlete-centred coaching looks like in one environment, or for any individual athlete, will never look the same as for any other.

Athlete-centred coaching: the theory

This section provides an introduction into the theoretical aspects of athlete-centred coaching and how these have evolved in the literature over the past 20 years. Where possible, we have made connections to the practical reflections in the previous sections in order to better understand the challenges of contemporary athlete-centred coaching approaches.

Kidman's (2001, 2005) original conception of athlete-centred coaching focussed on the concept of empowerment. She argued that an empowered athlete was actively engaged in the construction of their sporting environment, making decisions about what to do and how it should be done (Kidman, 2005). In her early work, the predominant focus was on coaching at an episodic level – i.e. what happened within the training/practice environment. Cassidy et al.

(2009) argued that an empowerment approach tackled some of the inherent problems arising from more linear, coach-led, approaches such as limited knowledge generation, a lack of cognitive involvement on behalf of the athletes, as well as participants' inhibited social development and creative problem solving ability. Therefore, an empowered athlete was considered to be a better decision maker, an independent thinker and a more rounded human being – concepts which inevitably appealed to almost all coaches (Mills & Denison, 2013). Kidman (2005) offered some pedagogically founded approaches to athlete-centred coaching, namely Teaching Games for Understanding (TGfU) (Bunker & Thorpe, 1982) and questioning. TGfU is one of a number of games-centred pedagogic models including, for example, Game Sense (Den Duyn, 1997) and Play Practice (Launder & Piltz, 2013). For the purposes of this chapter, we have used the umbrella term of GCA (Harvey & Jarrett, 2014) to represent all of these models. GCA-based research has commonly featured the term athlete-centred coaching as an over-arching term under which such models comfortably sit (Light & Evans, 2010; Renshaw, Chow, Davids & Hammond, 2010). It is beyond the scope of this chapter to describe GCAs in detail; however, the main premise of such approaches is that by enabling participants to engage with game-like practice environments, which are representative of the 'main/full' game and which exaggerate a particular tactical or technical solution, athletes will ultimately become more effective games-players.

Kidman's (2005) second principle of questioning holds even broader appeal than TGfU as it can potentially relate to every coaching context and not merely those focussed on games. Research into coach behaviour has found that, through questioning, coaches often strongly lead athletes to the 'desired' response and frequently require such an immediate answer that athletes have insufficient time to think (Cope, Partington, Cushion & Harvey, 2016). A more athlete-centred questioning approach encourages coaches to engage participants with strategically focused questions aimed at developing higher order thinking skills such as analysing and creating, rather than 'merely' checking for understanding (Cope et al., 2016). There are several useful ideas available for coaches such as The Debate of Ideas, Goal – Reality – Options – Way Forward (GROW) and the Reflective Toss (see Harvey, Cope & Jones, 2016). We find these basic principles of empowerment, GCA and question-led approaches to be relatively straightforward to apply within the NAGs environment.

Despite the widespread positivity surrounding athlete-centred coaching and empowerment, Nelson, Potrac and Marshall (2010) were concerned about over-simplification and misrepresentation. Nelson et al. (2010) reported that athlete-centred coaching was being viewed as synonymous with a questioning approach; a position which they felt was in danger of undermining the potential of the approach to benefit the athletes. Nelson et al. (2014) cautioned that many coaches' intentions to deliver an athlete-centred approach yielded nothing more than an illusion of empowerment. Nelson et al.'s (2014) position was influenced by their reading of Carl Rogers' contribution to Humanistic Psychology and is discussed in greater detail below. The interest in Carl Rogers emanated from Kidman and Lombardo's (2010) second edition of Kidman's (2005) earlier work which attempted to broaden the focus of athlete-centred coaching to even more prominently focus on the holistic development of the athlete. Kidman and Lombardo (2010) use the terms humanistic and athlete-centred coaching interchangeably, considering both to refer to the need to develop the 'whole' athlete. Kidman and Lombardo (2010) considered these 'whole' needs to include physical, cognitive, psychological, social and spiritual aspects. This latter focus on humanistic coaching has been considerably less pervasive than the earlier focus on empowerment. Cassidy (2010) argued that humanistic and athlete-centred practices are not synonymous and suggested that a simplistic understanding of the term 'holistic' could result in meaninglessness. However, recent texts appear to have retained the prominence of athlete-centred coaching but make no reference to Humanistic Psychology and either no (e.g. Gilbert, 2017; Pill, 2018), or nominal (e.g. Light, 2017), reference to holism.

Another principle which is worth examining at this stage is the extent to which coaching can be considered to be a principally educational endeavour (see Jones, 2006). It is through this educational lens that Nelson et al. (2014) critiqued the potential contribution of Carl Rogers' theoretical contribution whilst prompting coaches to fundamentally review their beliefs and values surrounding the broader purpose of coaching within their own contexts in order to establish the most appropriate approach to athlete-centeredness. Carl Rogers was a psychological theorist who was committed to understanding the realisation of human potential through client-centred therapy (Rogers, 1951). Rogers' educationally focused writings outlined the conditions through which human potential could be actualised through democratic principles, i.e. a reduced emphasis on learning via direct instruction and a re-modelling of the educator as a facilitator (Nelson et al., 2014). Key to Nelson et al.'s (2014) argument was the belief that democratic principles are not appropriate to all environments and that a universal, 'one size fits all' approach to athlete-centred coaching is both inefficient and ineffective. Rogers (1951) suggested that where the goal of the encounter was to produce efficient technical performers who did not question the authority of the educator, then his proposed democratic principles were not appropriate. Furthermore, Rogers (1969) posited that those individuals not desiring the kinds of freedom enabled by democratic principles should not be forced to engage and suggested the educator might then adopt a more directive approach. Adopting a democratic coaching approach requires, therefore, a consideration of the wishes of the individual and also whether the goal of the environment is to produce athletes who:

> are able to take self-initiated action and to be responsible for those actions; who are capable of intelligent choice and self-direction; who are critical learners, able to evaluate the contributions made by others; who have acquired knowledge relevant to the solution of problems; who, even more importantly, are able to adapt flexibly and intelligently to new problem situations.
>
> *(Rogers, 1951, p. 387)*

If the goal of a coaching environment is commensurate with the principles outlined by Rogers (1951), then the challenge to coaches becomes how to ensure athletes are engaged in appropriate tasks in order to facilitate learning. According to Rogers (1969), appropriate environments to facilitate learning are experiential by nature, requiring personal involvement on the behalf of the athlete, are self-initiated, pervasive and evaluated by the learner. Furthermore, the environments should be focused on something the athlete wants to learn and where the essence of the activity is 'meaning' itself. Whilst acknowledging the noble principles outlined by Rogers (1951, 1969), Nelson et al. (2014) questioned whether such altruistic notions were applicable in many coaching contexts, particularly those featuring a high degree of political control. A truly democratic environment would enable learners to help shape the technical areas of focus and tactical structures of the group. Within the NAGs environment, we are quite happy taking a pragmatic perspective on these issues and we are not convinced that this means we are guilty of misunderstanding or misrepresentation. Our perspective would be that we are implementing as democratic and as holistic a programme as we can facilitate within the constraints of the programme.

A further problem relates to the athletes' readiness to be empowered. Despite the prevalence of athlete-centred principles espoused within the literature over the past decade, studies of coaching behaviour have revealed that prescriptive, linear practice remains the dominant mode (e.g. Partington, Cushion & Harvey, 2013) – even in studies where the focus of the coach was reported to be holistic development and enhancing athletes' decision-making capabilities (Partington & Cushion, 2013). Nelson et al. (2014) suggested that assuming a democratic approach was always the best and most appropriate environment to create for all athletes was, at best, problematic and fraught with difficulties. Nelson et al. (2014) highlighted that many groups of athletes were unlikely to have been exposed to many coaching environments in which they were genuinely empowered. This poses a potential problem for coaches – if the athletes are not used to being empowered, are they going to be able to deal with the freedoms they are going to be exposed to in a democratic approach? Despite such concerns, further coach behaviour studies have identified some appropriately constructed democratic environments in both youth (Vinson, Brady, Moreland & Judge, 2016) and elite contexts (Croad & Vinson, 2018). These studies have revealed a utilisation of GCAs and extensive questioning, commensurate with an empowerment-focused athlete-centred approach (Kidman, 2005). However, neither the holistic focus nor the broader micro-political power relations evident within the environments were extensively problematised by the coaches featured within either of these investigations. We believe that part of the role of the skilful coach is to judge how best to offer the various freedoms with which we provide the athletes on as individual a level as we are able. For us this means we need to scaffold their learning in a bespoke manner and with different levels of freedom being granted to each individual.

Several recent articles have suggested that the micro-political power relations in coaching contexts could be better understood through the lens of social theory and, more specifically, the work of Michel Foucault (e.g. Denison et al., 2017; Denison, Pringle, Cassidy & Hessian, 2015; Piper, Garratt & Taylor, 2013). It is to this latter work that we now turn to illustrate how a number of contemporary coaching problems could be effectively framed and more critically problematised. Without denying that sports coaching is a pedagogic discipline, Denison et al. (2017) contended that acknowledging the centrality of the sociological power relations between coach and athletes could be an important tool in helping coaches to be more authentically athlete-centred. The principal concern highlighted within research viewed through a Foucauldian lens is that most coaching environments are founded on structures which make athletes subservient and through which they are pacified and controlled. Mills and Denison (2013) contend that this subservience, pacification and control is incredibly difficult, maybe even impossible, to tackle within our current sporting infrastructures. Going one step further, Denison et al. (2017) argued that coaches who assert that athlete empowerment can be facilitated through an athlete-centred coaching framework might even be limiting and constraining their participants – the exact opposite of their intent. Furthermore, without problematising the nature of the coach–athlete power relations more deeply, coaches might be in danger of merely echoing and repeating dominant discourses which resultantly make athletes subservient, not empowered. In order to tackle some of the difficulties which Foucauldian researchers have highlighted concerning power in the coach–athlete relationship, it is important to outline some of the key concepts which underpin these challenges, namely disempowerment, discipline and docility. We will address each of these concepts in turn.

Disempowerment can arise from coaching practices which are very well-intended and which sometimes seek to embrace technological innovation. For example, Vinson, Morgan, Beeching and Jones (2017) investigated the use of an online video-based platform which coaches engaged with in order to promote athlete autonomy through the medium of collaborative performance analysis. Vinson et al. (2017) found that the majority of athletes and coaches found such practices to be liberating to a degree, but also noted that most of the coaches were predominantly focused on ensuring their athletes arrived at a single, agreed, solution to any problem. Williams and Manley (2016) found even less freedom and autonomy within their case study of a professional rugby union club which utilised video analysis and a wide range of performance monitoring technology such as Global Positioning System (GPS). Williams and Manley (2016) concluded that the coaches' use of technological monitoring had enhanced players' perceptions of a controlling environment – this had led to enhanced conformity and a suspicion of how such technologies were being utilised. Foucault's (1977) contention was that many institutions, including prisons, schools and factories enforced and promoted discipline in order to make people more useful and productive. Similarly, the notion of sports teams promoting conformity through disciplined participation has long been established (see, for example, Parker, 2006). Mechanisms which promote conformity are often well-intended and designed to promote empowerment. The result is to create groups of athletes who are docile – who actively seek not to be seen to deviate from the norm but conform to what they come to understand to be the behaviours of a 'good athlete' (Tsang, 2000). The warnings of these writings surrounding disempowerment, discipline and docility serve as a warning to us as NAGs coaches – we use them as part of the balancing process to ensure that we provide the best possible developmental environment within the constraints of the programme whilst maintaining sufficient 'space' for the athletes feel genuinely empowered and authentically individual.

Conclusions

Few people would question the positively focussed and altruistic intent of coaches who want to be athlete-centred practitioners. There are also clearly a number of aspects of athlete-centredness, as we have illustrated in this chapter, which some coaches might be able to apply to their practice relatively unproblematically. However, there might also be other factors, beyond the scope of the coach, which might hinder their ability to be as authentically empowering as they would like. For us, the constraints of the programme and the inherent pressure of wanting to be selected for your country are factors beyond our control but that impact our practice. We would encourage practitioners who want to be athlete-centred coaches to continue to strive to facilitate environments which are as authentically empowering as possible within the constraints of their broader coaching context. We concur with Denison et al. (2017) that, as an industry, we need to more deeply problematise the concept of empowerment and investigate ways in which we can more authentically facilitate appropriate environments for our athletes. We also need further resources and support through coaches' learning communities to help each other to develop our practice as athlete-centred coaches.

Implications for practice

1) Coaches should continue to facilitate as empowering and question-led approach as they are able;
2) Coaches should embrace a pragmatic approach to adopting athlete-centred principles, acknowledging that these ideas will not be applied in a perfect, theoretically-pure, manner, but will require the careful consideration of what can best be done given the constraints of the environment. They should understand that every athlete-centred approach will look different to every other;
3) Coaches should continue to strive to get to know their athletes on an individual level as deeply as they possibly can – this probably requires as much one-to-one time simply talking to the athletes about their lives and will help facilitate genuinely bespoke and holistic approaches to their coaching practice;

4) Coaches should critically reflect on the constraints of their environment, which might serve to disempower the athlete or cause docility – addressing such factors as far as they are able.

References

Bunker, D., & Thorpe, R. (1982). A model for the teaching of games in the secondary school. *Bulletin of Physical Education*, *10*, 9–16.

Cassidy, T. (2010). Holism in sports coaching: Beyond humanistic psychology. *International Journal of Sports Science and Coaching*, *5*(4), 439–447.

Cassidy, T., Jones, R. L., & Potrac, P. (2009). *Understanding sports coaching: The social, cultural and pedagogical foundations of coaching practice* (2nd ed.). Abingdon: Routledge.

Cope, E., Partington, M., Cushion, C., & Harvey, S. (2016). An investigation of professional top-level youth football coaches' questioning practice. *Qualitative research in Sport, Exercise and Health*, *8*(4), 380–393.

Croad, A., & Vinson, D. (2018). Investigating games-centred pedagogies to enhance athlete decision making in elite coaching contexts. *International Journal of Coaching Science*, *12*(1), 35–68.

Den Duyn, N. (1997). *Game sense: Developing thinking players*. Canberra: Australian Sports Commission.

Denison, J., Mills, J. P., & Konoval, T. (2017). Sports disciplinary legacy and the challenge of 'coaching differently'. *Sport, Education and Society*, *22*(6), 772–783.

Denison, J., Pringle, R., Cassidy, T., & Hessian, P. (2015). Informing coaches' practices: Towards an application of foucault's ethics. *International Sport Coaching Journal*, *2*(1), 72–76.

England Netball. (2007). *Netball UKCC coach education programme level 2 coach qualification*. Loughborough: Author.

The Football Association. (2015). *Developing the developers*. Burton-upon-Trent: Author.

Foucault, M. (1977). *Discipline and punish: The birth of the prison*. London: Allen Lane.

Gilbert, W. (2017). *Coaching better every season: A year-round system for athlete development and program success*. Champaign, IL: Human Kinetics.

Great Britain Hockey. (2015). *Introduction to coaching hockey*. Bisham Abbey, Marlow: Great Britain Hockey.

Harvey, S., Cope, E., & Jones, R. (2016). Developing questioning in game-centred approaches. *Journal of Physical Eduction, Recreation and Dance*, *87*(3), 28–35.

Harvey, S., & Jarrett, K. (2014). A review of the game-centred approaches to teaching and coaching literature since 2006. *Physical Education & Sport Pedagogy*, *19*(3), 278–300.

Jones, R. L. (2006). How can educational concepts inform sports coaching? In R. L. Jones (Ed.), *The sports coach as educator: Re-conceptualising sports coaching* (pp. 3–13). London: Routledge.

Kidman, L. (2001). *Developing decision makers: An empowerment approach to coaching*. Christchurch, NZ: Innovative Print Communications.

Kidman, L. (2005). *Athlete-centred coaching: Developing inspired and inspiring people*. Christchurch, NZ: Innovative Print Communications.

Kidman, L., & Lombardo, B. J. (2010). *Athlete-centred coaching: Developing decision makers* (2nd ed.). Worcester: IPC Print Resources.

Launder, A., & Piltz, W. (2013). *Play practice: Engaging and developing skilled players from beginner to elite* (2nd ed.). Leeds: Human Kinetics.

Light, R. L. (2013). *Game sense: Pedagogy for performance, participation and enjoyment*. Abingdon: Routledge.

Light, R. L. (2017). *Positive pedagogy for sport coaching: Athlete-centred coaching for individual sports*. Abingdon: Routledge.

Light, R. L., & Evans, J. R. (2010). The impact of Game Sense pedagogy on Australian rugby coaches' practice: A question of pedagogy. *Physical Education & Sport Pedagogy, 15* (2), 103–115.

Mills, J. P., & Denison, J. (2013). Coach Foucault: Problematizing endurance running coaches' practices. *Sports Coaching Review, 2*(2), 136–150.

Nelson, L. J., Cushion, C. J., Potrac, P., & Groom, R. (2014). Carl Rogers, learning and educational practice: Critical considerations and applications in sports coaching. *Sport, Education and Society, 19*(5), 513–531.

Nelson, L. J., Potrac, P., & Marshall, P. (2010). Holism in sports coaching: Beyond humanistic psychology - a commentary. *International Journal of Sports Science & Coaching, 5*(4), 465–468.

Parker, A. (2006). Lifelong learning to labour: Apprenticeship, masculinity and communities of practice. *British Educational Research Journal, 32*(5), 687–701.

Partington, M., & Cushion, C. (2013). An investigation of the practice activities and coaching behaviors of professional top-level youth soccer coaches. *Scandinavian Journal of Medicine and Science in Sports, 23*(3), 374–382.

Partington, M., Cushion, C., & Harvey, S. (2013). An investigation of the effect of athletes' age on the coaching behaviours of professional top-level youth soccer coaches. *Journal of Sports Sciences, 32*(5), 403–414.

Pill, S. (Ed.). (2018). *Perspectives on athlete-centred coaching*. Abingdon: Routledge.

Piper, H., Garratt, D., & Taylor, B. (2013). Hands off! The practice and politics of touch in physical education and sports coaching. *Sport, Education and Society, 18*(5), 575–582.

Renshaw, I., Chow, J. Y., Davids, K., & Hammond, J. (2010). A constraints-led perspective to understanding skill acquisition and game play: A basis for integration of motor learning theory and physical education praxis? *Physical Education and Sport Pedagogy, 15*(2), 117–137.

Renshaw, I., Davids, K. W., Shuttleworth, R., & Chow, J. Y. (2009). Insights from ecological psychology and dynamical systems theory can underpin a philosophy of coaching. *International Journal of Sport Psychology, 40*(4), 540–602.

Richardson, B. (2015, 8th December). How high performance coach of the year Danny Kerry has put the Great into British hockey. Retrieved from www.connectedcoaches. org/spaces/10/welcome-and-general/blogs/general/181/how-high-performance-coach-of-the-year-danny-kerry-has-put-the-great-into-british-hockey

Rogers, C. R. (1951). *Client-centred therapy*. London: Constable and Robinson.

Rogers, C. R. (1969). *Freedom to learn*. Columbus, OH: Merrill.

Romar, J.-E., Sarén, J., & Hastie, P. (2016). Athlete-centred coaching using the sport education model in youth soccer. *Journal of Physical Education and Sport, 16*(2), 380–391.

Rugby Football Union. (2017). *Codes of conduct: Age grade rugby*. Twickenham: Author.

Tsang, T. (2000). Let me tell you a story: A narrative exploration of identity in high-performance sport. *Sociology of Sport Journal, 17*(1), 44–59.

Vinson, D., Brady, A., Moreland, B., & Judge, N. (2016). Exploring coach behaviours, session contexts and key stakeholder perceptions of non-linear coaching approaches in youth sport. *International Journal of Sports Science and Coaching, 11*(1), 54–68.

Vinson, D., Morgan, M., Beeching, K., & Jones, G. (2017). Collaborative evaluation of individual and team performance in training and match environments using the coach logic online platform. *International Sports Coaching Journal, 4*(1), 47–62.

Williams, S., & Manley, A. (2016). Elite coaching and the technocratic engineer: Thanking the boys at microsoft! *Sport, Education and Society, 21*(6), 828–850.

SECTION III

A guide to coach education and learning

5

MENTORING IN COACH EDUCATION

The importance of role models, context and gender

Rebecca Sawiuk, Ryan Groom and Lois Fidler

Introduction

The aim of this chapter is to explore the key mentoring experiences of Lois Fidler, a female international youth coach and UEFA Professional Licence (UEFA Pro) holder. In this chapter, we specifically focus upon Lois' mentee experiences in preparing to coach women's international youth football teams, as part of her learning journey. The chapter is divided into three sections. Section one briefly reviews contemporary literature in coach learning, coach education and mentoring in sports coaching. Section two examines Lois' mentoring experiences in practice. Section three outlines future recommendations for mentoring practice.

Review of literature

Coach learning and coach education

Sports coaches learn in a variety of learning scenarios, including formal coaching courses (e.g. governing body awards), non-formal educational activities (e.g. workshops, conferences, clinics and seminars) and informal daily experiences (e.g. previous experiences as an athlete, practical coaching experience, interactions with peer coaches and athletes and informal mentoring conversations; Mallett, Trudel, Lyle & Rynne, 2009; Nelson, Cushion & Potrac, 2006). Furthermore, coach learning situations can be characterised as mediated, where the learning material is prescribed to the coach (e.g. coach educator-led coaching certificates) or unmediated, where coaches decide what information they require to support their learning (e.g. personal reflection, coaching biography or seeking new information to solve practice dilemmas; Trudel, Culver & Werthner, 2013).

From an academic perspective, traditional mediated formal coach education courses have been subjected to a number of noteworthy criticisms by sports coaching scholars. For example, researchers have cautioned against the production of 'paint by numbers' coaches (Jones & Turner, 2006), through programmes that 'train' or 'indoctrinate' coaches into set ways of thinking and practising (Nelson et al., 2006), rather than developing critical and reflective thinkers (Jones & Turner, 2006). In addition, early research exploring formalised coach education programmes has been found to struggle with issues such as decontextualised learning (Cushion, Armour & Jones, 2003), as the programmes contradict candidates' personal experiences (Jones & Allison, 2014), encourages coach-learners to engage in 'studentship' to complete course assessments (Chesterfield, Potrac & Jones, 2010) and lacks impactful reflective practice (Leduc, Culver & Werthner, 2012), in a socio-cultural environment entrenched in gendered issues and authoritarian practices (Cushion, Griffiths & Armour, 2017; Lewis, Roberts & Andrews, 2018; Townsend & Cushion, 2017).

Unsurprisingly, coaches often report that unmediated informal learning situations that encourage social interactions with others are their most preferred and valued way to learn (Nelson, Cushion & Potrac, 2013; Stoszkowski & Collins, 2016; Wright, Trudel & Culver, 2007). Informal unmediated learning situations might include, for example, personal experiences as an athlete, observations of other coaches, self-directed learning utilising a variety of resources (e.g. books, online or social media), situated learning within the coach's own environment, critical discussions with a community of likeminded coaches and mentoring conversations with a more knowledgeable other (Cushion, 2006; Cushion et al., 2003; Cushion & Nelson, 2013; Gilbert & Trudel, 2001; Griffiths, Armour & Cushion, 2018; Nelson & Cushion, 2006; Nelson et al., 2006, 2013; Potrac, Nelson, Groom & Greenough, 2016; Stoszkowski & Collins, 2014; Wright et al., 2007).

These approaches to generating coach learning form an important part of the 'complex, idiosyncratic mix of learning experiences' which support the traditional mediated formal coach education pathways (Stodter & Cushion, 2014, p. 63). Indeed, our understanding of the social complexity of coach learning and the numerous theoretical considerations available to underpin coaching practice has significantly increased over the last decade (Allison, Abraham & Cale, 2015; Chambers, 2015, 2018; Jones, 2006; Jones, Potrac, Cushion & Ronglan, 2011; Lyle & Cushion, 2010, 2017; Nelson, Groom & Potrac, 2016; Potrac, Gilbert & Denison, 2013). Therefore, coach learning programmes require the space for quality interaction within an appropriate social context: for example, participation, development or elite domains, aligned to the coach learner's career development stage and allowing the coach to explore and develop their own biography, identity, philosophy and 'real-world' practice (Cushion et al., 2003, 2017; Cushion & Nelson, 2013; Griffiths et al., 2018; Jones & Allison, 2014; Jones, Armour & Potrac, 2004; Nelson et al., 2013; Phelan & Griffiths, 2018; Trudel et al., 2013; Watts & Cushion, 2017).

However, there is a dearth of useful work which explores how female performance coaches navigate their way through the coach education pathway and engage with a variety of knowledge sources, one of which is effective mentoring. The aim of this chapter is to go some way to addressing the dearth of useful work in this area, with a particular focus upon learning through elite female coach mentoring 'in context'. The following section will provide an overview of the field of contemporary mentoring practice.

Mentoring and career development

Mentoring occurs over a period of time and is often a mechanism used to support organisational change (Kram, 1985). Weaver and Chelladurai (2002, p. 25) suggest the process of mentoring is where a 'more experienced person (mentor) serving as a role model, provides guidance and support to a developing novice (protégé), and sponsors that individual's career progress'. Mentoring has been widely acknowledged as an important educational approach that can play a significant role in an individual's career development and advancement within an organisation (Allen & Eby, 2010; Chambers, 2018; Fletcher & Mullen, 2012; Ragins & Kram, 2007). The role of the mentor is to provide career-related, psychosocial and role model support, and to share knowledge and experience which aims to guide mentee learning in context (Higgins & Kram, 2001).

More recently, there has been an increase in empirical scholarly work examining mentoring within the field of sports coaching (Jones, Harris & Miles, 2009). This is because mentoring has the potential to support coach learning in real-world situations (e.g. Bloom, 2013; Bloom, Durand-Bush, Schinke & Salmela, 1998; Chambers, 2015, 2018; Cushion, 2006; Griffiths & Armour, 2012; Groom & Sawiuk, 2018; Potrac, 2015; Sawiuk, Taylor & Groom, 2016, 2017). Mentoring within sports coaching assumes informal unmediated discussion, where a coach may seek out the advice of a more experienced mentor to assist with a practice dilemma or as part of a mandatory formal mediated mentoring meeting, often as part of an assessment support activity (Sawiuk et al., 2016, 2017). Within the context of sports coaching, the 'practical wisdom' coaches gain from working *in practice* is often reported as being more popular than coaches' experiences of formal coach education (Stoszkowski & Collins, 2016). As a result of working with others, coaches are exposed to contextualised traditions, habits, rules, cultures and practices (Cushion et al., 2003; Merriam, 1983). In many formal coach mentoring programmes, which aim to develop coach learning, mentoring *in practice* often includes in-situ, episodic mentor observations of the mentee. However, even when coaches practise in their own environment, the assessment of the coach is still often aligned to the institutional agenda of the formalised coach education programme and mentoring scheme (Sawiuk et al., 2016). This may include, for example, perceived coaching workforce demographic needs (e.g. an increase in target populations), qualification targets (e.g. number of coaches holding certain awards), unrealistic assessment requirements (e.g. specific numbers of players involved within sessions, space requirements, systems of play and tactical decision making), notions of coaching effectiveness, prescriptive process models outlining the 'right ways to coach' and uncritical social reproduction (Cushion, 2006; Cushion et al., 2003; Jones et al., 2009; Sawiuk et al., 2016, 2017). Therefore, the need to critically challenge existing formal mentoring programmes, even with in-situ coaching observations and assessments, remains an important issue within coach education to improve the *education* of coaches.

Gender and mentoring: implications for sports coaching

Within the context of sports coaching, the development journey for a female coach is far from unproblematic and equitable. For example, female coaches experience a lack of coaching opportunities, developmental support, meaningful coach education and guidance from Governing Bodies (GB), as well as experiencing masculine cultural and behavioural norms, within an environment which oppresses gender ideology (Lewis et al., 2018; Norman, 2008, 2010). As a result, female coaches have reported a 'sense of being second best', where they are subjected to structural and practice inequality within the coaching profession (Lewis et al., 2018; Norman, 2008, 2010). Thus, female coaches in positions of power and leadership are scarce and overall there remains an underrepresentation of women in the coaching workforce (Norman, 2008, 2010). Norman (2008) and Lewis et al. (2018) explain that the current coaching profession and system of education within the UK are 'failing women coaches' and they demand an 'avenue for change'. In particular, female coaches who aspire to work at the highest level are met with the additional challenges of access to elite coaching environments and the problematic 'sense of isolation' in their coach development journey (Sawiuk & Groom, 2018; Lewis et al., 2018). In addition, female coaches need to navigate their way through a gendered and racialised discourse in coach education and coaching practice, which positions these 'surviving' female coaches as 'othered.' This subsequently highlights the importance of high profile, visible female coaches and educator role models to aspiring female coaches (Harvey, Voelker, Cope & Dieffenbach, 2018; Norman & Rankin-Wright, 2016; Rankin-Wright, Hylton & Norman, 2017).

Indeed, mentoring as an educational support mechanism is not without its gendered challenges. For example, the early work of Kram (1985) highlighted the complexity of managing cross-gendered mentorships, if the organisation wishes to benefit. Specifically, areas which might need to be considered are the commonalities between the mentee and mentor, shared experience and the manner in which the mentee–mentor relationship is initiated (Ragins, 1997; Scandura & Williams, 2001). Moreover, Acosta and Carpenter (2012) outlined the importance of female role models in leadership and mentor roles for female mentees, which may positively impact female coach career development. Currently, there is a lack of female high-performance coaches in comparison to the influx of male coaches within women's sport (White, Schempp, McCullick, Berger & Elliott, 2017). A contributing factor might be the lack of females in positions of power or leadership who can offer same-sex mentoring, guidance and support (Wickman & Sjodin, 1997). This may play a significant role in the lack of high-performance female coaches within sports coaching contexts. Furthermore, particularly within sports coaching, there is a lack of empirical attention examining the importance of gender in mentee-mentor pairing, and how this may influence the quality, development and outcomes of mentoring relationships (Ragins, 1997). Indeed, the work of Lockwood (2006) highlighted that female mentees acknowledge the desire for more vocational support, psychosocial support and role modelling than males in mentoring relationships. Moreover, within the business context, Gibson (2004) highlighted the importance for female mentees to have access to female mentors who are role models and are better able to simplify the translation of 'what works for me?' despite the fact that there are fewer women within these roles.

The following section provides an analysis of Lois' coach mentoring experiences as an elite coach, with the aim of illuminating the importance and effectiveness of different types of mentoring support on her learning journey.

Mentoring in practice: international youth football

Mentee biography

Lois Fidler, a UEFA Pro and FA Elite Licence holder, has accumulated a wealth of coaching knowledge and experience over her 25-year coaching career. In addition to this, she has completed a BSc Sport Science degree at the University of Greenwich and an MSc Sports Coaching degree at Brunel University. Her previous roles have included FA Women's National Player Development Centre Manager, FA Women's National Coach for the England U17, Hampshire FA Technical Director, Southampton FC Technical Director, Associate Lecturer in High Performance Coaching at Southampton Solent University and FA Coach Mentor. As the U17s National Head Coach, Lois led the team to their first FIFA World Cup semi-final in 2008. Whilst Lois was working towards her UEFA Advanced Licence (UEFA A) and learning her 'craft' within the elite female pathway at a London-based Centre of Excellence (now Regional Talent Clubs), she was identified by the FA Female Coach Mentoring programme as a 'female coach with potential'. As part of the formal FA mentoring initiative, Lois had regular exposure to international football across all age groups, from the U15s to the England senior team, where her contextualised learning and development were transformational. As a candidate on the FA Female Coach Mentoring programme, Lois was allocated two male mentors who provided in-situ support at her club.

Early experiences of mentoring: practice

I was allocated my first mentor, Walt (pseudonym). I didn't particularly enjoy it. I didn't really understand where I was at, which was understandable ... so I would go to meet him. Because of geography and accessibility it became quite difficult because he was based in east London and I was based in west London … I'm not sure that was really the right fit. I was then allocated my second mentor, David (pseudonym), and I found it pressured, not very organic when you have someone coming into your environment intermittently to watch you and assess you. I found that tricky. He was probably more on my level, more patient, a little bit less male; I hope I haven't just degenderised David there. He was a better fit for me. When I was working with Walt and David to try and deliver sessions that are topic based at my club, this is just my opinion, coaching courses, I don't feel capacity built me to understand about coaching philosophy or playing philosophy and about the technical detail that goes with that. It's more the design of the session, so those topics and themes I don't think I truly understood them; 'coach a team to defend deep to counter attack' or something, it's just a title.

Contextual mentoring and the importance of role models: practice

Hayley and Melissa (pseudonyms) were two significant role models to me, but there were bits and pieces I loved, really loved and respected about both of them, love is probably a strong word but admired, and it took me a while again to fathom that it's not about being the next Melissa or Hayley, it's about finding the best version of me in all of that … Both Melissa and Hayley had considerably more experience than me. Melissa's emotional intelligence and authenticity as a leader is incredible, her ability to read the group, intuition, technical detail, tactical knowledge, her ability to anticipate challenge, ahhh, just off the scale, just incredible. Hayley's tactical knowledge, her balls, I have to say she's got balls of steel, she protected us a lot for a while, she did a lot for us, in terms of getting us involved and being in that position of power and influence is not easy in an environment which was pretty unforgiving. She's a fantastic coach, knowledgeable, and I respect the fact she believed and invested in me. I got to be exposed to Hayley and Melissa on a regular basis as a national assistant coach, that more informal feedback, regularly … when I was on the road with the national team I was also learning about ways of playing, a formation, a strategy that made more sense in context of the titles I was given, for example 'defending from the front'. I was learning about defending from the front in the context of the under 19s defending from the front. But I was learning from Melissa and co about the international coaching and playing philosophy that was linked to that and the detail that came with it, and it made more sense to me, and I made mistakes but then I was able to have more time because I was with them 24/7 on the road, to actually sit down and unpick it with Melissa and the tactics board. I felt there was more patience and more opportunity for me to have that one-to-one time, that relationship with Melissa particularly. I didn't feel dumb by asking questions, when sometimes I do … Melissa and Hayley were present, I spent a huge amount of time with them; because of the opportunities I had, I got to go on the road and spend time with them, in different capacities. It's bigger than just going to a pitch and watching someone emotionlessly deliver a session, based on a topic. There was no context to it, coaches struggle in my environment to bring the curriculum to life. There is a difference between putting on a session and putting on a session that's for players and the coaches, to paint pictures and see pictures, and make decisions and bits and pieces that will impact. Those people, Melissa and Hayley, I got to see the session, I saw before the session, the problems, the games, the challenges in games, how we were going to solve the problem, the meetings before we went onto the pitch, the discussions, what was delivered on the pitch from a physical point of view. The way our information and feedback was framed, led, the meeting after the session, the detail on players, what next? Post-match briefings and their content.

I want to explore the word context again. The relationship and the context of what we were delivering and the emotions that are attached to it are grounded by that anchor which is 'you've got this group of players of which there are 18 who need to play in these 3 games or we have got 30 players or a broader squad or whatever and we have to take them on a journey to get to a point where we can qualify for this competition to give the players more exposure and give them the best chance of becoming a senior international'. There is that attachment emotionally to something that's bigger than you are, rather than a session in isolation. It also links to the journey you're on, why am I doing this? The what, the why the where and the how. I felt like I was part of something bigger than 'I've got to pass this course by being able to deliver this session'. For me personally I found I benefited from having that attachment; if I can better understand the playing philosophy and the technical detail that I can impart on these players and they can more effectively function as individuals and a team to provide a performance to give us the best possible chance of achieving whatever it is we want to achieve, then I know I'm heading in the right direction.

Early experiences of mentoring: theory

Lois problematised travel/geography, mentor–mentee matching and *'topic based'* in-situ visits, and commented on the nature of the gendered characteristics of the mentor. Importantly, the work of Norman (2008) highlighted the issues surrounding the development of female coaches within the UK (e.g. dominant masculine culture, not being adequately educated or supported, a lack of coaching opportunities, inappropriate female support structures) which contribute towards a gendered and unequal coaching structure. Thus, these environments can isolate the female coach, which creates a lack of confidence and demotivation to continue career development (Norman, 2013). Therefore, the formal mentoring programme can provide female coaches with much needed guidance and support. However, Lois discussed the *dysfunctional* and functional nature of mentee–mentor matching in the formal programme, which at times has largely been linked to availability rather than suitability (Fletcher, 2000). As a result, Lois experienced some *difficulty* during her mentoring relationship with *Walt*: for example, different personalities, work style and accessibility (Scandura & Pellegrini, 2007). Similarly, Ragins and Kram (2007) reported that the most effective mentoring relationships are built on similar interests or demographics, for example, gender, age, experience or commonalities. Therefore, if the mentee–mentor matching process is carefully considered, these mentorships are likely to have a stronger functional starting point within the initiation process. As a result, sports governing bodies must consider where the organisational aim coincides with the mentee-coach's personal ambition, which in turn will inform the allocation of right mentor and appropriate support at the right time in an attempt to satisfy the mentee's needs.

Additionally, Lois outlined how the institutional agenda and promotion of intermittent '*topic based sessions*' contributed to a lack of authenticity, detached from coaching philosophy and contextualised consideration. These findings reflect the work of Sawiuk et al. (2016) where the assessment-driven focus of the mentoring in practice had a negative impact on the mentee's bespoke learning and fulfilment.

Contextual mentoring and the importance of role models: theory

As part of the formal mentoring programme Lois was exposed to the international environment. 'Coaches of influence' Hayley and Melissa were described as informal mentors who were important role models. Lois acknowledges the importance of female role models within the international coaching environment and their accompanying attributes, although it took time to become the best version of herself. Additionally, the mentors in the multiple mentor framework possessed different skills which allowed Lois to access different types of knowledge from different mentors, for example Melissa's emotional intelligence and Hayley's tactical knowledge. Lois further discussed the importance of contextualised and authentic exposure to mentor role models. The mentoring relationship Lois had with Melissa and Hayley offered extensive amounts of time, with one-to-one bespoke support, open and honest in nature, built on mutual trust and respect, which Bloom (2013) and Colley, Hodkinson and Malcolm (2003) state are key components of successful mentoring. In addition, these relationships, within the context of working towards a common goal, encompassed an emotional, caring element. The power of effective mentoring in this case study was learner-centred situated learning. Chambers, Templin and McCullick (2015) stated 'effective mentoring relationships are reliant on context' (p. 13), although it is important to note that coaches can perhaps become socialised into a methodical culture, unwritten rules and expectations within an environment (Cushion, 2015), which at times can restrict personal coaching pedagogy. Lois highlights the significance of mentoring within the international environment from her role models, and acknowledges her emotional investment in the goal of 'long-term' player and personal development. The mentoring process here allowed Lois the opportunity to frame and re-frame her contextual experiences and develop wisdom-in-action (e.g. during pre-session briefings, practical delivery, post-session briefings and strategy meetings). This provided Lois with the opportunity to receive support and guidance through contextualised interactions with her mentors (Cushion, 2015). The mentors were, within context, able to provide appropriate and realistic challenges with guidance and support, which enabled Lois to constantly evaluate her coaching performance. As a result, the articulation of professional knowledge and international coaching experience provided an effective environment for situated learning.

Bandura's (1976, 1986) social learning theory suggests that modelling might consist of the psychological matching of cognitive skills, attitudes, actions and patterns of behaviour between a person and an observing individual. Lois described her mentors Hayley and Melissa as 'significant role models', which is considered an important element of the identification phase of mentoring. Role models within organisations can contribute to career success and individuals achieving their goals (Gibson, 2004, p. 268), although little research exists that explores the concept of role models and their contribution to personal develop-ment within mentoring relationships. Gibson (2004) defined role model as a cognitive construction based on the attributes of people in social roles that an individual perceives to be similar to himself or herself to some extent and desires to increase their perceived similarity to by emulating those attributes (p. 134).

Lois describes the attributes of both role models, Melissa and Hayley, whom she 'really loved' due to the quality of developmental support provided, and of the learning and self-actualisation (Higgins & Kram, 2001). Bandura's (1976, 1986) work outlined the importance of modelling in learning. In the inter-national coaching environment. Lois specifically identified the importance of seeing the actions of others (e.g. 'I got to see the session, I saw before the ses-sion, the problems, the games, the challenges in games'), rules of behaviour (e.g. 'emotional intelligence and authenticity as a leader is incredible, her ability to read the group, intuition, technical detail, tactical knowledge, her ability to anticipate challenge'), and guidelines (e.g. 'ways of playing, a formation, a strategy, playing philosophy and the technical detail'). Thus, this exposure and insight provided Lois with the confidence she was 'heading in the right direc-tion' on her coaching journey.

Recommendations for mentoring in practice

This chapter concludes with a number of considerations for effective and con-textualised mentoring in practice, although it is important to acknowledge that every coach's development journey within a high-performance environment is shaped by a unique, personal experience (Mallett, Rynne & Dickens, 2013):

1) This chapter illustrates the disadvantage of intermittent and decontextualised mentoring for the learning experience of a coach mentee. Lois highlighted a number of issues, which included assessment-driven mentoring and a lack of contextual understanding. They failed to take into account the coach/club philosophy and thus lacked meaningful impact upon coach development. Therefore, GBs deploying formal mentoring programmes must consider how

they can provide access for female coaches to high-performance coaching environments. This might, for example, include opportunities for shadowing senior coaches, acting as an assistant coach, study visits to high-performance clubs and national teams, and increasing the number of female coaches that are able to access international training camps.

2) GBs should consider how to overcome some of the current challenges female coaches face within coach mentoring programmes and initiate a strategic workforce drive to increase the number of qualified female coaches, female mentors and female coach educators. This chapter highlights the importance of female role models to Lois' learning, motivation, inspiration and process of discovering self-concept (Gibson, 2004), framed within the role of an international youth performance coach. Therefore, formal mentoring programmes must provide access to different types of mentors who can positively impact the mentee's ability to engage with the self-actualisation process and learning, and provide inspiration. This recommendation follows the guidance of Gunderman and Houk (2017) who suggest female role models allow other females to 'imagine themselves there', which can open career opportunities (p. 231).

3) GBs should carefully consider the process of mentee-mentor matching within formalised programmes. Perhaps the construction of informal 'meet and greets' would provide a space where powerful mentorships are formed on a foundation of mutual identification and value (Armour, 2015). Furthermore, mentoring relationships *in practice* are most effective when they are sensitive to individual and contextualised factors such as gender (Darling, Bogat, Cavell, Murphy & Sánchez, 2006).

4) Finally, this chapter highlights the importance of effective mentoring relationships which encompass high levels of psychosocial career support, where mentors use idiosyncratic mentoring pedagogy (Chandler, Kram & Yip, 2011). Therefore, within the context of sports coaching the mentor must consider the wider club or organisational philosophy, strategy and tactical focus, which will aid the mentee to draw meaningful contextual conclusions for their own practice.

References

Acosta, R. V., & Carpenter, L. J. (2012). Women in intercollegiate sport: A longitudinal, national study thirty-five year Update 1922–2012. Unpublished manuscript. Retrieved February 13, 2012, from www.acostacarpenter.org.

Allen, T. D., & Eby, L. T. (2010). *The Blackwell handbook of mentoring a multiple perspectives approach.* New Jersey: Wiley Blackwell.

Allison, W., Abraham, A., & Cale, A. (2015). *Advances in coach education and development: From research to practice.* London: Routledge.

Armour, K. (2015). Mentoring and professional development. In F. Chambers (Ed.), *Mentoring in physical education and sports coaching* (pp. 9–18). London: Routledge.

Bandura, A. (1976). *Social learning theory.* Englewood Cliffs, NJ: Prentice-Hall.

Bandura, A. (1986). *Social foundations of thought and action: A social cognitive theory.* Englewood Cliffs, NJ: Prentice-Hall.

Bloom, G. A. (2013). Mentoring for sport coaches. In P. Potrac, W. Gilbert, & J. Denison (Eds.), *Routledge handbook of sports coaching* (pp. 476–485). London: Routledge.

Bloom, G. A., Durand-Bush, N., Schinke, R. J., & Salmela, J. H. (1998). The importance of mentoring in the development of coaches and athletes. *International Journal of Sport Psychology, 29,* 267–281.

Chambers, F. (Ed.). (2015). *Mentoring in physical education and sports coaching.* London: Routledge.

Chambers, F. (Ed.). (2018). *Learning to mentor in sports coaching: A design thinking approach.* London: Routledge.

Chambers, F., Templin, T., & McCullick, B. (2015). Mentoring: A primer. In F. Chambers (Ed.), *Mentoring in physical education and sports coaching* (pp. 9–18). London: Routledge.

Chandler, D. E., Kram, K. E., & Yip, J. (2011). An ecological systems perspective on mentoring at work: A review and future prospects. *Academy of Management, 5*(1), 519–570.

Chesterfield, G., Potrac, P., & Jones, R. (2010). 'Studentship' and 'impression management' in an advanced soccer coach education award. *Sport, Education & Society, 15,* 299–314.

Colley, H., Hodkinson, P., & Malcolm, J. (2003). *Informality and formality in learning: A report for the learning skills research centre.* London: Learning and Skills Research Centre.

Cushion, C. J. (2006). Mentoring: Harnessing the power of experience. In R. L. Jones (Ed.), *Sports coach as educator: Re-conceptualising sports coaching* (pp. 128–144). London: Routledge.

Cushion, C. (2015). Mentoring for success in sport coaching. In F. Chambers (Ed.), *Mentoring in physical education and sports coaching* (pp. 155–162). London: Routledge.

Cushion, C. J., Armour, K., & Jones, R. (2003). Coach education and continuing professional development: Experience and learning to coach. *Quest, 55,* 215–230.

Cushion, C. J., Griffiths, M., & Armour, K. (2017 ifirst). Professional coach educators in-situ: A social analysis of practice. *Sport, Education & Society,* doi:10.1080/13573322.2107.1411795.

Cushion, C. J., & Nelson, L. (2013). Coach education and coach learning: Developing the field. In P. Potrac, W. Gilbert, & J. Denison (Eds.), *Routledge handbook of sports coaching* (pp. 359–374). London: Routledge.

Darling, N., Bogat, G. A., Cavell, T. A., Murphy, S. E., & Sánchez, B. (2006). Gender, ethnicity, development, and risk: Mentoring and the consideration of individual differences. *Journal of Community Psychology, 34*(6), 765–779.

Fletcher, S. (2000). *Mentoring in schools: A handbook of good practice.* London: Routledge.

Fletcher, S. J., & Mullen, C. A. (2012). *The sage handbook of mentoring and coaching in education.* London: SAGE.

Gibson, D. E. (2004). Role models in career development: New directions for theory and research. *Journal of Vocational Behaviour, 65,* 134–156.

Gilbert, W. D., & Trudel, P. (2001). Learning to coach through experience: Reflection in model youth sport coaches. *Journal of Teaching in Physical Education, 21,* 16–34.

Griffiths, M., & Armour, K. (2012). Mentoring as a formalized learning strategy with community sports volunteers. *Mentoring and Tutoring: Partnership in Learning, 20*(1), 151–173.

Griffiths, M., Armour, K. M., & Cushion, C. J. (2018 ifirst). Trying to get our message across': Successes and challenges in an evidence-based professional development programme for sports coaches. *Sport, Education & Society,* doi:10.1080/13573322.2016.1182014.

Groom, R., & Sawiuk, R. (2018). Making the transition from the UEFA Advanced Licence to the UEFA Professional Licence (or not). In F. Chambers (Ed.), *Learning to mentor in sports coaching: A design thinking approach* (pp. 56–76). London: Routledge.

Gunderman, R. B., & Houk, J. L. (2017). The importance of role models in increasing women in radiology. *Academic Radiology, 24*(2), 230–231.

Harvey, S., Voelker, D. K., Cope, E., & Dieffenbach, K. (2018). Navigating the leadership labyrinth: Barriers and supports of a woman collegiate coach in a 20-year leadership role. *Sports Coaching Review, 7*(1), 45–62.

Higgins, M. C., & Kram, K. E. (2001). Reconceptualizing mentoring at work: A developmental network perspective. *Academy of Management Review, 26*, 264–288.

Jones, R., & Allison, W. (2014). Candidates' experiences of elite coach education: A longitudinal study. *European Journal of Human Movement, 33*, 110–122.

Jones, R., Armour, K., & Potrac, P. (2004). *Sports coaching cultures: From theory to practice.* London: Routledge.

Jones, R. L. (2006). *Sports coach as educator: Re-conceptualising sports coaching.* London: Routledge.

Jones, R. L., Harris, R., & Miles, A. (2009). Mentoring in sports coaching: A review of literature. *Physical Education and Sport Pedagogy, 14*, 267–284.

Jones, R. L., Potrac, P., Cushion, C., & Ronglan, L. T. (2011). *The sociology of sports coaching.* London: Routledge.

Jones, R. L., & Turner, P. (2006). Teaching coaches to coach holistically: Can problem-based learning (PBL) help? *Physical Education & Sport Pedagogy, 11*, 181–202.

Kram, K. E. (1985). *Mentoring at work: Developmental relationships in organisational life.* Glenview, IL: Scott, Foresman.

Leduc, M., Culver, D., & Werthner, P. (2012). Following a coach education programme: Coaches' perceptions and reported actions. *Sports Coaching Review, 1*, 135–150.

Lewis, C. J., Roberts, S. J., & Andrews, H. (2018). 'Why am I putting myself through this?' Women football coaches' experiences of the Football Association's coach education process. *Sport, Education & Society, 23*, 28–39.

Lockwood, P. (2006). Someone like me can be successful: Do college students need same-gender role models. *Psychology of Women Quarterly, 30*(1), 36–46.

Lyle, J., & Cushion, C. (2010). *Sports coaching: Professionalization and practice.* Edinburgh: Church Livingston, Elsevier.

Lyle, J., & Cushion, C. (2017). *Sports coaching concepts: A framework for coaches' behaviour* (2nd ed.). London: Routledge.

Mallett, C. J., Rynne, S. B., & Dickens, S. (2013). Developing high performance coaching craft through work and study. In P. Potrac, W. Gilbert, & J. Denison (Eds.), *Routledge handbook of sports coaching* (pp. 463–475). London: Routledge.

Mallett, C. J., Trudel, P., Lyle, J., & Rynne, S. B. (2009). Formal vs. informal coach education. *International Journal of Sports Science & Coaching, 4*, 325–334.

Merriam, S. (1983). Mentors and protégés: A critical review of the literature. *Adult Education Quarterly, 33*(3), 161–173.

Nelson, L. J., & Cushion, C. (2006). Reflections in coach education: The case of the national governing body coaching certificate. *The Sport Psychologist, 20*, 174–183.

Nelson, L. J., Cushion, C. J., & Potrac, P. (2006). Formal, nonformal and informal coach learning: A holistic conceptualisation. *International Journal of Sports Science & Coaching, 1*, 247–259.

Nelson, L. J., Cushion, C. J., & Potrac, P. (2013). Enhancing the provision of coach education: The recommendations of UK coaching practitioners. *Physical Education & Sport Pedagogy, 18*(2), 204–218.

Nelson, L., Groom, R., & Potrac, P. (2016). *Learning in sports coaching: Theory and application*. London: Routledge.

Norman, L. (2008). The UK coaching system is failing women coaches. *International Journal of Sports Science and Coaching, 3*(4), 447–476.

Norman, L. (2010). Feeling second best: Elite women coaches' experiences. *Sociology of Sport Journal, 27*(1), 89–104.

Norman, L. (2013). The challenges facing women coaches and the contributions they can make to the profession. *International Journal of Coaching Science, 7*(2), 3–23.

Norman, L., & Rankin-Wright, A. J. (2016). Surviving rather than thriving: Understanding the experiences of women coaches using a theory of gendered social well-being. *International Review for the Sociology of Sport, 8*, 1–27.

Phelan, S., & Griffiths, M. (2018 ifirst). Reconceptualising professional learning through knowing-in-practice: A case study of a coaches high performance centre. *Sport Coaching Review*. doi:10.1080/21640629.2018.1424405.

Potrac, P. (2015). Delivering the FA grassroots club mentoring programme: Mentor's experiences of practice. In W. Allison, A. Abraham, & A. Cale (Eds.), *Advances in coach education and development: From research to practice* (pp. 76–86). London: Routledge.

Potrac, P., Gilbert, W., & Denison, J. (Eds.). (2013). *Routledge handbook of sports coaching*. London: Routledge.

Potrac, P., Nelson, L., Groom, R., & Greenough, K. (2016). Lev Vygotsky: Learning through social interaction. In L. Nelson, R. Groom, & P. Potrac (Eds.), *Learning in sports coaching: Theory and application* (pp. 101–112). London: Routledge.

Ragins, B. R. (1997). Diversified mentoring relationships in organizations: A power perspective. *Academy of Management Review, 22*, 482–521.

Ragins, B. R., & Kram, K. (2007). *The handbook of mentoring at work: Theory, research and practice*. Thousand Oaks, CA: SAGE.

Rankin-Wright, A. J., Hylton, K., & Norman, L. J. (2017). Negotiating the coaching landscape: Experiences of black men and women coaches in the United Kingdom. *International Review for the Sociology of Sport, 54*(5), 603–621.

Sawiuk, R., Taylor, W. G., & Groom, R. (2016 ifirst). Exploring formalized elite coach mentoring programmes in the UK: 'We've had to play the game. *Sport, Education & Society*. doi:10.1080/13573322.2016.1248386.

Sawiuk, R., Taylor, W. G., & Groom, R. (2017). An analysis of the value of multiple mentors in formalised elite coach mentoring programmes in the UK. *Physical Education & Sport Pedagogy, 22*(4), 403–413.

Scandura, T. A., & Pellegrini, E. K. (2007). Workplace mentoring: Theoretical approaches and methodological issues. In T. D. Allen & L. T. Eby (Eds.), *Handbook of mentoring: A multiple perspective approach* (pp. 1–38). Malden, MA: Blackwell.

Scandura, T. A., & Williams, E. A. (2001). An investigation of the moderating effects of gender on the relationships between mentorship initiation and protégé perceptions of mentoring functions. *Journal of Vocational Behavior, 59*(3), 342–363.

Stodter, A., & Cushion, C. (2014). Coaches' learning and education: A case study of cultures in conflict. *Sports Coaching Review, 3*(1), 63–79.

Stoszkowski, J., & Collins, D. (2014). Communities of practice, social learning and networks: Exploiting the social side of coach development. *Sport, Education & Society, 19*, 773–788.

Stoszkowski, J., & Collins, D. (2016). Sources, topics and use of knowledge by coaches. *Journal of Sports Sciences, 34*, 794–802.

Townsend, R., & Cushion, C. (2017). Elite cricket coach education: A Bourdieusian analysis. *Sport, Education & Society, 22*, 528–546.

Trudel, P., Culver, D., & Werthner, P. (2013). Looking at coach development from the coach-learner's perspective. In P. Potrac, W. Gilbert, & J. Denison (Eds.), *Routledge handbook of sports coaching* (pp. 375–387). London: Routledge.

Watts, D. W., & Cushion, C. J. (2017). Coaching journeys: Longitudinal experiences from professional football in Great Britain. *Sports Coaching Review, 6*, 76–93.

Weaver, M., & Chelladurai, P. (2002). Mentoring in intercollegiate athlete administration. *Journal of Sports Management, 16*(2), 96–116.

White, J. S., Schempp, P. G., McCullick, B. A., Berger, B. S., & Elliott, J. M. (2017). Mentoring relationships in sport from the protégé's perspective. *International Journal of Evidence Based Coaching and Mentoring, 15*(1), 152–168.

Wickman, F., & Sjodin, T. (1997). *Mentoring: The most obvious yet overlooked key to achieving more in life than you ever dreamed possible.* New York: McGraw-Hill Professional.

Wright, T., Trudel, P., & Culver, D. (2007). Learning how to coach: The different learning situations reported by ice hockey coaches. *Physical Education & Sport Pedagogy, 12*, 127–144.

6

REFLECTION AND REFLECTIVE PRACTICE

A theoretical and practical guide

Anna Stodter and Ian Minto

Introduction

The ability to reflect and to engage in reflective practice is accepted as a key characteristic of effective and 'expert' sport coaches (e.g. Côté & Gilbert, 2009). As sport coaching strives to become a more professionalised, accredited vocation, the role of reflective practice in enabling competent practitioners to function in a dynamic and complex domain has gained added importance (Huntley, Cropley, Gilbourne, Sparkes & Knowles, 2014). Although it is a ubiquitous feature of pedagogy and often promoted as central to learning and knowledge development in sports coaching, a 'beacon of hope' in solution to a multitude of challenging practice issues (e.g. Carson, 2008), not least in response to the limitations of formal coach education (Hall & Gray, 2016), reflection is a disputed concept. There is no one agreed definition to help practitioners pin down what it really is, what is involved and how to do it effectively. Coaching resources and literature borrow from well-established professions such as nursing and education, and interchangeably refer to reflection, self-reflection, reflective thinking, reflective skills, reflective logs or journals and reflective practice, sometimes alongside experiential learning, reviews and evaluations, with the effect of clouding the core meaning and purpose of reflection (Cushion, 2016; Huntley et al., 2014). Moreover, evidence suggests that the skill of reflecting on practice is hugely challenging for coaches, with limited guidance or exemplar education programmes (e.g. Knowles, Borrie & Telfer, 2005; Knowles, Gilbourne, Borrie & Nevill, 2001; Nelson & Cushion, 2006). Many coaches will likely be familiar with the experience of being expected to submit reflective portfolios as part of formal accreditation, with 'no perceptible support' (Hall & Gray, 2016, p. 367), potentially leading to cursory, superficial or even contrived engagement in the process (Burt & Morgan, 2014; Trelfa & Telfer, 2014). Accordingly, this chapter aims to aid coaching practitioners and students, firstly by examining the practice of a case study UKCC Level 4 qualified coach and coach educator (Ian) in exhibiting and developing reflection, both for himself and in others. Following this, the concept of reflection will be clarified, drawing upon examples from contemporary research to explain how reflective practice supports coaches' wider learning. The application of these key theoretical and practical aspects is integrated in the final section to provide evidence-based recommendations for coaching students and practitioners.

Reflections

The opening lyrics from the song 'Reflections' by Motown group The Supremes are about lost love, but I like to interpret 'you and me' as representing the various comparative versions of me in my professional capacity across the four decades I've been involved in Rugby Coaching and PE teaching. As a practitioner I consider reflective practice to be a very important tool in the learning necessary to examine and transform principles, philosophy, behaviours and conceptual understanding. The following five seminal 'experiences' have had (on reflection) maximum effect on these areas of my work, across my career.

Setting the context: 'unintended consequences of intended action'

I'm in primary school aged seven, and nervous about the impending lesson in the outdoor swimming pool. I hate swimming. The task is to go under water whilst holding the bar at the edge, to gain familiarity and confidence. I fail, and despite being shouted at, still don't do it. The teacher drops a rubber brick next to me and sternly orders me to 'fetch it'. I don't move, and she forcibly pushes my head underwater; I struggle, swallow water and resurface, shaking. For the next sixteen years, I don't go near a swimming pool. I gain a place at St Luke's PE College, but need a 25-metre swimming certificate to secure entry – so I enrol in an adult beginner class at a local pool. It involves eight public sessions, and the indignity and embarrassment I feel as a pretty confident and competent sportsman is only bearable due to my motivation to succeed. I eventually do succeed, and on reflection, across the years and in different contexts, I realise the whole episode shaped my teaching and coaching approach. Firstly, it enabled me to work with a great deal of empathy and understanding for those who are either nervous or have low self-concept in sporting situations. This, I reflect, is also a cornerstone of my preference for 'development coaching' as I refer to it. My 'role frame' in this respect influences which experiences I engage in and reflect upon, as well as pedagogical outcomes. For example, I consider various factors in lack of progress by participants and that these may well be within my control to change, by critically analysing my approach to setting an appropriate climate to maximise learning. This requires careful analysis of individual needs and knowledge required together with the pedagogical approach to be adopted.

Although the learning environment needs to be positive and safe, unlike my early experiences in the pool, I do feel that just being 'engaged' does not necessarily lead to learning or development, and that challenge and a degree of discomfort are vital to improvement. I've recently heard this described as striving to be 'uncomfortably excited', which can apply to coaches as well as athletes.

A roadmap to develop knowledge-in-action (learning)

Reflection offers a roadmap to examine experiences and responses as they occur (reflection-in-action), as well as consciously reviewing, describing, analysing and evaluating past practice, with a view to gaining insight to improve future practice (reflection-on-action). There is also a requirement to understand and connect with one's feelings to release intuition and creativity. As a novice PE teacher and coach I would happily cling to routines and habitual procedures which fulfilled perceived requirements or competencies, but I gradually became aware that 'to teach someone else's lesson or coach someone else's session' was not effective. Early coach education and continuing professional development (CPD) I attended somewhat reinforced this limited approach by offering demonstrations of good practice and to a degree expecting forms of replication. As I gained experience, my reflective discomfort with this led to research, experimentation, higher levels of self-critical analysis and a desire to re-examine practices of my own and others. This has enabled continuous development of personal knowledge-in-action that I can use in specific situations. I am pleased to see that coach education and CPD has now started to embrace this approach too, and consequently on attending such events I now mostly leave with creative and adaptive ideas to try out. Indeed, the championing of 'reflection' is itself a major advancement. Obviously after four decades I do have a huge amount of experience to reflect upon, but I have a continuous determination not to become what I call 'a slave to a drill' nor to 'revert to type'.

Using and adapting frameworks: I was schooled in the three R's, but now I believe in the five R's

The saying 'always be a learner' can summarise my thoughts around developing these links between the learning experience and the knowledge construction that follows it. I have found that reflective frameworks can help with this, albeit with some flexibility. For instance, Reading, (w)Riting and (a)Rithmetic were the staples of my school curriculum but as a 'staff development manager' in addition to teaching, and intent on expanding reflective practice, I was and continue to be influenced by the work of Zeichner and Liston (1996). They identified five levels of reflection for teachers, which I adapted for the context of my role as a rugby coach. This process was not linear and involved the production of notes on sessions and experiences both in teaching and coaching. I note in examining these that the reflections gradually increase in complexity and show evidence of an application of the 5R's below. Notes from CPD sessions attended either as a teacher or rugby coach also show a determination to consider how any knowledge gained might be utilised across situational contexts together with reflections on the actions taken. My role as a mentor and coach educator for a National Governing Body has also provided much material to stimulate iterative reflection, adaptation and critical analysis. The 5R's I use are:

- Rapid reflection – immediate, ongoing and automatic action by the teacher/ coach.
- Repair – in which a thoughtful teacher/coach makes decisions to alter their behaviour in response to learners' cues.
- Review – when a teacher/coach thinks about, discusses or writes about some element of their teaching.
- Research – when a teacher/coach engages in more systematic and sustained thinking over time, perhaps by collecting data or reading research. For example, the widespread use of video technology and performance data is one area that can impact greatly on coaching practice and the availability of feedback.
- Retheorizing and reformulating – the process by which a teacher/coach critically examines their own practice, behaviour and philosophy in the light of new academic theories or simply through communities of practice.

'Reflections of you and me': supporting reflective conversations

Mentoring coaches, and specifically encouraging and developing reflective practice, is an aspect of my current work in the wide field of coach and referee education that I really value. A mentor is often categorised as a 'critical friend' and in my experience can definitely assist in developing reflective practice by providing adequate support, resources, time and creating or highlighting opportunities and methods for reflection including the skills of critical analysis and the confidence to utilise it. I have supported reflective practice from all aspects of the process, including designing an action research scheme in a large sixth form college to encourage staff induction and mentoring, and the 'team/group' meetings engaged in were valuable in enabling collective reflective conversations. Translating this to rugby coaching, I have found the shared reflective process to significantly assist progress. Reflections are clearly internal processes to contemplate and develop cognitive structures leading to actions, but I have found the verbalising of these with another to be most valuable. The process falls on a continuum between formal and informal, with the aim of making sense of experiences and thus transforming coaching knowledge-in-action and behaviour. It is also applicable to the development of technical and tactical aspects of the coaching craft. However, I have learned that in order for this to occur, a crucial quality for critical friends or mentors is that of effective questioning and active listening. Key elements are the type, style, timing and frequency of questions, together with the ability to listen and give full attention to the answers received (e.g. Mitchell, 2014; UK Coaching, 2018). Clearly, questioning can be adapted for a variety of contexts, from challenging thinking through triggering self-awareness to developing self-expression. To paraphrase Kline (1999), most people aren't listening ... they are preparing to speak; so listening too needs to be authentic, non-judgemental and practised. For example, one question I use and reflect upon in my context is 'are there players in your squad you have not listened to?'

Problematising reflective practice ... where next?

My final thoughts on development as a reflective practitioner stem from studying an MSc in sports sociology. Reflective practice is interest-serving and it is important to consider what (and whose) interests might be served through the process (Ghaye, 2011). I therefore remain interested to investigate conceivable concerns about 'reflection' and its potential intended and unintended effects both on myself and my players. These can cover the realms of pedagogical, professional, conceptual and ethical issues. One example is the way that individual coaches' own self-awareness, knowledge and beliefs can limit their reflections, carrying the danger of perpetually reproducing practices and stifling innovation and progress (e.g. Hall & Gray, 2016). Critical reflection (retheorising and reformulating) is important in this regard. To extend this, it is worthwhile exploring how learning through reflective practice transfers into the development of a reflective practitioner. I have found that sports coaching is a work environment in which there can be a connection between learning (through reflection) and a conscious effort to apply this learning, but there remain many contextual and social constraints. In addition, reflective practice can be a written and cognitive process but there are clearly issues in recognising or indeed measuring the effects of reflective practice.

The key aspects of reflective practice for sports coaches illustrated in this reflective account will now be identified and explained in more theoretical detail, with links to the implications for coaches' wider learning.

Definitions of reflection

As alluded to above, the terms reflection and reflective practice generically refer to internal cognitive processes that act as a bridge between experience and learning (Lyle & Cushion, 2017). Although both reflection and practice are contested concepts, it is generally accepted that they are linked, as through reflection (often described as structured or organised thinking), we can develop new insights and understandings that help us to improve our actions (doing) (Ghaye, 2011). Theorising in the area draws significant influence from the work of educational pragmatist John Dewey (1910), who proposed that learning from experience occurs through a process of reflective thinking or inquiry; and later Donald Schön (1983, 1987), who introduced key ideas such as the temporal aspects of reflection-*in*-action (i.e. thinking while doing) and reflection-*on*-action (i.e. thinking after the event). Reflective practice is popularly promoted as a way of enhancing learning, knowledge and effective functioning in sports coaching, based on several years of research and practice in established professions where practitioners rely on experiential decision making and judgement, such as nursing, education and management (Knowles, Gilbourne, Cropley & Dugdill, 2014). Given these broad foundations from different domains, generating varying and at times contradictory interpretations, a number of myths and misunderstandings resonate around the concept of reflective practice. For instance, there is a tendency to see it as simply a matter of pausing for thought, conducting superficial reviews or 'navel gazing', yet reflective practice should go much further than these literal common-sense interpretations of loosely defined 'thinking about practice' (Ghaye, 2011; Thompson & Thompson, 2008). The following definition may be a useful starting point for sports coaches, as it brings together key characteristics commonly reported in definitions relevant to professionals working in sport and exercise. Knowles et al. (2014) proposed that reflective practice is:

> A purposeful and complex process that facilitates the examination of experience by questioning the whole self and our agency within the context of practice. This examination transforms experience into learning, which helps us to access, make sense of and develop our knowledge-in-action in order to better understand and/or improve practice and the situation in which it occurs.
>
> *(p. 10)*

Reflective practice and knowledge-in-action

Reflection is conceptualised as part of a learning process, and it appears at the heart of all experience-based learning theories (Gilbert & Trudel, 2001). A common thread among different theories is that reflective practice enables learning and knowledge construction embedded in the particular activity and context (i.e. knowledge-in-action). This is important for sports coaches because as Cropley, Miles and Nichols (2016, p. 13) put it, 'the map is not the territory'. In other words, theoretical, professional, technical-rational knowledge about things (the map) does not always match up neatly with the path required to negotiate the dynamic, ambiguous, situation-specific and socially derived practice issues that coaches encounter day-to-day (the territory). While the former, often found at the forefront of formal coach education programmes, provides clarity and a rational route 'from A to B' based on decontextualised knowledge, the latter requires that practitioners transform their experiences to develop tacit, situated knowledge that 'works' in context, bridging the gap between theory and practice (Cropley et al., 2016). Therefore reflective practice can generate understanding that enables coaches to implement relevant strategies directly resonating with their

personal practical needs in context. However, we cannot assume that such construction of coaches' knowledge 'just happens' (Knowles et al., 2001). For meaningful learning to take place, practitioners must actively engage in reflection that
results in the excavation of knowledge embedded within the experience (Cropley
et al., 2016). Indeed, it has been suggested that there are different levels or
'depths' of reflection, and investment in *critical reflection*, which questions and prob-
lematises social, political, moral and ethical meanings is required in order to effectively learn and change practices (Cassidy, Jones & Potrac, 2016; Hall & Gray,
2016; Knowles et al., 2005). As mentioned in the opening commentary, it seems
that some level of discomfort is needed for this to occur.

Reflective practice and learning

Despite the supposed benefits, there is limited direct real-world evidence linking
reflective practice with effectiveness in coach learning or practice (Hall & Gray,
2016; Lyle & Cushion, 2017). In the field of sports coaching, similar to wider
coach learning, reflection has tended to be dominated by uncritically recycled
definitions and simplified 'step-by-step' models or prescriptions *for* practice from
other domains (e.g. 'Plan-Do-Review'; Crisfield, 2009). Yet coaching and
learning to coach is increasingly understood as a complex and situation-specific
endeavour that consequently would benefit from context-specific and evidence-
based frameworks to more appropriately guide practice (Stodter & Cushion,
2017). Two relevant models *of* coaches' learning provide insights into the role of
reflection, grounded in empirical evidence from youth sport coaches (Gilbert &
Trudel, 2001; Stodter & Cushion, 2017). Both frameworks support Schön's
(1983) ideas in demonstrating the way that coaches learn from experiences
through cyclical 'reflective conversations', which consist of continuous adaptation of coaching strategies, experimentation and evaluation, framed by personal
biography, values or approaches to coaching. Through this research, coaches
were seen to 'try out' different coaching strategies or 'bits' of knowledge (i.e.
knowledge concepts, perhaps encountered through formal education), which
become conceptions as they are applied to a particular context meaningful to
the practitioner, their meanings becoming embedded in experiences of using it
(c.f. knowledge-in-action). Coaches then made judgements of 'what works' in
practice, and adopted, rejected, or adapted and experimented with refined strategies in a continuous reflective feedback loop (Stodter & Cushion, 2017).

Evidence suggests the importance of coaches' personal openness and contextual factors to the 'quality' of this often tacit reflective practice process. Individual
subscription to 'right' and 'wrong' ways of coaching, and more absolute ideas
about knowledge tend to go hand-in-hand with learning as simple reproduction
of accepted norms. As people begin to recognise knowledge as provisional and
relative, evidence is used to reason among alternatives (Entwistle & Peterson,
2004) – in other words, experimenting with and critically evaluating new ideas
in practice based on 'what works'. Moreover, since coaching practitioners may

be held accountable for maximising performance success and winning, it is perhaps understandable that they can be 'reluctant to take risks or depart too far from the status quo of accepted practice' (Light & Robert, 2010, p. 113). As alluded to above, coaches' reflective cycles of learning are bound up with practice that often takes place in contexts subject to power relationships and anti-intellectual beliefs. Consequently, while learning situated in everyday practice is essential, coaching environments are not often conducive to generating new ideas, supporting active experimentation or facilitating transfer from knowledge to implementation (Stodter & Cushion, 2016). Additionally, access to respected and trusted peers has been found to be critical in facilitating the reflective process (Gilbert & Trudel, 2001).

Recommendations

Despite some enduring concerns about adopting reflective practice without question, initial evidence from the sport and exercise literature does suggest that it is a highly skilled activity which can be developed over time, with benefits for coaching practitioners (Knowles et al., 2001, 2014). Based on the preceding discussion of literature and experiences from the field of sports coaching, we offer the following recommendations which, like reflective practice itself, sit at the interface between theory and practice:

1) Understanding personal biography and role frame is a valuable starting point, as this guides and influences what issues are seen as meaningful and worth reflecting on, as well as how they are interpreted (Stodter & Cushion, 2016).
2) Reflective practice needs to be authentically embedded in coaching practice (Cropley et al., 2016; Stodter & Cushion, 2016). Ideally, this can be enhanced with the development of contexts open to experimentation, as reflection is most likely to be found where there is 'a high priority on flexible procedures, differentiated responses, qualitative appreciation of complex processes, and decentralised responsibility for judgement and action' (Schön, 1983, p. 338).
3) Frameworks can help guide reflective practice, for example in providing a structure to examine reflective feedback loop processes of strategy generation, experimentation, evaluation and adaptation and/or rejection (Gilbert & Trudel, 2001; Stodter & Cushion, 2017). Nevertheless, models have their limitations and adaptations for individuals' own needs and contexts (through reflective practice!) may be most effective.
4) 'Making sense' of experiences is a key stage in most frameworks, which suggests that mere description is not effective as a means of learning. Reflection should be specific and where possible include a critical interpretation of actions (Lyle & Cushion, 2017). Central to the critical process is a need to question what coaches do and why (Knowles et al., 2001). This

can allow coaches to make judgements that are meaningful within particular situations and challenge, rather than reinforce accepted beliefs and practices (Partington, Cushion, Cope & Harvey, 2015).

5) Evidence consistently demonstrates that video-based feedback is a tool which provides powerful stimulation to recall events and potential for deep learning in coaching. With constant improvements in readily available portable technology, video can flexibly facilitate examination of 'what really works' and explicate tacit cognitive processes vital for the implementation of knowledge-in-action (Carson, 2008; Partington et al., 2015; Stodter & Cushion, 2017; Trudel, Gilbert & Tochon, 2001).

6) There are limits to learning alone. Reflection appears to be useful in combination with mentoring, for instance in facilitating open 'reflective conversations' on how to apply learning to specific contexts. The shared reflection process does depend on a shared vocabulary and underpinning understanding of the coaching process (Lyle & Cushion, 2017).

7) Effective involvement of others through reflective conversations relies on questioning (which directs growth) and listening, alongside discussions around professional values. Ghaye (2011) provides several useful ideas and examples around reflective conversations from the educational domain.

8) Reflection is one part of a wider learning process, and therefore practitioners should aim to make it a continuous, integrated activity (Lyle & Cushion, 2017).

Importantly, more direct evidence is needed to further our understanding of the impact of reflection *in* and *on* practice in coaching, in order to advance this taken-for-granted process and maximise effectiveness (Hall & Gray, 2016; Huntley et al., 2014; Lyle & Cushion, 2017). A principal challenge continues to be ensuring that individual coaches are supported to 'get' reflection and use it as intellectually curious professionals (Trelfa & Telfer, 2014).

References

Burt, E., & Morgan, P. (2014). Barriers to systematic reflective practice as perceived by UKCC level 1 and level 2 qualified rugby union coaches. *Reflective Practice, 15*(4), 468–480.

Carson, F. (2008). Utilizing video to facilitate reflective practice: Developing sports coaches. *International Journal of Sports Science & Coaching, 3*(3), 381–390.

Cassidy, T., Jones, R., & Potrac, P. (2016). *Understanding sports coaching: The pedagogical, social and cultural foundations of coaching practice* (3rd ed.). Abingdon: Routledge.

Côté, J., & Gilbert, W. (2009). An integrative definition of coaching effectiveness and expertise. *International Journal of Sports Science & Coaching, 4*(3), 307–323.

Crisfield, P. (2009). *Analysing your coaching*. Leeds: Coachwise Business Solutions/The National Coaching Foundation.

Cropley, B., Miles, A., & Nichols, T. (2016). Learning to learn: The coach as a reflective practitioner. In J. Wallis & J. Lambert (Eds.), *Becoming a sports coach* (pp. 11–25). Abingdon: Routledge.

Cushion, C. J. (2016). Reflection and reflective practice discourses in coaching: A critical analysis. *Sport, Education and Society*, *23*(1), 82–94.

Dewey, J. (1910). *How we think*. Boston: D.C. Health & Co.

Entwistle, N. J., & Peterson, E. R. (2004). Conceptions of learning and knowledge in higher education: Relationships with study behaviour and influences of learning environments. *International Journal of Educational Research*, *41*, 407–428.

Ghaye, T. (2011). *Teaching and learning through reflective practice: A practical guide for positive action* (2nd ed.). Abingdon: Routledge.

Gilbert, W., & Trudel, P. (2001). Learning to coach through experience: Reflection in model youth sport coaches. *Journal of Teaching in Physical Education*, *21*, 16–34.

Hall, E., & Gray, S. (2016). Reflecting on reflective practice: A coach's action research narratives. *Qualitative Research in Sport, Exercise and Health*, *8*(4), 365–379.

Huntley, E., Cropley, B., Gilbourne, D., Sparkes, A., & Knowles, Z. (2014). Reflecting back and forwards: An evaluation of peer-reviewed reflective practice research in sport. *Reflective Practice*, *15*(6), 863–876.

Kline, N. (1999). *Time to think: Listening to ignite the human mind*. London: Cassell Illustrated.

Knowles, Z., Borrie, A., & Telfer, H. (2005). Towards the reflective sports coach: Issues of context, education and application. *Ergonomics*, *48*(11), 1711–1720.

Knowles, Z., Gilbourne, D., Borrie, A., & Nevill, A. (2001). Developing the reflective sports coach: A study exploring the processes of reflective practice within a higher education coaching programme. *Reflective Practice: International and Multidisciplinary Perspectives*, *2*(2), 185–207.

Knowles, Z., Gilbourne, D., Cropley, B., & Dugdill, L. (2014). *Reflective practice in the sport and exercise sciences: Contemporary issues*. Abingdon: Routledge.

Light, R., & Robert, J. E. (2010). The impact of game sense pedagogy on Australian rugby coaches' practice: A question of pedagogy. *Physical Education and Sport Pedagogy*, *15*(2), 103–115.

Lyle, J., & Cushion, C. J. (2017). *Sport coaching concepts: A framework for coaching practice* (2nd ed.). Abingdon: Routledge.

Mitchell, J. (2014). Questioning to develop skill [Web log post]. Retrieved from https://coachgrowth.wordpress.com/2014/02/14/questioning-skill/

Nelson, L. J., & Cushion, C. J. (2006). Reflection in coach education: The case of the national governing body coaching certificate. *The Sport Psychologist*, *20*, 174–183.

Partington, M., Cushion, C. J., Cope, E., & Harvey, S. H. (2015). The impact of video feedback on professional youth football coaches' reflection and practice behaviour: A longitudinal investigation of behaviour change. *Reflective Practice*, *16*(5), 700–716.

Schön, D. A. (1983). *The reflective practitioner: How professionals think in action*. Farnham: Ashgate.

Schön, D. A. (1987). *Educating the reflective practitioner*. San Francisco: Jossey-Bass.

Stodter, A., & Cushion, C. J. (2016). Effective coach learning and the processes of coaches' knowledge development: What works? In P. A. Davis (Ed.), *The psychology of effective coaching and management* (pp. 35–52). New York: Nova Science Publishers.

Stodter, A., & Cushion, C. J. (2017). What works in coach learning, how, and for whom? *A Grounded Process of Soccer Coaches' Professional Learning*, *9*(3), 321–338.

Thompson, S., & Thompson, N. (2008). *The critically reflective practitioner*. Basingstoke: Palgrave Macmillan.

Trelfa, J., & Telfer, H. (2014). Keeping the cat alive: 'Getting' reflection as part of professional practice. In Z. Knowles, D. Gilbourne, B. Cropley, & L. Dugdill (Eds.), *Reflective practice in the sport and exercise sciences: Contemporary issues* (pp. 48–53). Abingdon: Routledge.

Trudel, P., Gilbert, W., & Tochon, F. V. (2001). The use of video in the semiotic construction of knowledge and meaning in sport pedagogy. *International Journal of Applied Semiotics*, 2(1–2), 89–112.

UK Coaching. (2018). Let's play 20 questions: Top tips for using questions for athlete-centred coaching [Web log post]. Retrieved from www.ukcoaching.org/blog/let's-play-20-questions-top-tips-using-questions-athlete-centred-coaching

Zeichner, K. M., & Liston, D. P. (1996). *Reflective teaching: An introduction*. Abingdon: Routledge.

7

THE THINK-ALOUD PROGRAMME

Developing reflection in coaches – from practice to theory

Amy Whitehead and Craig Richards

Introduction

Reflection and reflective practice have been criticised within coach education as something that is often neglected or misunderstood (Cushion, 2018; Huntley, Cropley, Gilbourne, Sparkes & Knowles, 2014). Approaches to reflection have also been under scrutiny, with researchers and practitioners calling for more novel and innovative approaches to reflection that emphasise participation (Dixon, Lee & Ghaye, 2013). For example, Dixon et al. (2013), call for more innovative technologies through online social networks, blogs and content sharing sites. Furthermore, Nelson and Cushion (2006) acknowledge that the coaching environment is complex and socially-derived, therefore it may be important to consider how we engage the coach to in reflection-in-action, in addition to reflection-on-action. Such methods to engage in reflection-in-action during live coaching practice may involve reflective conversations or think-aloud (TA) (Stoll, Mullem, Mullem & Beller, 2018).

As reflection and reflective practice has already been covered within Chapter 6, this chapter aims to provide or suggest an alternative approach to reflective practice (the TA programme) by presenting an outline of this approach. A coach's experience of this approach will then be provided, followed by a theoretical explanation to support how this approach can provide coaches with more meaningful learning, where practitioners actively engage in reflection that is directly embedded within their experience.

Think-aloud

TA as a protocol (see Ericsson & Simon, 1993) stems from cognitive psychology. Since the time of Aristotle, 'thinking has been viewed as a temporal sequence of mental events' (Ericsson & Simon, 1993, p. xiii). From this perspective, thought processes can be seen as a sequence of states, which are made up of cognitive processes. This information is retrieved from the long-term memory, and this information is then verbalised and reported orally. Therefore, TA requires a participant to verbalise their thoughts concurrently out loud. TA protocol has been used to understand cognition and cognitive differences between expert and novices in events such as chess (Chase & Simon, 1973), and more recently within a variety of different sports such as golf (Whitehead, Taylor & Polman, 2015, 2016b), cycling (Whitehead et al., 2018), running (Samson, Simpson, Kamphoff & Langlier, 2015), tennis (Swettenham, Eubank, Won & Whitehead, 2018) and snooker (Welsh, Dewhurst & Perry, 2018).

Within coaching, however, the use of TA as a reflective tool is something that is under-explored (Whitehead et al., 2016a). Prior to Whitehead et al. (2016a), TA has been found to support individuals' experiential learning in other disciplines. For example, TA has been used previously implemented in domains such as nursing (Banning, 2008), medicine (Borleffs, Custers, van Gijn & Ten Cate, 2003) and physiotherapy (Atkinson & Nixon-Cave, 2011) to develop clinical reasoning and decision making within these settings. Banning (2008) used TA as an educational tool to develop and assess clinical reasoning in undergraduate nursing students. Banning (2008) adopted the 'think-aloud' seminar (Lee & Ryan-Wenger, 1997), where student nurses were encouraged to verbalise their thoughts as they problem solved a case study or interpreted a statement. This process allowed nurses to become more aware of their decision-making processes, promoted their 'thinking about thinking' (metacognition) and in turn developed their cognitive reasoning skills.

The think-aloud programme

In response to the above, Whitehead et al. (2016a) adopted TA as a tool to develop a coach's ability to reflect-in-action. Kemmis (1985) proposed that reflection is:

> A dialectical process: it looks inwards at our thoughts and thought processes and outward at the situation in which we find ourselves; when we consider the interaction of the internal and external, our reflection orients us for further thought and action. Reflection is thus 'meta thinking' (thinking about thinking) in which we consider the relationship between our thoughts and action in a particular context.
>
> *(p. 141)*

Therefore, it was proposed that asking a coach to verbalise thoughts and think aloud, could in fact promote this very essence of 'meta thinking'. Therefore, Whitehead et al. (2016a) conducted a study with six rugby league coaches, where coaches were trained to use TA within a workshop setting. Following this they were then asked to use TA whilst coaching during one of their usual coaching sessions (over a two-week period). This study aimed to encourage coaches to explain and reflect-in-action as they coached, as described,

> Participants were instructed to verbalize their thoughts as much as possible (Level 3 verbalization) throughout their one-hour coaching session. This included their normal coaching session with additional reflections throughout. For example, participants would give instructions and feedback to their athletes and then step back and verbalize their own thoughts and reflections in action, whenever they felt the need to do so.
>
> *(Whitehead et al., 2016b, p. 272)*

Coaches listened back to their TA audio file and discussed their thoughts and reflections of this in a second workshop. Coaches then used TA a second time as an opportunity to develop this ability to reflect in action further. Please see Whitehead et al. (2016a) for a full overview of this study.

Craig Richards is the Coaching and Education Manager for Saints Helens RFC. Craig leads on the community, junior academy and pathway coaches, in addition to being the current England Women's Rugby League Head coach. Craig is a UKCC level 4 coach and has coached for 18 years at club, regional, national and international level. Previously Craig worked as a national coach education manager for the Rugby Football League and also spent three years as a Coaching systems lead for Olympic Team GB Taekwondo.

Craig has been involved in a TA programme, both as a coach and in a second programme as the Coach Development Manager. The following section of this chapter shows Craig's experiences of this programme.

Craig's reflection of using TA: from a coach and coach developer perspective

Craig as a coach

As a coach, when the TA programme was first introduced to me, I thought it was a refreshing change to see a programme, where a small number of coaches would be delivered to, and receive individualised feedback which is also directly related to their own coaching environment.

I feel reflective practice is a very important part of the coaching process. I truly believe efforts and experiences are wasted if, as a professional, you don't make sense of why you act and behave the way you do. I knew I had some knowledge of reflective practice and its importance to growing as a coach or individual, but I wasn't convinced that it was a strength of mine. In particular, I struggled to take feedback from others unless I perceived them to be a true expert or very experienced practitioner. I have very strong values and beliefs and I always trust my gut feelings, which I also realise can be a weakness as I know I don't know everything, but as a coach I constantly want to learn but only off the best (I very often see experienced coaches make really simple mistakes and offer wrong information, I also see experienced coaches attempt to deliver stuff they don't understand or believe in but don't have the strength to be honest with themselves and challenge). It's in my nature to not accept feedback that goes against my gut feelings and beliefs, this can even be not accepting praise if I don't think it's warranted, needed or evidenced. But with the TA programme, there is no escaping feedback, as I'm actually listening back to myself and critiquing myself, there's no one else to blame in that situation and no way of ignoring some of the mistakes I might make or the ways in which I communicate.

It [the TA programme] made the coaching process more about me, my behaviours my thoughts, why I react the way I do, rather than almost just managing practice and feeding back to and on players, it made me aware and accountable for my coaching practice. I found myself having more silent and focused observation, I was less likely to interrupt the flow of the session now I was reflecting more in the practice.

In one of my sessions it rationalised to me why one player who was struggling to perform at this level, would get more attention off me and nothing but positive feedback, I realised that this individual would often receive constant corrective feedback off others in a bid to improve his performance, so I made an extra effort to adjust my approach and almost be more emotionally supportive. I had never really consciously thought about this until I started using TA.

The key part of the process for me was the feedback that I received from members of the group on my coaching. I am a big advocate of sharing coaching practices and inviting feedback from relevant people. By allowing others to view and listen to my coaching session [this was something Craig implemented himself], this allowed me to receive some rich feedback from the group, which I then implemented within my future sessions. Without the feedback from the group I believe that I may have continued to coach the way I was coaching, with 'rose tinted glasses' on.

Craig as a coach developer

When introducing TA to our coaches, I tried to be particular and get a good mix of coaches with different challenges to attend, but I wasn't convinced the whole group of coaches would fully engage in the programme as previous attempts to have reflective sessions as an academy group have been very challenging. This could be due to coaches' perceptions of reflection and previous reflective practice education has been quite generic.

Culturally I think as a sport we are very poor at reflecting on our own practice: generally coaches become very defensive, almost aggressive, in group or guided reflections. Discussion can turn to banter which leads to coaches feeling as though it's a personal attack when the spotlight is on them. Also convincing coaches it's a development tool to improve their performance and not a disciplinary process of highlighting they are not good enough to coach at this level is something to contend with.

The TA process seemed to first increase knowledge of reflective practice, then in a simple way get the coaches to better understand the TA protocol and be more open to interrogating the what, why and how they coach. It's initially tough for them, as coaches are normally only thinking about the players' performance, we are taught to be player centred so the focus naturally becomes about the players.

Over a number of weeks following the TA programme, it became possible to have short informal interventions during practice where coaches would be more comfortable reflecting in action. Prior to the TA programme the challenges that were evident were linked to getting coaches to reflect on the positives of their delivery. I found coaches more open to talk about what they did wrong and became less fearful of other coaches doubting their ability.

Since the TA Programme, coaches are able to identify both their strengths and weaknesses but also see this as a positive an open process. For example, one of the coaches has commented on his monotone pitch and how this is impacting his session. He has been able to see how to improve and change this and has reported the positive impact this has had on his delivery. Another coach, Sam, has reflected on his role in the coaching group and how the players perceive him as a coach. He is 'Mr. Nice' but he is now questioning whether he is taken seriously by the players and if he should change his approach. He has been able to step back and evaluate both the positives and negatives of this approach of coaching and the impact it has on the group of players he is coaching.

The whole process has definitely helped with the coaches in terms of growing as a coach. Sometimes in coaching, coaches can start to stagnate and deliver the same things in the same way. The programme has now allowed us to have open discussions about what a good coach looks like and what certain players in the squad need from coaches. This was also evidenced in the workshops, where the coaches supported each other and provided feedback on their strengths.

One of the coaches is now doing his Level 3 qualification, and he was originally always defensive if you tried to discuss how he had performed as a coach and would be quite confrontational, but it's notable when I work with him, he now leads a lot of discussion without me prompting or guiding him. I don't think he notices the change but I know it's a massive shift in him. I can also be more critical of his delivery and he now engages in discussing his coaching and his own coaching processes, and seems really aware of other coaches' ways. It is important to note that within the Level 3 RFL coaching qualification there is no longer a reflective practice delivery from an expert, which for me is criminal. This was where I first bought in to how important it is as a coach so as a sport some of our best coaches are now missing a key part of their essential learning.

The workshops (built into the TA programme) promote a non-threatening environment, and its great how coaches actually open up and start to discuss themselves, but also comment on each other's coaching behaviours in the group. As a coach development manager, I work closely with the coaches and try and develop them on a regular basis. This process has also allowed a couple of coaches to challenge (vent) parts of my philosophy and for me to discuss and explain (e.g. some coaches don't believe you can be honest), I also used it to get certain points across (e.g. don't walk past bad practice) coaches were able to challenge this and I was able to explain that this particular point has been a frustration of mine as I feel our job is to improve player performance not babysit players. This may have been a difficult discussion outside of the workshop.

The coaches really seemed to have opened up on their own practices and areas of improvement; though heated at times there has been some honest comment, in particular from the women's coaches. One of the coaches who opened up on how he feels the players perceive him and how it makes him feel. He has experienced a situation in training where a player has been really disrespectful to him. This allowed him to bring his feelings and thoughts to the group and as a group, he was given advice and support.

In Rugby League coach education, reflective practice is almost nonexistent, though it is touched upon with simple models based on Plan, Do, Review, its importance is lost in a qualification that focuses on what to coach and how to coach. The TA processes and feedback felt really personalised to me and the coaches, and furthermore feedback was subjective and detailed. Thinking aloud then listening back to this forces honest self-reflection, it provides some truths both good and bad but ultimately it then makes us accountable to what we do about these findings. The workshop then allows a chance to review the importance of reflecting on and in action and how as a coaching group we could support and drive a reflective group.

The key themes that are evident within Craig's experiences of the TA programme will now be discussed and explained from a theoretical perspective.

Synthesizing Craig's reflections and experiences

Throughout the previous section Craig has highlighted a number of key mechanisms of learning and development that he himself has experienced as a coach, and also as a coach developer through his engagement in the TA programme. Some of these mechanisms are clearly evidenced in previous research within coach education and they will be discussed within this section. The mains themes that have developed from Craig's discussions are how the TA programme has provided him with individualised learning, challenged his (and the coaches he develops) perceptions of reflection, and allowed for a community of practice to develop within the club.

Individualised learning

Craig clearly articulates how being part of the TA programme has enabled him to receive a more individual approach to learning. Craig discussed how he is not entirely comfortable receiving feedback. However, by engaging with TA, 'there is no escaping feedback, as I'm actually listening back to myself and critiquing myself, there's no one else to blame in that situation and no way of ignoring some of the mistakes I might make or the ways in which I communicate'.

Kemmis (1985) proposes that reflection is concerned with looking inwards at our thoughts and outward at the situation we find ourselves in. In turn, we are thinking about thinking. Throughout the TA process, we are encouraging the coach to 'suspend' himself above the coaching environment, this is allowing the coach to break this autonomous thinking process and 'zoom in' – to look inwards on themselves and their thought processes from the outside. This in turn, may also allow for some of these non-conscious processes to be challenged and made conscious, which can promote a more accurate self-evaluation.

From a theoretical perspective, this processes of 'suspending' the self within the situation using TA, is disrupting the natural cognitive process of decision making and coaching during a session. Masters (1992) proposed that if an individual has an inward focus on attention, within a task, this could lead to the breakdown of the performance within that task. Masters (1992) names this Reinvestment, and has subsequently produced many empirical papers to support this theory (e.g. Masters, Paul, MacMahon & Eves, 2007; Masters, Poolton, Maxwell & Raab, 2008). This inward focus of attention acts as distraction to the previously natural process. However, the process of TA is to purposely promote an inward focus of attention, which will create a heightened sense of awareness within the coach. Although this may lead to some level of disruption of the task of coaching, it is something that can be developed if a coach practises this process. This may be why previous research has highlighted that coaches find the process of reflection and specifically reflection-in-action difficult (Cropley, Miles & Nichols, 2016; Knowles, Borrie & Telfer, 2005; Nelson & Cushion, 2006).

By using TA, coaches can potentially reduce self-bias by making the decision-making process more conscious, becoming aware of some of these biases, which in turn may allow for coaches to develop their coaching practice.

Challenging the perceptions of reflection

As previously mentioned in Chapter 6, many coaches may be familiar with reflection and reflective practice in the forms of reflective portfolios or diaries as part of a formal accreditation (Hall & Gray, 2016). Dixon et al. (2013) have even gone as far as suggesting that these types of exercises may actually be detrimental as these written forms of reflection often provides a structure which is 'fictionalizing the life of practitioners and therefore weakening coaches' emotional awareness' (p 588). These types of reflection may have also been detrimental to how National Governing Bodies see reflection and how they adopt them within their own coach education programmes. It is evident throughout Craig's section how coach education within rugby league does not and has not adopted the notion of reflection and reflective practice,

> In Rugby League coach education, reflective practice is almost nonexistent, though it is touched upon with simple models based on Plan, Do, Review, its importance is lost in a qualification that focuses on the what to coach and how to coach.

Again, this is emphasizing that what is covered within this National Governing Body may be more focused on reflection-on-action, rather than reflection-in-action. This reflection-on-action is what has typified the reflective practice element within coach education (Dixon et al., 2013). Therefore, it is refreshing to see how Craig's perception of TA moves away from this rigid process of reflection-on-action and allows him to explore his reflections-in-action, which is situated within his practice. Cropley et al. (2016) emphasise this importance of practitioners actively engaging in reflection, which is embedded within the experience.

Another challenge or preconception that coaches may have with reflection or reflective practice is the notion that this process acts as some form of surveillance (Mackey, 2007). That is, their reflections or ability to articulate these reflections are being judged by others or, in the case of Craig, by him as a coach development officer. This also links to the notion of power (Cushion, 2018); given that Craig is the coach development manager, he potentially creates this sense of surveillance within his position. Although the TA programme promotes individualised learning where coaches are reflecting on their own reflection-in-action, these discussions within a workshop setting may perceived by some coaches as a form of surveillance. However, what is evident from Craig's section is that coaches may have developed a feeling of 'safeness' or comfort throughout the TA programme, and feel safe to have these open discussions about their own reflections with other coaches within their club and their coach development manager.

Developing a community of practice

Communities of practice involve a group of people who share a common set of problems or a passion for a topic, and who then deepen their knowledge and expertise in this area by interacting on an ongoing basis (Wenger, McDermott & Snyder, 2002). It is evident throughout Craig's section that the TA programme has been able to promote some sort of community of practice. From his own perspective Craig acknowledges that he has been able to develop from others, as he states 'without the feedback from the group I believe that I may have continued to coach the way I was coaching, with "rose tinted glasses" on'. In addition, he acknowledges that others have also been able to learn from this process, when writing about another coach he stated, 'this [the workshop] allowed him to bring his feelings and thoughts to the group and as a group, he was given advice and support'.

By promoting a community of practice via workshops, the TA programme is incorporating both individualised learning in the form of TA and reflection-in-action during an actual coaching section (coaches own practice) and the opportunity for coaches to bring their own learning into their community in the form of a workshop.

Recommendations

It must be made clear that although this chapter is painting the TA programme in a very positive light, we are not advocating that it is the panacea to all forms of reflective practice. The TA programme is still in the very early stages of development within coach education and therefore we hope that this chapter and the following recommendations provide some loose guidelines for other practitioners and academics to adopt, critique and develop further.

Based on the content of this chapter and Craig's perceptions of the TA programme we provide the following recommendations:

- It is important that researchers and practitioners implementing TA take into consideration the types of reflection and reflective practice that coaches Programme have engaged in previously. A comprehensive understanding of the context and the national governing body is also important.
- TA on its own is only one part of the programme. Although the TA process promotes reflection-in-action and on its own can develop a coach's learning and ability to reflect (Stephenson, Cronin & Whitehead, under review), throughout the last three years of developing this programme, the workshop has become an integral part of this process. Specifically, previous TA programmes have involved three workshops. This involves an introductory workshop and two reflective workshops where coaches bring their own reflections of their TA reflection-in-action to discuss within these workshops. However, this process can be modified and extended, depending on the needs to the group.
- Having an awareness of the possible power dynamics that can occur when implementing the TA programme. For example, coaches may feel that the TA itself is being used as a surveillance mechanism and they are being judged within their coaching environment. It could be argued that power is something that is unavoidable (Cushion, 2018). Therefore, the power dynamics within groups of coaches during coach education and the implementation of the TA programme is something to be aware of and consider. Consider the impact of power and how it affects what and how a coach reflects within their specific environment.

References

Atkinson, H. L., & Nixon-Cave, K. (2011). A tool for clinical reasoning and reflection using the International Classification of Functioning, Disability and Health (ICF) framework and patient management model. *Physical Therapy*, *91*(3), 416–430.

Banning, M. (2008). A review of clinical decision making: Models and current research. *Journal of Clinical Nursing*, *17*, 187–195. doi:10.111/j.1365-2702.2006.01791.x

Borleffs, J. C., Custers, E. J., van Gijn, J., & Ten Cate, O. T. (2003). 'Clinical reasoning theatre': A new approach to clinical reasoning education. *Academic Medicine*, *78*, 322–325.

Chase, W. G., & Simon, H. A. (1973). The mind's eye in chess. In W. G. Chase (Ed.), *Visual information processing* (pp. 215–281). New York: Academic Press.

Cropley, B., Miles, A., & Nichols, T. (2016). Learning to learn: The coach as a reflective practitioner. In J. Wallace & J. Lambert (Eds.), *Becoming a sports coach* (pp. 11–26). London: Routledge.

Cushion, C. J. (2018). Reflection and reflective practice discourses in coaching: A critical analysis. *Sport, Education and Society, 23*(1), 82–94. doi:10.1080/13573322.2016.1142961

Dixon, M., Lee, S., & Ghaye, T. (2013). Reflective practices for better sports coaches and coach education: Shifting from a pedagogy of scarcity to abundance in the run-up to rio 2016. *Reflective Practice, 14*(5), 585–599.

Ericsson, K. A., & Simon, H. A. (1993). *Protocol analysis.* Cambridge, MA: MIT press.

Hall, E., & Gray, S. (2016). Reflecting on reflective practice: A coach's action research narratives. qualitative research in sport. *Exercise and Health, 8*(4), 365–379.

Huntley, E., Cropley, B., Gilbourne, D., Sparkes, A., & Knowles, Z. (2014). Reflecting back and forwards: An evaluation of peer-reviewed reflective practice research in sport. *Reflective Practice, 15*(6), 863–876.

Kemmis, S. (1985). Action research and the politics of reflection. In D. Boud, R. Keogh, & D. Walker (Eds.), *Reflection: Turning experience into learning* (pp. 139–163). Kogan Page: London.

Knowles, Z., Borrie, A., & Telfer, H. (2005). Towards the reflective sports coach: Issues of context, education and application. *Ergonomics, 48*(11–14), 1711–1720.

Lee, J. E. M., & Ryan-Wenger, N. (1997). The 'think aloud' seminar for teaching clinical reasoning: A case study of a child with pharyngitis. *Journal of Paediatric Health Care, 11*(1), 105–110.

Mackey, H. (2007). 'Do not ask me to stay the same': Foucault and the professional identities of occupational therapists. *Australian Occupational Therapy Journal, 54*, 95–102.

Masters, R. S. W. (1992). Knowledge knerves and know-how: The role of explicit versus implicit knowledge in the breakdown of a complex motor skill under pressure. *British Journal of Psychology, 83*, 343–358.

Masters, R. S. W., Pall, H. S., MacMahon, K. M. A., & Eves, F. F. (2007). Duration of Parkinson disease is associated with an increased propensity for 'reinvestment'. *Neurorehabilitation and Neural Repair, 21*, 123–126.

Masters, R. S. W., Poolton, J. M., Maxwell, J. P., & Raab, M. (2008). Implicit motor learning and complex decision making in time constrained environments. *Journal of Motor Behavior, 40*, 71–79.

Nelson, L. J., & Cushion, C. J. (2006). Reflection in coach education: The case of the national governing body coaching certificate. *The Sport Psychologist, 20*(2), 174–183.

Samson, A., Simpson, D., Kamphoff, C., & Langlier, A. (2015). Think aloud: An examination of distance runners' thought processes. *International Journal of Sport and Exercise Psychology*, 1–14. doi:10.1080/1612197x.2015.1069877

Stephenson, J., Cronin, C., & Whitehead, A. E. (under review). 'Suspended above, and in action': An interpretative analysis of using think aloud as a reflective practice tool within amateur Women's Soccer Coaching. *International Sport Coaching Journal.*

Stoll, S. K., Mullem, H. V., Mullem, P. V., & Beller, J. M. (2018). The missing science: Ethics in practice. *Sport and Exercise Science, Intech Open.* 55–68.

Swettenham, L., Eubank, M., Won, D., & Whitehead, A. E. (2018). Investigating stress and coping during practice and competition in tennis using think aloud. *International Journal of Sport and Exercise Psychology.* doi:10.1080/1612197X.2018.1511622

Welsh, J. C., Dewhurst, S. A., & Perry, J. L. (2018). Thinking aloud: An exploration of cognitions in professional snooker. *Psychology of Sport and Exercise, 36*(1), 197–208. doi:10.1016/j.psychsport.2018.03.003

Wenger, E., McDermott, R., & Snyder, W. M. (2002). *Cultivating communities of practice.* Boston: Harvard Business School Press.

Whitehead, A. E., Cropley, B., Miles, A., Huntley, T., Quayle, L., & Knowles, Z. (2016a). 'Think aloud': Towards a framework to facilitate reflective practice amongst rugby 776 league coaches. *International Sport Coaching Journal, 3*, 269–286.

Whitehead, A. E., Jones, H. S., Williams, E. L., Rowley, C., Quayle, L., Marchant, D., … Polman, R. C. (2018). Investigating the relationship between cognitions, pacing strategies and performance in 16.1 km cycling time trials using a think aloud protocol. *Psychology of Sport & Exercise, 34*, 95–109.

Whitehead, A. E., Taylor, J. A., & Polman, R. C. J. (2015). Examination of the suitability of collecting in event cognitive processes using think aloud protocol in golf. *Frontiers in Psychology, 6*, 1–12.

Whitehead, A. E., Taylor, J. A., & Polman, R. C. J. (2016b). Evidence for skill level differences in the thought processes of golfers during high and low pressure situations. *Frontiers in Psychology, 6*, 1–12.

SECTION IV

A guide to sport science support

8

THE ANALYSIS PROCESS

Applying the theory

Benjamin Stanway and Philip Boardman

Introduction

The purpose of this chapter is to provided information on the role of an analyst and the process that an analyst must go through to provide reliable and efficient support for the team or individual in question. The chapter aims to bridge the gap between academia and the elite support environment, for analysis, drawing upon experience and guidance of an analyst, with nine years' experience.

Performance analysis (PA) as a scientific discipline can be dated back to the work of Chadwick (1861) and Remley (1931), who started to use hand notation in sport with the aim of summarising and impacting performance (Eaves, 2015). Consequently, the application of PA in professional sport is constantly evolving, as is the requirement for individual athletes, teams, coaches and owners to acquire competitive advantage over their competitors. Due to the fact that the main aspect of a coach's job is to analyse performance to provide feedback and develop subsequent coaching sessions (James, 2006a; Wright, Atkins, Jones & Todd, 2013), performance analysis practitioners are and should be considered an integral part of any sporting organisation's athlete support network, whether this be part of a National Governing Body, where practitioners may work across a multitude of sports, employed by professional clubs to support multiple athletes and coaches or as part of a team behind a specific individual, in sports such as tennis and golf. Not only has the prominence of performance analysts within a range of sports increased, but the breadth and depth of work within these organisations has also grown (Figure 8.1).

PA is needed because objective feedback in sports performance is required as a coach may only remember 40–59 per cent, depending on their experience and the part of performance they are recollecting (Laird & Waters, 2008). This objective data is needed to enhance the subjective thought process of a coach.

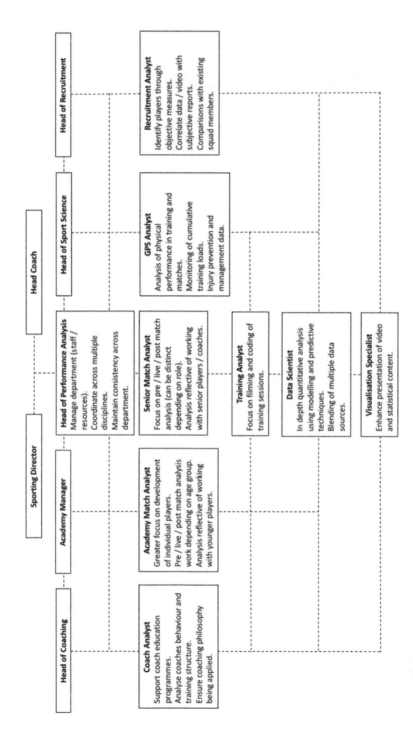

Head Coach

Sporting Director

Head of Coaching

Head of Recruitment

Head of Sport Science

Academy Manager

Coach Analyst
Support coach education programmes.
Analyse coaches behaviour and training structure.
Ensure coaching philosophy being applied.

Academy Match Analyst
Greater focus on development of individual players.
Pre / live / post match analysis work depending on age group.
Analysis reflective of working with younger players.

Head of Performance Analysis
Manage department (staff / resources).
Coordinate across multiple disciplines.
Maintain consistency across department.

Senior Match Analyst
Focus on pre / live / post match analysis (can be distinct depending on role).
Analysis reflective of working with senior players / coaches.

Training Analyst
Focus on filming and coding of training sessions.

Data Scientist
In depth quantitative analysis using modelling and predictive techniques.
Blending of multiple data sources.

Visualisation Specialist
Enhance presentation of video and statistical content.

GPS Analyst
Analysis of physical performance in training and matches.
Monitoring of cumulative training loads.
Injury prevention and management data.

Recruitment Analyst
Identify players through objective measures.
Correlate data / video with subjective reports.
Comparisons with existing squad members.

FIGURE 8.1 Structure

When looking into the memory recall of elite coaches within youth football, Nicholls and Worsfold (2016) concluded a lower mean observation accuracy of 38.8 per cent, with 20 per cent more effective observation for unsuccessful actions. Stemming from the work initially completed by match analysts, directly involved in delivery and feedback of objective information on a match day, Governing Bodies and professional teams now look to apply the tools and skill sets of performance analysts to inform and complement the decision-making process within differing levels of their organisations.

As an analyst, the dissemination of results can be completed in a number of different ways (in a one to one situation or in front of a group) and can include several different data formats such as numerical data or video (Fernandez-Echeverria, Mesquita, González-Silva, Claver & Moreno, 2017). In one study conducted by Wright, Atkins and Jones (2012) they emphasise that a large proportion of coaches (86 per cent of the sample in professional and semi-professional rugby, hockey, football and basketball coaches) utilised video-based performance analysis to aid the delivery of feedback. Using this type of video-based performance analysis can assist with identifying the strengths and areas to exploit in an opposition analysis report, whilst also aiding in the creation of tactical strategies and improving the provision of augmented feedback (Groom, Cushion & Nelson, 2011; Nelson & Groom, 2012; O'Donoghue, 2009). In an individual sport such as golf, Guadagnoli, Holcomb and Davis (2002) indicate a need for the athlete to progress through their development of skill performance. Coaches would achieve this using the knowledge of their results to improve learning of a golfer's performance. This demonstrates the need for video instruction in order to improve the distance and consistency of a golfer's swing. With video-based feedback being an important tool for players and coaches, Reeves and Roberts (2013) have found there to be three developmental areas which video feedback can contribute towards. These areas include:

1)   Team and individual performance
2)   Reflection
3)   Psychological associations with performance

When taking on an athlete's perspective, in provision of feedback in ice hockey, Nelson, Potrac and Groom (2014) suggested that there is not a clear answer for the delivery of video-based feedback. One of the most important aspects, from their research, is the fact that the athlete's understanding of and responses to the video-based feedback were related to the respect they had for the coach (Nelson et al., 2014). Therefore, it is important to consider the person delivering video-based feedback and the target audience as this can be a significant influencer in retention and learning of information, for an athlete or team. Reeves and Roberts (2013) interviewed eight academy football players; along with other professionals, they suggest an argument for the individualisation of performance analysis provision as players wanted to know 'what' of their own individual performance should be analysed. If the video-based performance analysis is specific to the target audience, then it is important to consider the ability of the video to replicate match situations to give a stronger relationship between the analysis presented and future performance. Affecting future performance is the fundamental underpinning of the job for any practitioner.

In elite sport, where short term results are often a priority, the time pressures influencing the type of analytical work can be significant. Whilst both academic research and work carried out by practitioners seeks to improve performance, the nature of this work can be quite different.

Applied example (working on a tight timescale)

The example of a match analyst in a club setting may involve preparatory work of the opposition's previous six performances. Their work would be extremely focused on providing a detailed analysis of the opposition ahead of a forthcoming fixture. However, once that fixture has been completed, the work of those six matches is largely irrelevant. An evaluation of the pre-match work should be used to affect future pre-match information; however, the type of analysis is still relatively short-term. To improve this process, the creation of an automated statistical report would save manually entering data each time. Using this additional time may lead to creating video examples that reinforce the insights highlighted in the report. As a result, the analysis the match analyst provides has improved in terms of efficiency and in terms of depth of information for the coach to review. Under strict time pressures it is easy for practitioners to continue to produce the same level of information and become specialists in their specific role.

In contrast, academic research is largely reflective, analysing previous performances over a larger sample size. In terms of the sample size and type, the number of wins, draws and losses for unsuccessful and successful teams should be considered. Jones, Mellalieu and James (2004) suggest that successful teams have more wins than unsuccessful teams, therefore, the number of wins, draws and losses should be considered. As this may not be a true representation of the successful team, the number of games selected for each of the three categories is of great importance. A sample used by Castellano et al. (2012) incorporated match location with different opponents and an equal number of wins, draws and losses (n=6), to minimise the effect of situational variables. Some studies (Higham, Hopkins, Pyne & Anson, 2014; Lago-Ballesteros & Lago-Peñas, 2010; Mikołajec, Maszczyk & Zając, 2013) have looked to establish trends and benchmarks from a season's worth of results in order to ensure results are significant to the competition. Whilst this research affects performance by educating practitioners, it cannot have the immediate impact on performance that analysts in a practical setting are tasked to do. In addition, as Potter and Carter (2001) emphasise, the greater the database the more accurately you will be able to compare future performances. On the other hand, Hughes, Evans and Wells (2001) suggested that the critical number of matches, to make a comparison between performances, is dependent on the type of data and variables analysed. For example, when conducting analysis on passing in football, the mean may stabilise earlier than a cross or shot due to the number of instances and the way the data is analysed. In this example a pass may only need a sample of five games, whereas a shot's mean may stabilise after more games (Hughes et al., 2001). There should also be consideration for how recent the game is – more recent games will be more valuable than earlier games in the competition (Mosteller, 1979). Lastly, more consideration is needed for the normalisation of performance indicators to benefit analysis and coaching (Bartlett, 2001). For example, this could be in the form of a ratio, for shots on target against shots attempted or turnovers per possession rather than simple frequencies.

Time pressures not only influence the type of analysis that is carried out, but also the different levels of information available to practitioners and researchers. A performance analyst working in an applied environment will experience short and strict deadlines with acute time pressures defined by the date of the next tournament or the fixture schedule (Hughes et al., 2001). Consequently, a practitioner may not be afforded the time to research over a complete competition period whilst using performance indicators with definitions that are exclusive to their organisation. As well as technical performance data, physical and well-being information are also significant impactors on performance. This type of data, being heavily sensitive in professional sport, is not always made available to researchers.

As Figure 8.1 highlights, the domain of performance analysis in professional sport is a broad one. As sports organisations look to improve the provision and service they provide to their athletes and coaches, the support networks behind them have become more specific. It is therefore important that practitioners are able to develop skill sets that focus on their job role, whilst having an awareness of their position in a multi-disciplinary subject.

Applied example (working together as a multidisciplinary team)

An example of this in a club setting could be the relationship between analysts in the production of an age-appropriate coaching drill book. With reference to Figure 8.1, the Coach Analyst, Academy Match Analyst, Training Analyst, GPS Analyst and Head of Performance Analyst could all be involved in such a project. Whilst all the individual job roles have their specific focus, they should all contribute to a more global development of how the drill book can be most beneficial to the coach and athlete. In this instance the Coach Analyst would look to evaluate the instruction style or session structure employed by the coach. The Training Analyst would be able to give quantitative comparisons on how similar training sessions were carried out by different coaches at different age groups, thus ensuring consistency and a development to the session as players moved through different age groups. In addition to comparisons in training, the Academy Match Analyst would look to link how the training sessions were then implemented in a more competitive environment to analyse the extent of learning within more pressurised situations. Finally, within more senior age groups, the GPS Analyst would look to provide a physical assessment of what each individual drill should look like in terms of effort and intensity, therefore allowing the coach to adapt the training session as part of the players' physical training load. Whilst all these individual practitioners are providing specific support to the project, the Head of Performance Analysis would coordinate and liaise with other key figures to ensure the drill book is consistent with club's philosophy and reflective of the expectations of the Sporting Director.

The example highlighted above illustrates how large sporting organisations can utilise an expansive support staff to provide a more holistic level of information. Whilst the individual practitioner is focused on their own job role, the key principles of working as a Performance Analyst remain a constant. As explained below in this chapter, the importance of the analyst's relationship with coaching staff, a consistent process for evaluating performance and a commitment to innovation and development of technical skills should underpin any job role. Huggan et al. (2015) place importance on knowing and understanding the different roles that stakeholders have and the type of support they provide. This will enable the analyst to interact effectively and make measured decisions when communicating with the manager, who controls the analyst's time, resources and opportunities of development (Huggan et al., 2015). In reality, the key stakeholders should act in relation to the good of the team and go beyond their self-interests to achieve the team or individual's goals (Macquet et al., 2015). Furthermore, Macquet et al. believe that the key to success is having a shared vision of the team performance and what aspects each individual can add to implementation of the game plan.

Establishing the analysis process: an applied perspective

Previously, within the academic literature, dynamic analysis models have been devised (Carling, 2005; Duckett, 2012; O'Donoghue, 2006) to inform analysts and coaches in professional practice. Within this section the analysis process will be discussed with ideas from research and experience from professional practice. For us as practitioners the first set of questions, when establishing an analysis process, are all simple. The analysis process will be split into four distinct stages; What, How, When and Where are we going to analyse in order to have the biggest impact on improving performance. Explanations and applications as to why each of these stages exist will be established and evidenced, from industry and research. Whilst answering those questions, it is vital that the process is underpinned by a consistent approach, which is flexible enough to meet the demands of coaches and athletes. The analysis process developed (Figure 8.2) closely corresponds with the current sports performance literature of Wright, Collins and Carling (2014) with the inclusion of reliability and operational definitions for the system created, based on the philosophy of the team or athlete involved.

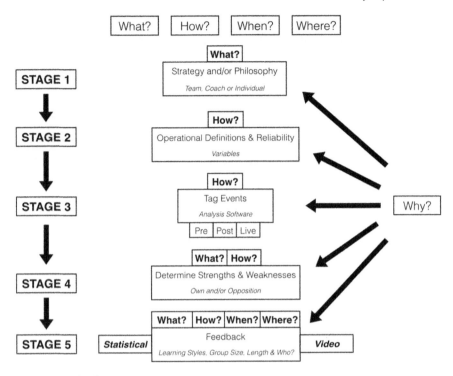

FIGURE 8.2   Analysis process

Stage 1: devising the system

Establishing what you are going to analyse requires a clear understanding of the strategy employed by the coach or individual athlete. It is important to note that in best practice the playing strategy should remain consistent to facilitate the best performance from the team. Hughes and Franks (2007) and Carling et al. (2005) suggest the following simple schematic flow chart (Figure 8.2) which includes Player, Position, Action and Time. From professional practice, team performance is usually analysed by looking into four distinct areas; in possession, out of possession, attacking transitions and defensive transitions. By including both team performance and playing strategy, a thorough analysis can be developed to reflect the philosophy and strategy of the team or athlete. Rather than just looking at outcome, a simple consideration of how that outcome is achieved and why it has happened would gather more valuable information of sports performance.

   This allows the coach and analyst to devise tactics that complement the overall strategy of the team. For instance, in football, the team may employ a high pressing strategy out of possession. As an analyst, with this understanding, it is possible to identify the strengths and weaknesses of the opposition in matches when they are being pressed high. This may lead to developing tactics such as directing the ball to a specific opposition player before pressing aggressively. A comprehension of the playing strategy allows the practitioner to gain a stronger insight into what a successful or unsuccessful performance should look like and as a result the analysis they conduct can be more specific to the requirements of the coach.

Stage 2: reliable system

How we are going to analyse how performance underpins the type and level of information that is delivered to the coach or athlete. Using performance indicators to analyse performance requires a clear set of operational definitions that are consistent between the practitioner and those receiving the information. Once definitions are established for each variable, they become quantifiable and can be recorded over multiple performances. Within current research, there is a lack of consensus and openness when developing and displaying variables as part of an analysis. Mackenzie and Cushion (2013) found that 79 per cent of the current literature lacks definitions for the technical variables analysed, with other definitions being too simplistic. Williams (2012) indicated that 38.9 per cent of articles in the *International Journal of Performance Analysis in Sport* did not fully define or disregarded their operational definitions. If such articles had detailed definitions, the results would be meaningful to the population of elite sports clubs/individuals and therefore give an insight into sports performance. Fundamentally, the analysis must be accurate, accessible to those who need it and be interpretable by the target audience.

O'Donoghue (2007) suggests following the below procedure during the development and operation of a performance analysis system. Steps 1 to 4 are to aid the creation of a reliable system and steps 5 to 7 should apply when a new operator uses the system.

1) Identify the variables of interest and define these as precisely as possible. Video instances may be created to help operators understand the more subjective variables. An example of an operational definition, for possession, would be sufficient control over the ball to enable a deliberate influence on its direction (Jones et al., 2004, p. 100).
2) Identify the measurement of each performance indicator for type of performance. For example, this may be tactical or technical performance.
3) Select a reliability test which suits the current sample of operators. The test may look for agreement between operators (inter-operator reliability) or the consistency of an individual (intra-operator reliability) for the performance analysis system.
4) Determine what value of each performance indicator represents an acceptable level of reliability – this might be percentage error or a weighted kappa value, for example.
5) Train the operators using intra-operator reliability studies. Examples of a test to use could be a Pearson's product-moment correlation coefficient or percentage error for each variable (Cooper, Hughes, O'Donoghue & Nevill, 2007; Hughes et al., 2001).

6) Undertake an inter-operator reliability test. This stage could be to compare reliability of performance indicators using a system with commercial or elite data sources, or between internal analysts to search for consistent bias (James, Taylor & Stanley, 2007).

7) If the level of reliability achieved by the operator(s) is poor, consider teaching the operator(s) within the performance analysis department, using video instances or explaining each definition thoroughly.

(O'Donoghue, 2007)

When testing the reliability of system there are three sources errors that may occur; observational, operational and definitional (James et al., 2007). When tagging events in sports performance, an observational error would consist of the operator missing a particular action, Secondly, an operational error is when the operator presses the wrong button in error. Lastly, a definitional error occurs when the operator does not fully understand the definition for the action taking place.

Stage 3: gathering data

Once the practitioner has a strong understanding of the playing strategy and the process for how performances are going to be recorded and analysed, the next step is to determine where this information is going to have the biggest impact. In terms of match analysis, work is generally split into pre-match, live and post-match analysis external data sets and primarily capturing bespoke data as a performance analysis team. Through communication with coaching staff it should be decided what level of analysis is required within each of these broad areas. This allows the analyst to structure their work timetable, so they are efficient in meeting the demands of the coaches and athletes. Factors such as athlete type, competition schedule, team standard, previous analysis experience and resources available could all influence where analysis is going to have the biggest impact on performance. For example, when working with younger athletes, the competition schedule may be less intense in terms of number of fixtures and less results-orientated. Therefore, the practitioner may focus the majority of their work on analysing the performance of their own players retrospectively. However, the greatest performance gains could be through analysing individual player development rather than focusing on the strengths and weaknesses of the upcoming opposition.

Analysts often use commercial and elite data sets to inform their practice: therefore, it is important to understand the reliability of this data to use as an insight into sports performance. Commercial data sets have previously been analysed and tested for reliability. Worsfold and Macbeth (2009) found between 10 per cent and 59.51 per cent mean percentage error between companies such as BBC, ESPN, Sky Sports, Eurosport, whilst also measuring against a post-match analysis for six performance indicators. This has resulted in the need for clarification of terminology and operational definitions to understand the variables that are being analysed. Using a weighted kappa statistical test to calculate reliability, Liu, Hopkins, Gómez and Molinuevo (2013) concluded that the OPTA client system had very good agreement for coded team events (kappa values between 0.92 and 0.94) between independent operators. This suggests that the difference between commercial data and elite performance data is one of reliability. Therefore, more research, calculating the reliability between the commercial system data and elite performance data is needed if this data is going to be used to enhance and develop performance, within the elite environment.

Stage 4: analysing data

It is at this point that methods to archive and benchmark performances in relation to different situational variables become important. By consistently recording specific Key Performance Indicators (KPIs) throughout every performance, more immediate forms of feedback (i.e. the last match) can lead to the creation of more longitudinal type of analysis, such as player development over a whole season. A consistent process for recording and benchmarking performance through databases allows practitioners to automate as much of their work as possible, thus saving time and making the presentation of their analysis much easier. In turn this should flag variations in performances over the short, medium and long term that can highlight trends that may affect the coaching process. How performances are recorded and analysed has a significant impact on how this information is presented.

When analysing data, analysts and researchers are able to establish benchmarks and highlight trends in performance that can be interpreted by analysing the information from a number of different circumstances. For example, such techniques include the creation of normative performance profiles (Butler & Hardy, 1992; Hughes et al., 2001; James, Mellalieu & Jones, 2005; Lago-Peñas & Lago-Ballesteros, 2011; Liu, Gomez, Lago-Peñas & Sampaio, 2015; O'Donoghue, 2005) to establish differences between individual or team performance, representative of a population. These normative profiles can be related to the Key Performance Indicators (KPIs) that have been established, following the application of statistical tests to determine the differences between winning and losing sports performance (Lago-Ballesteros & Lago-Peñas, 2010; Jones et al., 2004; Lago-Peñas, Lago-Ballesteros & Rey, 2011; Lago-Peñas, Lago-Ballesteros, Dellal & Gómez, 2010; Castellano et al., 2012; Csataljay, O'Donoghue, Hughes & Dancs, 2009; Mikołajec et al., 2013; O'Donoghue, 2008; Hughes et al., 2012; Vaz, Van Rooyen & Sampaio, 2010; Higham et al., 2014; Wright, Atkins, Polman, Jones & Sargeson, 2011). In addition to creating a normative performance profile, in relation to KPIs, the addition of situational variables (Carron, Loughhead & Bray, 2005; O'Donoghue, 2008; Taylor, Mellalieu, James & Shearer, 2008) to the aforementioned theories can bring the performance into context. These theories can be analysed in isolation or in relation to the other theories, to determine the strengths and weaknesses of the opposing team/individual or your own performance(s). This type of information and analysis is required to understand more about the sports performance taking place. Sarmento et al. (2014) put forward the notion of considering the situational and contextual variables and their dynamic influence on sports performance, as did Mackenzie and Cushion (2013) and Gómez, García-de-Alcaráz and Furley (2017).

Stage 5: feedback techniques

The final stage of establishing an analysis process in a practical environment is the scheduling of when analysis work needs to be delivered. One example from academic literature, in futsal, indicated that coaches usually organise two short weekly meetings, with players, to analyse multiple aspects of performance (Sarmento et al., 2016). The first of the meetings usually includes an analysis of the opposing team's strategies and the second developing and delivering the plan to combat the strategy of the opposing team (Sarmento et al., 2016). It is vital that information is provided to meet the demands of coaches and athletes, whilst creating the best circumstances for this information to be translated into performances during competition. As previously highlighted, for analysts working in a practical environment the deadlines for producing information can lead to high time pressures on a day to day basis. Therefore, it is important to utilise the 'what', 'how', 'where' and 'when' part of the process as efficiently as possible. Generally, this involves clear communication pathways with coaches and athletes for it affects the coaching process and ultimately performance. Formulating the game strategy ahead of the next match is an example of where analysts need to be organised to have started preparatory work, often before the previous match has occurred in busy competition schedules, therefore providing coaching staff with analysis that can influence forthcoming training sessions immediately after the previous fixture. Deciding when analysis is presented can have a big effect on how this information is processed by athletes. In support, Wulf, Shea and Lewthwaite (2010) recommend normative feedback (informational and motivational) to be produced and delivered after successful trials, to enhance the performance of learning. Notably, the type of analysis, group size, athlete experience, presentation length and competition schedule should all influence when analysis interventions take place. For example, analysis sessions early in the training week may involve small groups or team units, with specific information that reinforces coaching points made during training sessions. In the lead up to match day, the analysis session may be presented to the whole team, which reviews the overall playing strategy and combines the key coaching points made earlier in the week. Work developed and concluded by Wright, Carling, Lawlor and Collins (2016), on player engagement in football, found 53 per cent (n=48) of players from three different English Championship sides to prefer a 11–20 minute presentation, with this feedback being given one to two days prior to performance being completed. It is important to highlight that there is no specific length of time that fits every feedback session. This is why it is important to consider the group size, athlete age, participating sport, feedback topic and method of feedback.

When providing analysis support to younger athletes, it may be beneficial for those athletes to take ownership of reviewing their own performance. The analyst may play the role of a facilitator, providing information that promotes questions around reviewing performance rather than simply presenting the results of their work. The delivery of this information is likely to be more interactive to introduce analysis material as a way of reviewing performance. Liebermann et al. (2002) state that feedback can slow down the learning process by athletes being dependent on the immediate provision of information. To combat this, athletes need to be able to detect the errors themselves and then correct those errors, by not being reliant on the information provided to them (Liebermann et al., 2002). Conversely, a senior player may want to analyse their performance independently in their own time. Therefore, the analyst should be able to provide ways athletes can securely access information remotely. The type of information an analyst is likely to directly provide to an athlete is often different to that of a coach. Again, the analysis should be specific to the athlete and presented in a way that is suited to their preferred learning style. Millar, Oldham, Renshaw and Hopkins (2017) analysed the athlete and coach roles in a rowing environment, with the primary role of a coach being facilitator of knowledge and to improve the outcome of the athlete. They provide evidence that rowers were more accurate than coaches at knowing when their performance was successful, as a coach cannot identify all the small changes in performances. As a consequence, to succeed and develop athletes, a consideration of the athlete's experience during the performance should come before the coach applies their own coaching knowledge (Millar et al., 2017). Whilst this provides a rationale for a contemporary approach to guide the learner towards a solution, this may only be correct for the sport of rowing.

Generally, improvements are either through becoming more efficient at existing processes or an ability to provide a new form of analysis that previously wasn't possible. In reality a greater efficiency is required before new work can be implemented into the analysis process; however, it is important to consider how these changes will affect the overall work load when tight deadlines are already in place. As a practitioner, improving your understanding of the technology you use on a day to day basis can have long term effects on reducing work time for specific tasks.

Conclusion

Alongside the technical skills of being an analyst, it is also important to continue to improve game understanding. This again reinforces the coach–analyst relationship and allows a better application of the technical skills that analysts provide. Whilst improvements in game understanding can come directly from coaches, referring to academic literature can provide an additional source of information that may cover a broader range of tactical insights. At this point it is necessary to introduce differences between working in a practical setting compared to academic research-based projects. Mackenzie and Cushion (2013) suggested that the questions asked and the research undertaken may be of little use within an applied setting. Consequently, the findings have little impact and become less transferable, producing a gap between the practitioner and researcher. In addition, Fernandez-Echeverria et al. (2017) introduce the notion of existing research being ignored by coaches, and therefore not being transferred into professional practice. This suggests that a practitioner may not utilise the information gathered and analysed by researchers, which may be a consequence of working to tight timescales, as discussed above. To bridge the gap between the practitioner and researcher it would be beneficial for researchers to have a stronger rationale for their research to develop a clearer understanding of sports performance, which will impact professional practice.

This chapter has highlighted the need for feedback and how sports performance analysis may need to be implemented in an elite sporting environment, to have an impact on the coaching process. Importance has been placed on the analysis process and working as a multi-disciplinary team, with professional practice examples shared.

References

Bartlett, R. (2001). Performance analysis: Can bringing together biomechanics and notational analysis benefit coaches? *International Journal of Performance Analysis in Sport*, *1*(1), 122–126.

Butler, R. J., & Hardy, L. (1992). The performance profile: Theory and application. *The Sport Psychologist*, *6*(3), 253–264.

Carling, C., Reilly, T., & Williams, A. M. (2005). *Handbook of soccer match analysis: A systematic approach to improving performance*. London: Routledge.

Carron, A. V., Loughhead, T. M., & Bray, S. R. (2005). The home advantage in sport competitions: Courneya and Carron's (1992) conceptual framework a decade later. *Journal of Sports Sciences*, *23*(4), 395–407.

Castellano, J., Casamichana, D., & Lago, C. (2012). The use of match statistics that discriminate between successful and unsuccessful soccer teams. *Journal of Human Kinetics*, *31*, 137–147.

Cooper, S. M., Hughes, M., O'Donoghue, P., & Nevill, M. A. (2007). A simple statistical method for assessing the reliability of data entered into sport performance analysis systems. *International Journal of Performance Analysis in Sport*, *7*(1), 87–109.

Csataljay, G., O'Donoghue, P., Hughes, M., & Dancs, H. (2009). Performance indicators that distinguish winning and losing teams in basketball. *International Journal of Performance Analysis in Sport*, *9*(1), 60–66.

Duckett, J. (2012). *Objectivity in analysis: Performance analysis of football*. London: The Football Association.

Eaves, J. S. (2015). A history of sports notational analysis: A journey into the nineteenth century. *International Journal of Performance Analysis in Sport*, *15*(3), 1160–1176.

Fernandez-Echeverria, C., Mesquita, I., González-Silva, J., Claver, F., & Moreno, M. P. (2017). Match analysis within the coaching process: A critical tool to improve coach efficacy. *International Journal of Performance Analysis in Sport*, *17*(1–2), 149–163.

Gómez, M. Á., García-de-Alcaráz, A., & Furley, P. (2017). Analysis of contextual-related variables on serve and receiving performances in elite men's and women's table tennis players. *International Journal of Performance Analysis in Sport, 17*(6), 1–15.

Groom, R., Cushion, C., & Nelson, L. (2011). The delivery of video-based performance analysis by England youth soccer coaches: Towards a grounded theory. *Journal of Applied Sport Psychology, 23*(1), 16–32.

Guadagnoli, M., Holcomb, W., & Davis, M. (2002). The efficacy of video feedback for learning the golf swing. *Journal of Sports Sciences, 20*(8), 615–622.

Higham, D. G., Hopkins, W. G., Pyne, D. B., & Anson, J. M. (2014). Performance indicators related to points scoring and winning in international rugby sevens. *Journal of Sports Science & Medicine, 13*(2), 358–364.

Huggan, R., Nelson, L., & Potrac, P. (2015). Developing micropolitical literacy in professional soccer: A performance analyst's tale. *Qualitative Research in Sport, Exercise and Health, 7*(4), 504–520.

Hughes, M., Caudrelier, T., James, N., Redwood-Brown, A., Donnelly, I., Kirkbride, A., & Duschesne, C. (2012). Moneyball and soccer-an analysis of the key performance indicators of elite male soccer players by position. *Journal of Human Sport and Exercise, 7*(2), 402–412.

Hughes, M., Evans, S., & Wells, J. (2001). Establishing normative profiles in performance analysis. *International Journal of Performance Analysis in Sport, 1*(1), 1–26.

Hughes, M., & Franks, I. (2007). *The essentials of performance analysis: An introduction.* London: Routledge.

James, N., Mellalieu, S., & Jones, N. (2005). The development of position-specific performance indicators in professional rugby union. *Journal of Sports Sciences, 23*(1), 63–72.

James, N., Taylor, J., & Stanley, S. (2007). Reliability procedures for categorical data in performance analysis. *International Journal of Performance Analysis in Sport, 7*(1), 1–11.

Jones, N. M., Mellalieu, S. D., & James, N. (2004). Team performance indicators as a function of winning and losing in rugby union. *International Journal of Performance Analysis in Sport, 4*(1), 61–71.

Lago-Ballesteros, J., & Lago-Peñas, C. (2010). Performance in team sports: Identifying the keys to success in soccer. *Journal of Human Kinetics, 25,* 85–91.

Lago-Peñas, C., & Lago-Ballesteros, J. (2011). Game location and team quality effects on performance profiles in professional soccer. *Journal of Sports Science & Medicine, 10*(3), 465–471.

Lago-Peñas, C., Lago-Ballesteros, J., Dellal, A., & Gómez, M. (2010). Game-related statistics that discriminated winning, drawing and losing teams from the Spanish soccer league. *Journal of Sports Science & Medicine, 9*(2), 288.

Lago-Peñas, C., Lago-Ballesteros, J., & Rey, E. (2011). Differences in performance indicators between winning and losing teams in the UEFA Champions League. *Journal of Human Kinetics, 27,* 135–146.

Laird, P., & Waters, L. (2008). Eyewitness recollection of sport coaches. *International Journal of Performance Analysis in Sport, 8*(1), 76–84.

Liebermann, D. G., Katz, L., Hughes, M. D., Bartlett, R. M., McClements, J., & Franks, I. M. (2002). Advances in the application of information technology to sport performance. *Journal of Sports Sciences, 20*(10), 755–769.

Liu, H., Gomez, M. Á., Lago-Peñas, C., & Sampaio, J. (2015). Match statistics related to winning in the group stage of 2014 Brazil FIFA World Cup. *Journal of Sports Sciences, 33*(12), 1205–1213.

Liu, H., Hopkins, W., Gómez, A. M., & Molinuevo, S. J. (2013). Inter-operator reliability of live football match statistics from OPTA Sportsdata. *International Journal of Performance Analysis in Sport, 13*(3), 803–821.

Mackenzie, R., & Cushion, C. (2013). Performance analysis in football: A critical review and implications for future research. *Journal of Sports Sciences, 31*(6), 639–676.

Macquet, A. C., Ferrand, C., & Stanton, N. A. (2015). Divide and rule: A qualitative analysis of the debriefing process in elite team sports. *Applied ergonomics, 51,* 30–38.

Mikołajec, K., Maszczyk, A., & Zając, T. (2013). Game indicators determining sports performance in the NBA. *Journal of Human Kinetics, 37*(1), 145–151.

Millar, S. K., Oldham, A. R., Renshaw, I., & Hopkins, W. G. (2017). Athlete and coach agreement: Identifying successful performance. *International Journal of Sports Science & Coaching, 12*(6), 807–813.

Mosteller, F. (1979). A resistant analysis of 1971 and 1972 professional football. In J. H. Goldstein (Ed.), *Sports, games and play* (pp. 371–401). New Jersey: Laurence Erlbaum Associates.

Nelson, L. J., & Groom, R. (2012). The analysis of athletic performance: Some practical and philosophical considerations. *Sport, Education and Society, 17*(5), 687–701.

Nelson, L. J., Potrac, P., & Groom, R. (2014). Receiving video-based feedback in elite ice-hockey: A player's perspective. *Sport, Education and Society, 19*(1), 19–40.

Nicholls, S. B., & Worsfold, P. R. (2016). The observational analysis of elite coaches within youth soccer: The importance of performance analysis. *International Journal of Sports Science & Coaching, 11*(6), 825–831.

O'Donoghue, P. (2005). Normative profiles of sports performance. *International Journal of Performance Analysis in Sport, 5*(1), 104–119.

O'Donoghue, P. (2006). The use of feedback videos in sport. *International Journal of Performance Analysis in Sport, 6*(2), 1–14.

O'Donoghue, P. (2007). Reliability issues in performance analysis. *International Journal of Performance Analysis in Sport, 7*(1), 35–48.

O'Donoghue, P. (2008). Principal components analysis in the selection of key performance indicators in sport. *International Journal of Performance Analysis in Sport, 8*(3), 145–155.

O'Donoghue, P. (2009). *Research methods for sports performance analysis.* London: Routledge.

Potter, G., & Carter, A. (2001). The 1995 world cup finals. The four-year cycle: A comparison of the 1991 and 1995 Rugby World Cup Finals. In M. Hughes (Ed.), *Notational Analysis of Sport III* 216–219. Cardiff: UWIC.

Reeves, M. J., & Roberts, S. J. (2013). Perceptions of performance analysis in elite youth football. *International Journal of Performance Analysis in Sport, 13*(1), 200–211.

Sarmento, H., Bradley, P., Anguera, M. T., Polido, T., Resende, R., & Campaniço, J. (2016). Quantifying the offensive sequences that result in goals in elite futsal matches. *Journal of Sports Sciences, 34*(7), 621–629.

Sarmento, H., Marcelino, R., Anguera, M. T., CampaniÇo, J., Matos, N., & LeitÃo, J. C. (2014). Match analysis in football: A systematic review. *Journal of Sports Sciences, 32*(20), 1831–1843.

Taylor, J. B., Mellalieu, S. D., James, N., & Shearer, D. A. (2008). The influence of match location, quality of opposition, and match status on technical performance in professional association football. *Journal of Sports Sciences, 26*(9), 885–895.

Vaz, L., Van Rooyen, M., & Sampaio, J. (2010). Rugby game-related statistics that discriminate between winning and losing teams in IRB and Super twelve close games. *Journal of Sports Science & Medicine, 9*(1), 51–55.

Williams, J. J. (2012). Operational definitions in performance Analysis and the need for consensus. *International Journal of Performance Analysis in Sport, 12*(1), 52–63.

Worsfold, P., & Macbeth, K. (2009). The reliability of television broadcasting statistics in soccer. *International Journal of Performance Analysis in Sport, 9*(3), 344–353.

Wright, C., Atkins, S., & Jones, B. (2012). An analysis of elite coaches' engagement with performance analysis services (match, notational analysis and technique analysis). *International Journal of Performance Analysis of Sport, 12*(2), 436–451.

Wright, C., Atkins, S., Jones, B., & Todd, J. (2013). The role of performance analysts within the coaching process: Performance Analysts Survey 'The role of performance analysts in elite football club settings'. *International Journal of Performance Analysis in Sport, 13*(1), 240–261.

Wright, C., Atkins, S., Polman, R., Jones, B., & Sargeson, L. (2011). Factors associated with goals and goal scoring opportunities in professional soccer. *International Journal of Performance Analysis in Sport, 11*(3), 438–449.

Wright, C., Carling, C., Lawlor, C., & Collins, D. (2016). Elite football player engagement with performance analysis. *International Journal of Performance Analysis in Sport, 16*(3), 1007–1032.

Wright, C., Collins, D., & Carling, C. (2014). The wider context of performance analysis and it application in the football coaching process. *International Journal of Performance Analysis of Sport, 14*(3), 709–733.

Wulf, G., Shea, C., & Lewthwaite, R. (2010). Motor skill learning and performance: A review of influential factors. *Medical Education, 44*(1), 75–84.

9

PHYSICAL DEVELOPMENT OF THE YOUTH ATHLETE

Theoretical considerations and practical implications of growth and maturation

Greg Doncaster and Chris Towlson

Introduction

There has been a ~633 per cent increase in annual youth athlete focussed published research in the last 20 years, with many youth athletes now being exposed to talent identification and talent development programmes (e.g. British Cycling, British Swimming, British Tennis Association, English Cricket Board, English Football Academies Elite Player Performance Plan, The Royal Ballet, etc.) from ever-earlier ages. The effectiveness of such programmes, however, requires an appropriate level of understanding (and application) of child growth and maturation. Indeed, rapid changes in physiological and anthropometric characteristics during adolescent (~10 to 19 years) years can make it very difficult to provide appropriate physical support (Unnithan, White, Georgiou, Iga & Drust, 2012).

Setting the context: physical development of youth athletes

The need to recognise and accommodate the individual athlete, when working with youth populations, is arguably more pertinent than when working with adult athletes. We are all likely to have had experiences of being (or being subjected to) the more physically dominant individuals excelling in sports performance, particularly within team sports. Indeed, within the chronologically derived age groups (U12, U13, U14, etc.), such individuals are seen as the quicker, stronger and more powerful athletes who outperform their age-matched counterparts. Conversely, the smaller and less 'physically' developed individuals are viewed as slower, weaker and therefore inferior to the bigger athletes. Often, we have been involved in the talent identification (fitness testing) processes for identifying elite youth football players but despite the variances in aspects of growth and maturation within adolescent populations, the application of age group benchmarks still remained. As such, players were commonly assessed in relation to their age-group, not their (more appropriate) respective stage of growth and maturation. To what extent should we base ourselves on the week-to-week results (i.e. score-lines) that our youth team achieves? Or do we take a more developmental focused approach, in which we look at the individual athlete's performance in relation to their own stage of physical development?

As we will argue, research clearly demonstrates the extent to which aspects of growth and maturation can affect youth athletes' physical performance. Therefore, with the varying rates of growth and maturation within youth populations, there is a clear requirement to account for, and acknowledge, the implications of 'growth' and 'maturation' within athletic practice. We have a responsibility for the holistic development of our players and must ensure that all elements of our development programme are complementary. We must always seek to ensure that individual athletic needs are acknowledged and accommodated whenever possible. It also needs to be reiterated that patience and monitoring with regards to growth and maturation is highly important, especially phases that precede puberty.

For example, when providing aspects of strength and conditioning to youth athletes, it is important to consider growth and maturation because both of these factors affect the players' movement efficiency and quality. Regular assessment of players' maturity status can allow for the development and prescription of (strength) training programmes that accommodate the needs of the individual athlete. Once this information is known, effective planning of players' programmes in a greater level of detail can take place. While the majority of players may work through a physical continuum of movement competency, being aware of the stage of maturation and potential issues is of great importance, as we can make small changes to exercises or sessions that accommodate this. This helps us to (continually) develop players through periods of growth and maturation. Indeed, following the occurrence of peak height velocity, there are known to be increases in youth athletes' body mass, which are a result of increased muscle mass and commonly referred to as a period of peak weight velocity. While the exact time points and rate of change in peak height velocity and weight velocity are difficult to predict, early indication of these phases of growth and maturation can aid training prescription. For example, during periods of peak height velocity, alterations to training programmes can be adapted to focus on maintaining limb coordination, whereas during peak weight velocity, increases in muscle mass may be able to be accommodated through a (controlled) exposure to heavy loads and/or increased levels of power production.

In addition, a holistic approach to athlete development in which a multidisciplinary team communicate and collaborate is of paramount importance. The goal is to develop the improved all-round athlete but in practice there can be occasions in which expert practitioners (coaches, sports scientists, psychologists, etc.) work in their own respective silos, failing to recognise and align their approach with the rest of the team. As sports science support staff (Strength & Conditioning coaches, physiotherapists and analysts), the first responsibility is to safeguard the health and wellbeing of all players. In this regard, the systemic and systematic challenges associated with periods of growth and development in young players contribute to overall stresses experienced, and also impact on capacity to tolerate load. During these periods of accelerated growth, we work closely with technical coaches to deliver programmes which still have a technical and physical input, but are carefully controlled and monitored to minimise injury risk and maximise player availability and therefore development. An example of this is the development of continual monitoring systems in which players' growth and maturation can be tracked. This process will provide more detailed insights into individual athlete's current rates of growth and maturation, which will then inform training prescription. For example, during rapid periods of growth (e.g. peak height velocity) athletes' training load may be reduced to minimise the risk of growth-related injuries.

Theoretical underpinning: appreciation for growth and maturation

'Growth' refers to the process by which something has increased in size as a whole (e.g. increase in height or increase in leg length) whereas, 'maturation' refers to the process towards a mature state and can be established using indicators of maturity, which include skeletal maturation, somatic maturation and sexual maturation (Malina, Bouchard & Bar-Or, 2004). However, individual differences in both the timing and rate of growth and maturation within physically developing athletes only confound this area of research and athlete development. Therefore, to deliver suitable and specific physical development programmes, practitioners should consider individuals' maturity status in relation to their chronological age, often referred to as biological age (Unnithan et al., 2012). This will provide an indication of each individual athlete's maturity status, which subsequently informs both the design and delivery of individualised holistic development (Balyi & Hamilton, 2004; Lloyd & Oliver, 2014) and talent identification (Reilly, Williams, Nevill & Franks, 2000; Unnithan et al., 2012) programmes.

   The application of determining athlete maturity is of relevance given that children mature at a tempo that is individual to them and independent of chronological age groupings (U10's, 11's etc.) that are often used in competition. As established in ice-hockey (Sherar, Baxter-Jones, Faulkner & Russell, 2007), rugby (Till et al., 2011; Till, Cobley, O'Hara, Cooke & Chapman, 2014), gymnastics (Baxter-Jones et al., 1995) and football (Malina et al., 2000) young athletes tend to be categorised by chronological age, resulting in a varied range of maturity status within the same age group. Given the practicalities and complexities of practice within elite youth sport, non-invasive somatic (height, body-mass and age) measures (Khamis & Roche, 1994; Mills, Baker, Pacey, Wollin & Drew, 2017; Mirwald, Baxter-Jones, Bailey & Beunen, 2002; Moore et al., 2015) have often been a preferred method for practitioners and national governing bodies (English Football Association, Rugby Football League, Rugby Football Union) for estimating maturity status. This has subsequently elicited an abundance of research that seeks to investigate the impact and use of maturity status measures on the physical responses, development and (de)selection process within youth athlete populations.

Complexities of working with physically maturing athletes

Due to the added complexities of growth and maturation within youth populations, research examining adult training programmes and exercise physiology cannot simply be extrapolated to youth athletes (Matos & Winsley, 2007). For example, processes of growth and maturation are in themselves associated with improvements in physical performance, hence when considering the physical development of the youth athlete it is important to keep this in mind (Lloyd & Oliver, 2014). For example, research examining the anaerobic processes to energy production suggests that younger populations have a reduced glycolytic enzyme activity (Ratel, Duche & Williams, 2006; Tonson et al., 2010), which manifests itself in inferior levels of speed, strength and power (Gil et al., 2014; Lovell et al., 2015). Dotan et al. (2012) discuss the role of muscle activation when accounting for difference in physical performance capabilities in line with growth and maturation. In particular, Dotan et al. (2012) highlight the lower type-II (fast-twitch) fibre composition, reduced maximal volitional muscular force and increased levels of muscle co-contraction (simultaneous contraction of agonist and antagonist) within pre-adolescent populations, resulting in inferior levels of muscular performance.

The consequence of these physical differences is likely to transcend into physical performance. Indeed, within team sports, multiple studies have highlighted and demonstrated the (unintended) preference for individuals who are of an advanced stage of maturity (e.g. early maturers) (Malina et al., 2000; Till et al., 2014; Towlson et al., 2017). The preference for early maturing players is likely to be a result of their improved levels of strength and power (De Ste Croix, Deighan & Armstrong, 2003), which result in faster and stronger players, as well as their physical height and weight advantages (Malina et al., 2000; Malina et al., 2004; Philippaerts et al., 2006). Similarly, enhancements in such physical abilities have been shown to contribute to specific playing position allocation (Deprez et al., 2015; Towlson et al., 2017). For example, Towlson et al. (2017) found that maturation and anthropometric characteristics (height and weight) bias the allocation of more mature, taller and heavier English academy football players into key defensive roles from an early age. In addition, wide-sided (full-back and wide midfield) English academy football players have been identified as having developed greater sprint capacity than their central (central defence and midfield) playing team-mates, within U15–U18 age groups. These differences, however, were not evident preceding the adolescent growth spurt (prepubescent) and it is likely that this development of anaerobic capacity mirror the professional match-play characteristics of wide-sided players rather than an early maturity selection phenomenon (Towlson et al., 2017).

Whereas maturation has been shown to have a positive impact upon aspects of strength, power and speed (e.g. anaerobic energy systems), the research regarding cardio-respiratory fitness and oxidative metabolism (aerobic fitness) requires further consideration. In this regard, research has demonstrated a preference for aerobic energy provision in less mature individuals (Doncaster, Iga & Unnithan, 2017; Loftin, Sothern, Abe & Bonis, 2016; Tonson et al., 2010). Reviews by Ratel et al. (2006) and Ratel and Blazevich (2016) both highlight the preference for aerobic energy production within younger populations, with Ratel et al. (2006) also discussing the increased capacity for anaerobic energy production with advances in maturity status. Despite an inferior one-off sprint ability, the preference for aerobic metabolism within less mature (prepubescent) populations has particular advantages for an individual's ability to withstand fatigue (e.g. maintenance of sprinting performance during repeated sprints). This improved ability to maintain performance and withstand fatigue may be attributed to a greater percentage of type-I muscle fibres, higher levels of aerobic enzyme activity, enhanced mitochondrial volume density and an improved ability for phosphocreatine re-synthesis and muscle by-product clearance rates, post exercise (Ratel & Blazevich, 2016). The preference for aerobic energy provision may, however be due to an underdeveloped anaerobic system in pre-adolescent individuals (Ratel et al., 2006).

Finally, practitioners should seek to address (or at least acknowledge) whether or not a prescribed training programme has resulted in physical improvements which are independent of influences of growth and maturation. Furthermore, practitioners need to be aware of the impact growth and maturation can have upon both the physical and physiological capabilities of youth athletes, as this will have implications for training prescription and periodization. Here, research, which has compared the impacts of long-term systematic training against expected changes in physical development, can be particularly useful (Wright, Hurst & Taylor, 2016; Wrigley, Drust, Stratton, Atkinson & Gregson, 2014). Wrigley et al. (2014) compared 3-year changes in indicators of physical performance between elite academy football players, aged between 12–16 years and age-matched controls. Within the control group, there were improvements of 15.5 per cent, 4.5 per cent, 3.7 per cent and 48.2 per cent for counter-movement jump, 10m sprint, 20m sprint and an anaerobic endurance test (Yo-Yo Intermittent Recovery Level 2 test). Improvements within the elite academy football players were 22.4 per cent, 8.6 per cent, 9.5 per cent and 85 per cent for the same physical tests. As such, the changes incurred within the elite academy players were beyond expectations (i.e. greater than the age-matched controls) and independent of change in maturation. This is a particularly good example that highlights the need to consider the impact of growth and maturation on physical performance, and whether or not the training imposed upon the athlete has a positive impact, beyond expected (maturity related) developments. Therefore, when designing and implementing a training programme for youth athletes, practitioners should look to consider; (1) the length of the training programme, (2) the expected (natural) changes in physical performance and (3) the aspects of physical performance they intend to target and subsequently improve. In addition, practitioners need to consider the impact growth and maturation can have upon injuries, and the potential risk factors. Research by van der Sluis et al. (2014) suggests an increased vulnerability for traumatic injuries (i.e. injuries which resulted from a specific, identifiable event) during the adolescent growth spurt (peak height velocity: PHV) and a susceptibility to overuse injuries after PHV. Reasons for this include; less resistant articular surfaces (bone or cartilage which makes normal direct contact with another skeletal structure) to tensile, shear or compressive forces, decrease in bone-mineral density, lack of lean tissue mass, increase in joint hypermobility as well as growth and strength imbalances, which are a result in rapid growth during PHV (DiFiori et al., 2014).

Youth physical development models

Through the available scientific research there have been attempts to develop longitudinal models designed to optimise the physical development of youth athletes, in-line with the processes of growth and maturation (Balyi & Hamilton, 2004; Lloyd & Oliver, 2012). The traditional 'Long-term Athlete Development (LTAD)' model from Balyi and Hamilton (2004) focuses on 'windows of opportunity', during an athlete's physical development, despite limited evidence to support such an approach. Lloyd and Oliver (2012)'s more recent 'Youth Physical Development', in line with the research (Philippaerts et al., 2006; Towlson et al., 2017), suggests that the wide array of fitness components (e.g. strength, power, speed, etc.) can be trained from childhood, through adolescence, to a fully mature state. The specific focus (e.g. movement competency vs. strength development) and resultant mechanisms that lead to training adaptations and improved performance however, are likely to differ according to maturity status. Indeed, research by Till, Cobley, O'Hara, Chapman and Cooke (2013) tracked both anthropometric and fitness characteristics, once per year, for a 3-year period (U13s–U15s) and demonstrated that there was a clear variance in the development of both anthropometric and fitness characteristics players of differing maturity status. This emphasises the need to adopt an individual approach when working with youth athletes.

More recently, however, the International Olympic consensus statement on long-term youth athletic development (Bergeron et al., 2015) demands that athlete development frameworks should be holistic and representative of the multidimensional nature of athlete development and that 'best practice' should be realised for each development phase rather than prescriptions of training based on age and maturity based factors. Such sentiment is echoed by the British Association of Sport and Exercises Scientists (BASES), who state that a maturational threshold for enhanced sensitivity to athletic training (i.e. 'windows of opportunity') is unlikely to occur at a distinct point – rather, they should be viewed as a continuation throughout childhood (Lloyd & Oliver, 2012; McNarry et al., 2014). Therefore, following these recommendations (Bergeron et al., 2015; McNarry et al., 2014), there is a necessity for further research and in particular, controlled longitudinal investigations of physical development within youth athletes. Despite the given complexities of longitudinal research, such research should help clarify the optimal training prescription that will elicit the greatest rates of development for distinct physical attributes with respect to maturation.

While, research regarding 'windows of opportunity' have in large been discredited (Ford et al., 2011; Lloyd & Oliver, 2012; Wrigley et al., 2014), research has revealed contrasting effects of systematic training within youth athletes, in relation to maturity status (Meylan, Cronin, Oliver, Hopkins & Contreras, 2014; Wright et al., 2016). In particular, Wright et al. (2016) found that 8 weeks of high-intensity interval training had a positive impact on endurance capacity for those within their peak height velocity (PHV) (31 per cent) and those post-PHV (28 per cent) but only moderate individual differences evident within those identified as pre-PHV. In addition, decrements in repeated-sprint ability (6.5 per cent) were also evident within those identified as pre-PHV (Wright et al., 2016). Moreover, Meylan et al. (2014) examined the effect of maturation on adaptations to 8 weeks of strength training and found that strength training was less effective before PHV (pre-PHV vs. mid-PHV & post-PHV), with regards to 1 repetition maximum and estimations of maximal force and power. There was no impact of maturation, however, on movements that were of a high-velocity (e.g. 30m sprint and horizontal jump). Although cross-sectional studies, these results do suggest that there may be incidences within an individual's physical development when there is an opportunity to expose them to particular types of training. Nevertheless, further longitudinal research, which considers or controls for extraneous variables, is required to establish whether such 'opportunities' are related to maturation.

Impact of energy provision on physical performance

As previously discussed, the processes of maturation will have an impact upon the energy provision during sporting performance, particularly during high-intensity intermittent exercise. A more mature metabolically active anaerobic energy system will correspond to improvements in one-off sprint and power activities (e.g. jumps, throws, etc.) but it will also have implications for recovery time. In contrast, pre-adolescent athletes demonstrate a prevalence for aerobic energy provision and therefore a potentially reduced susceptibility to muscular fatigue (Ratel et al., 2006; Tonson et al., 2010), resulting in improved rates of recovery. In relation to sporting performance, however, research from Buchheit and Mendez-Villanueva (2014) demonstrated, in a cohort of U15 football players, that players advanced in maturation presented systematically greater match running performances than their less mature teammates, as evidenced by a greater amount of high intensity activity (distance covered above a speed threshold of > 19 km/h^{-1}). This is likely to be a result of their improved sprinting ability (anaerobic capacity, increase in leg length and explosive leg strength), rather than their ability to maintain their sprinting ability (Valente-dos-Santos et al., 2012). Nevertheless, researchers should consider the impact of absolute speed thresholds within maturity-affected groups and the associated limitations. Indeed, relative and individualised speed thresholds may be more appropriate when assessing physical performance during match play, in relation to maturity status (Abt & Lovell, 2009; Doncaster, Marwood, Iga & Unnithan, 2016). In addition, the maturity status of youth athletes will have implications for the prescription and delivery of fatigue inducing training drills (e.g. high intensity interval training, repeated sprint drills, small-sided games), as the allocated recovery time may need to be adapted in respect to an athlete's current maturity status.

Practical recommendations

Despite the plethora of growth and maturation related research, the transfer from theory to practice can often be ambiguous and confusing. As a result, the following section aims to highlight practical recommendations, based upon the previous discussions of the literature, thus aiding in the development of evidenced-based practice. Practical implications and recommendations which should be considered when working with youth athletes are;

1) Specific to team sports, there is a wealth of evidence to show that early-maturing youth athletes are over-selected compared to later-maturing players in many professional leagues throughout the world (Helsen, van Winckel & Williams, 2005). Firstly, we recommend that you seek to assess if there is such a bias within your groups of athletes. Are those born earlier in the year favoured in comparison to those born later in the selection year? If so, one solution to this problem, is to categorise young players according to their maturity status (commonly referred to as 'bio-banding') (Cumming, Lloyd, Oliver, Eisenmann & Malina, 2017b) rather than their chronological age. The International Centre for Sports Studies and the introduction of the English Premier League's 'bio-banding' programme have given increased recognition to this matter. Several methods can be used to 'bio-band' (group) athletes, a common method employed within EPL academies is to categorise players based on a percentage of estimated adult stature attainment (Cumming et al., 2017a). In addition, you may also seek to adjust the (age) grouping of athletes at certain times within training, giving athletes the experience of training with relatively older and relatively younger athletes throughout their development.

2) If implementing bio-banding approaches, we would advise that you seek to monitor players' development in relation to this method of grouping players.

This may be via simple subjective based measures (e.g. session RPE) or (if available) through the use of advanced technological systems (e.g. Global Positioning Systems). Indeed, there is a paucity of evidence on the application of bio-banding and its long-term effectiveness for exposing the technical, physical, psychological and social determinants for ongoing talent development.

3) Encourage the use of resistance training for developing aspects of muscular strength in both children and adolescents (Behm, Faigenbaum, Falk & Klentrou, 2008; Lloyd et al., 2014). As noted previously, youth athletes should not be viewed as mini-adults (Matos & Winsley, 2007), and any practitioners who are involved in the physical development of youth athletes need to have the requisite knowledge and skills to provide safe and effective training (Behm et al., 2008). In this regard, strength training should not be simply viewed as 'lifting heavy weights', instead consider the individual athlete's maturity status and their current needs and developmental stage, adopting an approach to strength training that incorporates and acknowledges the sport-specific movement competencies (with a strong coaching/technical element). In such an approach you can then systematically integrate and implement additional exercises, which emphasise key aspects relating to sport performance, such as force production, by adapting the exercise and/or load in relation to the individual's stage of development and technical capabilities (Lloyd & Oliver, 2014).

4) Increases in strength appear to be related to maturation, with enhancements in neural, structural and hormonal changes occurring during adolescence (Lloyd et al., 2014). Indeed, if a young athlete has both the physical and physiological capacities (and proficiency) to perform heavy resistance exercise (e.g. maximum strength or power training), and provided there is an appropriate environment and rationale to do this, such training should be encouraged. Conversely, if your athlete is experiencing a period of volatile growth (rapid increases in limb length) or does not yet have the physical and physiological capacities, then a programme which has a dominantfocus on either movement competency, neural development, co-ordination or technical proficiency (Lloyd et al., 2014), may be preferred.

5) Be assured that there is no evidence to suggest that resistance training will have a negative impact upon an athlete's growth and maturation during childhood and adolescence (Faigenbaum et al., 2009). Rather, the targeted provision of resistance training should be encouraged to aid and enhance an athlete's development. Similarly, with regard to sport-specific conditioning, an indication of a player's current rate of growth, as well as their maturity status can help to guide and inform both training prescription and training practices. Therefore develop methods and process which will allow you to regularly monitor your athlete's growth and development (e.g. height measurements and maturity status; Moore et al., 2015).

6) Develop protocols which are appropriate for the individual athlete (e.g. recovery times, power outputs, expected levels of fatigue). Maturity status also has an impact upon the contribution from anaerobic and aerobic energy sources (Ratel et al., 2006), in addition to improved levels of strength, power and speed (Lloyd & Oliver, 2014). When devising conditioning drills you should, again, consider the athlete's current rate of growth and maturity status. Athletes that are regarded as prepubescent (pre-PHV), may be given less time during the recovery periods, due to their (likely) increased reliance upon the aerobic energy system and underdeveloped anaerobic system. Conversely, more mature athletes who are regarded as post-PHV, may be allocated a greater amount of recovery due to their improved ability to activate the anaerobic system and the subsequent feelings of fatigue that are associated with anaerobic energy production. Admittedly, however, this will depend upon the current training focus and intended adaptations but it should give you an insight into how an appreciation of maturity status can inform training practices.

7) Consider whether or not the training you are prescribing is appropriate your athlete's current stage of physical development. Certain periods of growth and maturation (i.e. PHV) are potentially susceptible periods for injury (DiFiori et al., 2014; van der Sluis et al., 2014) due to rapid increase in limb length. As a result, a focus toward movement competencies, technique and inter- and intra-muscular co-ordination is advisable at this stage of an athlete's development. Indeed, while an athlete may still undertake a holistic training programme during their period of PHV, the distribution and focus of key aspects may be altered at this stage of volatile growth, thus aiding their development. For example, with the dramatic increases in limb length (i.e. leg length) a reduced exposure to sprinting and an increased focus on developing players' inter- and intra-muscular co-ordination through plyometric, co-ordination based exercises, may be beneficial. DiFiori et al. (2014) provide a number of recommendations within their position statement, including; (a) limited weekly and yearly participation times, with scheduled rest periods, (b) careful monitoring of training workload during periods of PHV, (c) design and implementation of appropriate conditioning programmes to help target areas of potential vulnerability and (d) execution of pre-practice neuromuscular training exercises (prehab) prior to training sessions and competitive matches.

Evidence and research in relation to athlete's (physical) development is ongoing and with this growing base of knowledge it is the task of the sports practitioner to synthesise, analyse, disseminate and apply such information, where appropriate, into practice. In doing so, researchers should seek to support those working in practice by communicating and cooperating with each other to provide evidence (and analyse existing evidence) which helps to improve future practice.

Acknowledgements

The authors would like to acknowledge all practitioners who helped to provide insights into the practical relevance of growth and maturation, in particular Jamie Goldsmith, Chris Barnes, Paul White and Robert Fox.

References

Abt, G., & Lovell, R. (2009). The use of individualized speed and intensity thresholds for determining the distance run at high-intensity in professional soccer. *Journal of Sports Sciences*, *27*(9), 893–898.

Balyi, I., & Hamilton, A. (2004). *Long-term athlete development: Trainability in childhood and adolescence.* Windows of opportunity, optimal trainability, Victoria: National Coaching Institute British Columbia and Advanced Training and Performance Ltd.

Baxter-Jones, A., Helms, P., Maffulli, N., Baines-Preece, J., & Preece, M. (1995). Growth and development of male gymnasts, swimmers, soccer and tennis players: A longitudinal study. *Annals of Human Biology*, *22*(5), 381–394.

Behm, D., Faigenbaum, A., Falk, B., & Klentrou, P. (2008). Canadian society for exercise physiology position paper: Resistance training in children and adolescents. *Applied Physiology Nutrition, and Metabolism*, *33*, 547–561.

Bergeron, M., Mountjoy, M., Armstrong, N., Chia, M., Cote, J., Emery, C. A., Faigenbaum, A., et al. (2015). International Olympic Committee consensus statement on youth athletic development. *British Journal of Sports Medicine*, *4*, 843–851.

Buchheit, M., & Mendez-Villanueva, A. (2014). Effects of age, maturity and body dimensions on match running performance in highly trained under-15 soccer players. *Journal of Sports Sciences*, *32*(13), 1271–1278.

Cumming, S., Brown, D., Mitchell, S., Bunce, J., Hunt, D., Hodges, C., Crane, G., et al. (2017a). Premier League academy soccer players' experiences of competing in a tournament bio-banded for biological maturation. *Journal of Sports Sciences*, *19*, 1–9.

Cumming, S., Lloyd, R. S., Oliver, J. L., Eisenmann, J. C., & Malina, R. (2017b). Bio-banding in sport: Applications to competition, talent identification, and strength and conditioning of youth athletes. *National Strength & Conditioning Association*, *39*(2), 34–47.

De Ste Croix, M., Deighan, M., & Armstrong, N. (2003). Assessment and interpretation of isokinetic muscle strength during growth and maturation. *Sports Medicine*, *33*(10), 727–743.

Deprez, D., Fransen, J., Boone, J., Lenoir, M., Philippaerts, R., & Vaeyens, R. (2015). Characteristics of high-level youth soccer players: Variation by playing position. *Journal of Sports Sciences*, *33*(3), 243–254.

DiFiori, J., Benjamin, H., Brenner, J., Gregory, A., Jayanthi, N., Landry, G., & Luke, A. (2014). Overuse injuries and burnout in youth sports: A position statement from the American Medical Society for Sports Medicine. *British Journal of Sports Medicine*, *24*, 3–20.

Doncaster, G., Iga, J., & Unnithan, V. (2017). Assessing differences in cardio-respiratory fitness with respect to maturity status in highly trained youth soccer players. *Pediatric Exercise Science*, *30*(2), 216–228.

Doncaster, G., Marwood, S., Iga, J., & Unnithan, V. (2016). Influence of oxygen uptake kinetics on physical performance in youth soccer. *European Journal of Applied Physiology*, *116*, 1781–1794.

Dotan, R., Mitchell, C., Cohen, R., Klentrou, P., Gabriel, D., & Falk, B. (2012). Child – adult differences in muscle activation – a review. *Pediatric Exercise Science*, *24*, 2–21.

Faigenbaum, A., Kraemer, W., Blimkie, C., Jeffreys, I., Micheli, L. J., Nitka, M., Rowland, T. W. (2009). Youth resistance training: Updated position statement paper from the National Strength and Conditioning Association. *Journal of Strength and Conditioning Research, 23*(4), S60-S79.

Ford, P., De Ste Croix, M., Lloyd, R., Meyers, R., Moosavi, M., Oliver, J., Till, K., et al. (2011). The long-term athlete development model: Physiological evidence and application. *Journal of Sports Sciences, 29*(4), 389–402.

Gil, S. M., Badiola, A., Bidaurrazaga-Letona, I., Zabala-Lili, L., Gravina, L., Santos-Concejero, J., … Granados, C. (2014). Relationship between the relative age effect and anthropometry, maturity and performance in young soccer players. *Journal of Sports Sciences, 32*(5), 479–486.

Helsen, W. F., van Winckel, J., & Williams, M. (2005). The relative age effect in youth soccer across Europe. *Journal of Sports Sciences, 23*(6), 629–636.

Khamis, H. J., & Roche, A. F. (1994). Predicting adult stature without using skeletal age: The Khamis-Roche method. *Pediatrics, 94*(4), 504–507.

Lloyd, R., Faigenbaum, A., Stone, M., Oliver, J. L., Jeffreys, I., Moody, J. A., Brewer, C., et al. (2014). Position statement on youth resistance training: The 2014 International Consensus. *British Journal of Sports Medicine, 48*, 498–505.

Lloyd, R. S., & Oliver, J. L. (2012). The youth physical development model: A new approach to long-term athletic development. *Strength and Conditioning Journal, 34*(3), 61–72.

Lloyd, R., & Oliver, J. L. (2014). *Strength and conditioning for young athletes: Science and application.* London: Routledge.

Loftin, M., Sothern, M., Abe, T., & Bonis, M. (2016). Expression of VO2peak in children and youth, with special reference to allometric scaling. *Sports Medicine, 46*, 1451–1460.

Lovell, R., Towlson, C., Parkin, G., Portas, M., Vaeyens, R., & Cobley, S. (2015). Soccer player characteristics in English lower-league development programmes: The relationships between relative age, maturation, anthropometry and physical fitness. *PLOSone, 10*(9), e0137238.

Malina, R., Pena Reyes, M., Eisenmann, J., Horta, L., Rodrigues, J., & Miller, R. (2000). Height, mass and skeletal maturity of elite Portuguese soccer players aged 11-16 years. *Journal of Sports Sciences, 18*(9), 685–693.

Malina, R. M., Bouchard, C., & Bar-Or, O. (2004). *Growth, maturation, and physical activity.* Champaig, IL: Human Kinetics Publishers.

Matos, N., & Winsley, R. J. (2007). Trainability of young athletes and overtraining. *Journal of Sports Science and Medicine, 6*, 353–367.

McNarry, M., Barker, A., Lloyd, R., Buchheit, M., Williams, C., & Oliver, J. (2014). The BASES expert statement on trainability during childhood and adolescence. *Sport and Exercise Scientist, 41*, 22–23.

Meylan, C., Cronin, J., Oliver, J., Hopkins, W., & Contreras, B. (2014). The effect of maturation on adaptations to strength training and detraining in 11-15 year-olds. *Scandinavian Journal of Medicine and Science in Sports, 24*, e156-e164.

Mills, K., Baker, D., Pacey, V., Wollin, M., & Drew, M. (2017). What is the most accurate and reliable methodological approach for predicting peak height velocity in adolescents? A systematic review. *Journal of Science and Medicine in Sport, 20*, 572–577.

Mirwald, R. L., Baxter-Jones, A., Bailey, D. A., & Beunen, G. P. (2002). An assessment of maturity from anthropometric measurements. *Medicine and Science in Sports and Exercise, 34*(4), 689.

Moore, S. A., McKay, H. A., Macdonald, H., Nettlefold, L., Baxter-Jones, A. D., Cameron, N., & Brasher, P. M. (2015). Enhancing a somatic maturity prediction model. *Medicine and Science in Sports & Exercise, 47*(8), 1755–1764.

Philippaerts, R., Vaeyens, R., Janssens, M., Van Renterghem, B., Matthys, D., Craen, R., Bourgois, J., et al. (2006). The relationships between peak height velocity and physical performance in youth soccer players. *Journal of Sports Sciences, 24*(3), 221–230.

Ratel, S., & Blazevich, A. J. (2016). Are prepubertal children metabolically comparable to well-trained adult endurance athletes? *Sports Medicine, 47*(8), 1477–1485.

Ratel, S., Duche, P., & Williams, C. A. (2006). Muscle fatigue during high-intensity exercise in children. *Sports Medicine, 36*(12), 1031–1065.

Reilly, T., Williams, A., Nevill, A., & Franks, A. (2000). A multidisciplinary approach to talent identification in soccer. *Journal of Sports Sciences, 18*, 695–702.

Sherar, L. B., Baxter-Jones, A. D., Faulkner, R. A., & Russell, K. W. (2007). Do physical maturity and birth date predict talent in male youth ice hockey players? *Journal of Sports Sciences, 25*(8), 879–886.

Till, K., Cobley, S., O'Hara, J., Brightmore, A., Cooke, C., & Chapman, C. (2011). Using anthropometric and performance characteristics to predict selection in junior UK Rugby League players. *Journal of Science and Medicine in Sport, 14*(3), 264–269.

Till, K., Cobley, S., O'Hara, J., Chapman, C., & Cooke, C. (2013). An individualized longitudinal approach to monitoring the dynamics of growth and fitness development in adolescent athletes. *Journal of Strength and Conditioning Research, 27*(5), 1313–1321.

Till, K., Cobley, S., O'Hara, J., Cooke, C., & Chapman, C. (2014). Considering maturation status and relative age in the longitudinal evaluation of junior rugby league players. *Scandinavian Journal of Medicine and Science in Sports, 24*(3), 569–576.

Tonson, A., Ratel, S., Le Fur, Y., Vilmen, C., Cozzone, P. J., & Bendahan, D. (2010). Muscle energetics changes throughout maturation: A quantitative 31P-MRS analysis. *Journal of Applied Physiology, 109*, 1769–1778.

Towlson, C., Cobley, S., Midgley, A. W., Garrett, A., Parkin, G., & Lovell, R. (2017). Relative age, maturation and physical biases on position allocation in elite-youth soccer. *International Journal of Sports Medicine, 38*, 201–209.

Unnithan, V., White, J., Georgiou, A., Iga, J., & Drust, B. (2012). Talent identification in youth soccer. *Journal of Sports Sciences, 30*(15), 1719–1726.

Valente-dos-Santos, J., Coelho-e-Silva, M., Severino, V., Duarte, J., Martins, R. A., Seabra, A. T., Philippaerts R. M., et al. (2012). Longitudinal study of repeated sprint performance in youth soccer players of contrasting skeletal maturity status. *Journal of Sports Science and Medicine, 11*, 371–379.

van der Sluis, A., Elferink-Gemser, M., Coelho-e-Silva, M., Nijober, J., Brink, M., & Visscher, C. (2014). Sport injuries aligned to peak height velocity in talented pubertal soccer players. *International Journal of Sports Medicine, 35*, 351–355.

Wright, M. D., Hurst, C., & Taylor, J. M. (2016). Contrasting effects of a mixed-methods high-intensity interval training intervention in girl football players. *Journal of Sports Sciences, 39*(19), 1808–1815.

Wrigley, R., Drust, B., Stratton, G., Atkinson, G., & Gregson, W. (2014). Long-term soccer-specific training enhances the rate of physical development of academy soccer players independent of maturation status. *International Journal of Sports Medicine, 35*(13), 1090–1094.

10

PSYCHOLOGICAL CHARACTERISTICS OF DEVELOPING EXCELLENCE IN YOUTH COACHING

Áine Macnamara and Iain Simpson

Introduction: equipping young athletes for challenge and choice

As practitioners working on the talent development pathway, both in a school setting and in the pre-academy space, we recognise the importance of developing psycho-behavioural characteristics as 'part and parcel' of the coaching process. Indeed, our experience in both these settings has shown that many of the most promising young athletes do not progress to the next level and either drop out of sport completely, or compete at lower levels than would be expected because they don't have the skills and capabilities to cope with the inevitable challenges of development. Interestingly, we have also observed the opposite with some players who might not have shown early signs of talent but through sheer commitment, determination and hard work progress through to high levels of sport. As a result of these observations, and reflecting the evidence from research, we have more and more begun to appreciate how an athlete's potential to develop depends on physical ability, an appropriate physical profile *and* other determinants such as commitment, motivation and determination. Reflecting this, some of the approaches we have taken within our coaching environment have centred around *Psychological Characteristics of Developing Excellence (PCDEs)* and embedding these into our coaching structures in a very practical, player-centred and coach-delivered manner. Embedding the teaching, development and refinement of PCDEs *within* the coaching process was a deliberate decision and a very important consideration in a school and youth sport setting. A decision to focus on a new element of coaching will almost certainly never coincide with a greater allocation of time or resource. Therefore, a pragmatic approach to including PCDEs must be to work within an existing timescale and to incorporate interventions within an existing coaching framework necessitating buy-in from coaches, athletes and other support staff to optimise the process. In this chapter, we will offer an overview of the PCDE framework, drawing on evidence from literature and research before discussing the operationalisation of this in a school sport environment.

Psychological characteristics of developing excellence

There is a robust evidence base for the importance of psychological characteristics as determinants of both performance and development. In talent development terms, and as introduced above, we propose that a range of psychological factors have been shown to play a key role in the realisation of potential. Termed *Psychological Characteristics of Developing Excellence* (PCDEs; MacNamara, Button & Collins, 2010a, 2010b), these encompass both the trait characteristics (the tendency to …) and the state-deployed skills (the ability to … when …) shown to play a crucial role in the realisation of potential. Importantly, PCDEs are not just the mental skills, such as imagery or goal setting that are a traditional part of a Mental Skills Training (MST) package, but also include attitudes, emotions and desires such as commitment (see Table 10.1) that are essential for negotiating the development pathway. PCDEs allow young performers to optimise development opportunities (e.g. first time appearances at a new level of competition, significant wins and losses), adapt to setbacks (e.g. injury, slumps in performance) and effectively negotiate key transitions (e.g. selection, demands for increased practice) encountered along the pathway to excellence. Simply, PCDEs equip young athletes with the capacity and competencies to strive to reach their potential, at whatever level that is.

The importance of emphasising psychological skills and behaviours as a key part of the developmental diet of young athletes reflects a multiplicative appreciation of talent development (Simonton, 1999). Even if a young athlete looks like the 'real deal' and is performing at a high level as a youth, they must possess and systematically develop the PCDEs that allow them to interact effectively with the developmental opportunities encountered along the pathway. As such, the systematic development of PCDEs in youth coaching is a crucial step in

TABLE 10.1 Psychological characteristics of developing excellence

- Commitment
- Focus & distraction control
- Realistic performance evaluation
- Self-awareness
- Coping with pressure
- Planning & self-organisation
- Goal setting
- Quality practice
- Effective imagery
- Actively seeking social support

supporting the translation of potential into talent and ensuring young athletes can be 'the best they can be'. Of course, there is not a causative relationship between PCDEs and high-level performance; the route to the top is far too complex! However, ensuring that young athletes have a 'toolbox' of mental skills, and the ability to draw on these to cope with developmental challenge, will provide aspiring elites with the capacity and competencies to strive to reach their potential. PCDEs appear to be the mechanism to allow young athletes strive for challenge and choice on their developmental journey.

This approach might be especially important for the 'best performing' young athletes in schools and academy settings; after all, natural ability and certain physical and anthropometric profiles can bring significant early success but an overly smooth pathway may be the worst preparation for senior success (Pearson, Naughton & Torode, 2006). If a young performer hasn't had to invest considerable effort to achieve, cope with any setbacks or deal with disappointments during their early years, it is unlikely that they have had the opportunity to develop the psycho-behavioural skills, work ethic, or commitment to cope with the (almost) inevitable challenges that await them later on in the pathway. The real-world experiences of young athletes follow a non-linear and dynamic trajectory (Abbott, Button, Pepping & Collins, 2005; Bridge & Toms, 2013; MacNamara et al., 2010a, 2010b) and there is growing recognition that facing and overcoming a degree of challenge is desirable for aspiring elites and as such, should be recognised and employed. Indeed, in the 2016 paper 'Super champions, champions and almosts: Commonalities and differences on the rocky road' (Collins, MacNamara & McCarthy, 2016), super champions – athletes who had achieved the highest level in their sport – were differentiated from their less successful counterparts by their use of positive proactive coping and a 'learn from it' approach to challenge. This skill-based, PCDE focus to talent development is supported extensively in the literature (e.g. Gould, Dieffenbach & Moffett, 2002; MacNamara et al., 2010a, 2010b) and suggests that the differences between levels of adult achievement relate more to what performers *bring to* the challenges than *what* they experience.

The rocky road to success

Interestingly, however, many talent development pathways (whether these are schools, clubs, or academies) do not provide an optimum environment for developing PCDEs. In an effort to accelerate young athletes' progress, talent development environments often minimise the number and certainly the impact of developmental challenges on young athletes. For example, independent schools in the UK certainly provide young athletes with significant financial, coaching, academic and sport science assistance in a supportive environment. Indeed, many talent development pathways purposefully try to smoothe the pathway for their most talented performers. 'Helicopter coaches', or 'snowplough parents', tend to try and soften the journey for performers, removing challenges, doing things 'for' and 'to' the athlete in an effort to expedite success. The problem is further exacerbated since, due to their early ability, many young athletes may often not encounter many challenges until late in their career. Providing early opportunities to develop and refine PCDEs that help performers overcome developmental challenges should be one of the key aspects of youth coaching. Teaching PCDEs and providing opportunities to deploy these appropriately appears to be an appropriate way to prepare performers for what is ahead.

Of course, without experiencing a degree of challenge during development many young athletes will not have the opportunity to develop, test and refine the PCDEs required for progression and performance in sport. As such, there have been calls for the inclusion of structured challenge, designed and implemented as part of the pathway, as an essential feature of talent development and young coaching systems (Collins & MacNamara, 2012) and something that should be recognised and employed. For young athletes, these structured challenges might include experiences such as playing up an age-group, out of position, de-selection or selection for particular competitions, different roles or responsibilities, or increases in training load (Collins & MacNamara, 2012). Essentially, this approach requires coaching to design experiences that require athletes to learn, deploy and then tweak PCDEs to negotiate a 'challenge-filled' pathway. There appears to be considerable merit in the teaching of PCDEs and offering opportunities to test and refine these skills against real-life challenges. As such, the explicit teaching of PCDEs, implemented and supported against developmental challenges along the pathway has been shown to equip athletes with the generalisable skills, and the ability to deploy them appropriately to cope with challenge (Collins & MacNamara, 2012). The crucial factor is that the challenge experiences should be preceded by PCDE skills training, and fully supported and debriefed, if the benefits of this approach are to accrue (Collins & MacNamara, 2012).

In this section, we have identified the importance of PCDEs as part of the 'toolbox' young athletes require to progress in sport. Having identified this, the next logical step is to look at how PCDEs can be developed and deployed (see Gould et al., 2010) in talent development environments. In the following section, Iain will discuss how he designed a PCDE framework and embedded this into the coaching curriculum in an independent school sport environment.

What do PCDEs look like in youth coaching?

Defining PCDE behaviours

Incorporating PCDEs into the coaching environment is a key step in encouraging young athletes to behave like champions and make the most of the opportunities they are afforded. The first step in this process is to understand exactly what these 'champion behaviours' entail and what performers should be doing to demonstrate each PCDE both generally *and* in response to specific events and challenges. In this section, I offer some examples of how we have incorporated PCDEs into our coaching programme in a school environment. Ensuring the pragmatic application of this concept was a priority and we followed a series of practical guidelines to ensure that the process was as effective, authentic, systematic and practical as possible.

To begin, we defined each PCDE that we wanted the players to display. We ensured that each of the PCDEs were defined as clear and observable behaviours so that the player recognised what was expected from them and progress could be monitored by the athlete themselves as well as the coach. To illustrate this process, let's use 'commitment' as the first example. If we asked different coaches athletes, or teachers in a school what commitment was, they would likely respond with a variety of answers. For example, a committed athlete may be one who never misses practice, or who engages in lots of independent training or someone that 'never gives up' (see Table 10.2). However, in order to increase clarity, each PCDE needs to be broken down into observable and objectively defined behaviours that are important for *that* athlete(s) at *that* particular point in their development. By doing this, the coach, teacher and, of course, the athlete themselves can easily assess, monitor, measure and reinforce progress and behaviour. This joined-up thinking is critical to make sure everyone is on message: all concerned must understand what behaviours are important for their particular activity and consistently model and/or reinforce them.

It is also important that each PCDE is defined in a manner that is meaningful to both the young athlete and the context in which they perform. The main consideration here is that each PCDE must be operationalised with the specific needs of the individual in mind. As such, Table 10.3 illustrates how the behaviours might differ for young athletes at different stages or at different ages within a school environment. Essentially, as young athletes progress there are levels of commitment that can be built on and layered. At the basic level, young athletes are encouraged to realise their level of competence and to self-reinforce. At the intermediate level, young athletes are encouraged to begin to take responsibility for their own development. At the advanced level, young athletes are encouraged to aspire to excellence by achieving autonomous development (Abbott

TABLE 10.2 Commitment behaviours (adapted from Abbott, Collins, Sowerby & Martindale, 2007)

- Arrives early to training
- Keeps going hard in practice
- Trains independently away from the rest of the team
- Shows a consistent effort and good preparation
- Works hard at their own level
- Understands and is responsible for both training and rest where appropriate
- Is resilient when faced with obstacles and setbacks

et al., 2007). A key point in our PCDE curricula was to remember that the behaviour should be *visual* (something that can be seen and measured), *behavioural* (something that can be promoted) and *positive* (i.e. not a lack of …). Simply, we want to emphasise the development of skills and characteristics that will improve performance and the athlete's mental skills profile.

The same process and guidelines can then be followed for each PCDE, starting with defining the behaviours and then considering a staged approach across the age-groups. Tables 10.4 and 10.5 outline some of the PCDE behaviours that were incorporated into our coaching curriculum and embedded across sports.

As we discussed earlier in the chapter, the development of PCDEs is embedded within the day-to-day coaching practices rather than an 'extra' element of the coaching curriculum. As such, this required coaches to consider how their session design supports the development and testing of the PCDE behaviours. In the case of 'focus and distraction control', for example, we emphasised the importance of players remaining engaged during training and focusing on the objectives of the session: this can be facilitated through short intense periods of training incorporating a cognitive element such as decision making. Clearly articulating the focus of the session – technical, tactical *and* PCDE – to the players was an important element of the session design. In the competitive and training environment, we

TABLE 10.3 A developmental approach to commitment behaviours

- *Basic*: Punctuality, correct kit, water bottle, timekeeping
- *Intermediate*: Positive engagement with extra practice, off field sessions; S&C, video analysis and pathways
- *Advanced*: Demonstrates attention to technical detail, engagement with improving weaknesses and making sacrifices (social life, etc.)

TABLE 10.4 A developmental approach to coping with pressure behaviours

- *Basic*: Trains with freedom when time and space are constrained. Copes with academic, family and sport pressures.
- *Intermediate*: Maintains performance level despite situation, circumstance (crowd, opposition, score-line)
- *Advanced*: Effective problem solving under pressure in matches. Uses techniques to stay in the moment when pressure is high (breathing, centring etc.)

TABLE 10.5 A developmental approach to focus and distraction control behaviours

- *Basic*: Eye contact when listening to coach, engaging in training, remains on task
- *Intermediate*: Understanding of internal and external distractions
- *Advanced*: Use of focus techniques – self-talk, centring etc.

emphasised the importance of focusing on positive performance and relevant cues. One of the techniques that we have used successfully in training to prepare for this is *freezing*. By stopping play, in the moment, it not only checks and reviews decision-making and understanding but checks the picture that players are seeing and any irrelevant cues/distractors that they are attending to. This checking can be as simple as *'what picture are you seeing right now?'* or *'what are you thinking right now?'* To check these PCDE behaviours in matches we ensured that this questioning and reflection was part of the video analysis process; *'what were you thinking when XXXXX happened? Was that the most effective thought? Did you notice that …?'* We have also used a method when one player is removed from a training game and stands in a good vantage point with a coach. The coach asks the player to commentate on the game with perhaps a particular theme in mind. An example of this would be a hockey player commentating on the formation of an opposition team; we are looking for the player to be able to pick up big pictures, in terms of the shape of the formation as well as smaller pictures, such as an individual player's body shape or skill levels. Again, we are checking if internal or external distractors are being attended to. This can be progressed so that the player carries out the same exercise whilst playing either commenting aloud or internally.

Embedding PCDEs into coaching

Once key PCDEs, and the behaviours associated with them, have been identified, the next step is to consider how these are promoted, developed and reinforced in training and competitive settings. A series of *coach behaviours* and *coach systems* that encourage, prime and reinforce the desired behaviours is an effective framework and we adopted some guidelines to increase the effectiveness of these behaviour modification techniques. Firstly, as outlined in the previous section, it is important to target and define the behaviours that need to be addressed. It is essential to limit this focus to only a couple of behaviours at a time, otherwise both the athlete and coach can get overwhelmed by attempting to change too much too quickly. For example, in our school setting we target two or three PCDEs as a focus over a term of activities. Delimiting our focus made it easier to reinforce the desired behaviours effectively and consistently and was an effective way to establish change.

Secondly, as coaches and teachers we recognise the importance of positive feedback and reinforcement that clearly indicates to the young athlete the progress s/he is making towards achieving the desired behaviours. These *coach behaviours*, provided they occur within a supportive environment, not only increase motivation but also increases the likelihood of the desired behaviour occurring again in the future. Finally, young athletes must have a clear understanding of what behaviour is required and coaches must clearly state the outcomes of performing, or not performing, these targeted behaviours. Essentially, the coach/teacher employs *coach systems* to clarify what behaviours are expected and what the consequences are of engaging or not engaging in those behaviours. These systems act as 'setting conditions' that encourage, teach and promote the desired behaviour. It is important to keep these principles in mind as we now consider what these coaching practices looked like in a school coaching environment.

Coaching behaviours and coaching systems

This section will discuss how we practically implemented a combination of *coach behaviours* and *coach systems* to effectively promote the PCDEs in our coaching environment. It is important that coaches consider how both their own behaviours, and the system within which they work, promote desired (and, unfortunately, dysfunctional) behaviours. Coaches must carefully consider their interactions with athletes if these specific behaviours are going to be promoted and strengthened and thus likely to reoccur. For example, if a coach wishes the athlete to behave in a *committed* manner by 'addressing weaknesses in training' they must reinforce this through coach behaviours such as goal orientated feedback based on individual performance and progression related to their goals. It is also important to consider how the coaching system increases the likelihood of the desired behaviour occurring. In this case, the coach system could take the form of regular goal setting and progress meetings between the player and coach. Through the interaction of coach behaviours and coach systems the athlete is encouraged to engage in the desired behaviour. If these practices are continually adhered to, the athlete will accept and internalise these behaviours to the point where they occur as a matter of course, to the benefit of athlete's performance.

To illustrate how we approached this process in our school environment, a number of examples are presented. Essentially, we first identified the behaviours associated with each PCDE and then designed coach behaviours and systems to encourage athletes to act in the manner desired and then positively reinforce 'good' behaviour. In Table 10.6 we have outlined the behaviours associated with realistic performance evaluations that we selected as important.

The *coach systems* to drive these behaviours included 'review and reflection' sessions both individually and collectively. As a part of the review and reflection

TABLE 10.6 A developmental approach to realistic performance evaluations behaviours

- *Basic*: Ability to talk through performance with coach - understanding of good and not so good elements of performance – Avoids over-emotional response to win/loss
- *Intermediate*: Understand the *techniques, structures, standards and expectations* that have been put in place by the coach – compares own performance to these
- *Advanced*: Be performance/process driven rather than outcome driven – micro analysis rather than macro, is aligned with coach in evaluation of performance

process we stressed the importance of players understanding the techniques, strategies and positional responsibilities required from them using clear performance indicators. It was important from a developmental perspective that links were made between process and outcome; that reflections and performance evaluations were process centred and that performance evaluation was realistic.

Coaching behaviours such as personal feedback and conversations were key to this process. A basic reflection process could start with a prompt such as, '*Let's both individually rate your performance from 1–10 under the following headings (e.g. defence, attack, breakdown, kicking etc.). You talk through your reasons for your ratings then we can compare them to mine*'. As the player develops their ability to realistically evaluate their performances, the coaching behaviours (e.g. the prompts) change to give more ownership and responsibility to the player: '*I want you to lead a 10 minute post-match video review before training on Tuesday. Can you focus on the elements of the game that you feel were critical?* As players get better and more comfortable, the *coach systems* can also evolve so that players can be challenged to take the lead in post-match reviews.

An important feature of this process was how all three aspects – athlete behaviour, coach behaviour and coach systems – had to interact effectively with the coach reinforcing appropriate behaviour and providing appropriate setting conditions that supported the development and deployment of PCDEs. In the introduction, we discussed how resources are limited within a school setting and therefore care must be taken in ensuring this approach is embedded as effectively and efficiently as possible to get optimum results. Critically, we employed similar methods (e.g. coach systems and coach behaviours) to encourage a range of behaviours – team meetings, reviews, debriefs, game scenarios were all used for multiple outcomes. This has a number of benefits – it simplified the coaching process and increased the probability of each system and behaviour being appropriately implemented. By embedding the development of PCDEs into coaching (rather than as an added-on extra), we found that the athlete was more likely to accept and internalise these behaviours to the point where they will automatically engage in them. Essentially, we regard PCDE as 'part and parcel' of our coaching approach and design our sessions with this in mind. Coaching sessions were designed with 'explicit' (improving a technique, working on a game-plan, improving fitness) reasons but also for 'implicit' outcomes (increasing confidence, self-regulation, commitment).

Bridging the research-practice divide

In the first section of this chapter, and reflecting the importance of psychological skills as determinants of development, Iain has outlined how he has embedded PCDEs into his youth coaching practice. Of course, there is a difference between knowing that psychological skills are an important part of the development process and systematically developing PCDEs as part of the coaching process. As youth coaches and practitioners working in youth sport, we want to focus on supporting young athletes to proactively develop a comprehensive skillset that underpins their ability to make the most of the developmental opportunities they are afforded. In short, understanding the *skills* that athletes need to achieve a growth mindset, show resilience or be gritty.

In regard to this skills development approach, we have tested for, refined and proposed (see Collins & MacNamara, 2017) the systematic teaching, testing and tweaking of PCDEs as a logical way to prepare young people for the 'ups and downs' of development. This set of empirically derived skills (MacNamara et al., 2010a) are proactively developed through a 'teach, then test, then refine' approach, offering young athletes a toolbox with which they have practised and are confident in using to counter the range of challenges that are a feature of sport (Collins & MacNamara, 2017). The PCDE skill set has been shown to be comprehensive enough to help athletes cope with, and optimally benefit from, the range of challenges inherent in their pathway (Collins & MacNamara, 2017).

The benefits of the PCDE approach

In this chapter we have outlined the evidence and rationale of PCDEs and provided exemplars of how they have been operationalised in a school sport setting. In closing, there are a number of principles that we would like to emphasis, which we list below:

1) The approach is skills-based ensuring that young athletes are taught the skills and then supported to test and tweak them as they progress in sport.
2) The skills are taught through a combination of formal, informal and procedural methods (what we have described in this chapter as coach systems) and then tested against realistic challenges in the athlete's environment. As Iain has outlined, this approach is most effective when PCDEs are integrated as part of your coaching; athletes will have to deploy PCDEs in response to challenges in their environment and 'coach behaviours' such as feedback will refine and reinforce the application of the skill. After each coaching episode, coaches and other practitioners engage the athletes in review – what happened and why – developing their own capacity to evaluate and self-manage in tandem with structured feedback. Given the need for reflection and refinement, and recognising that this will differ depending on the age and maturity level of your athlete, you must allow sufficient time for athletes to learn from, develop and refine and, crucially, secure confidence in their capacity to use the skills.
3) It is important to recognise the need for an individualised and gradual approach to the development and deployment of PCDEs as another important feature of this approach. This is backed up by a variety of informal interactions, with coach, teacher, parent, other support specialists and even fellow players modelling effective application of the skills. The procedural part – the coach systems – also helps to keep the skills at the forefront, and embed them within the culture of life for the young player.
4) The skills are taught, deployed and culturally encouraged as part of everyday practice.

The generality of PCDEs is also a positive feature of this approach – the same PCDEs seems to be important regardless of domain or stage of development. From a talent transfer perspective this is important as it enables the cross-fertilisation of talent; athletes will have the skills to successfully transfer from one domain to another. Even if the athlete remains in their sport, they will have the skillset to cope with developmental challenges and the range of 'other stuff' challenges that are a feature of development

References

Abbott, A., Button, C., Pepping, G. J., & Collins, D. (2005). Unnatural selection: Talent identification and development in sport. *Nonlinear Dynamics, Psychology, and Life Sciences*, *9*(1), 61–88.

Abbott, A., Collins, D., Sowerby, K., & Martindale, R. (2007). Developing the potential of young people in sport. In *A Report for Sportscotland by University of Edinburgh*.

Bridge, M. W., & Toms, M. R. (2013). The specialising or sampling debate: A retrospective analysis of adolescent sports participation in the UK. *Journal of Sports Sciences*, *31*(1), 87–96.

Collins, D., & MacNamara, Á. (2012). The rocky road to the top. *Sports Medicine*, *42*(11), 907–914.

Collins, D., & MacNamara, A. (2017). *Talent development: A practitioner guide*. London: Routledge.

Collins, D., MacNamara, Á., & McCarthy, N. (2016). Super champions, champions, and almosts: Important differences and commonalities on the rocky road. *Frontiers in Psychology*, *6*. Online. Available at: www.frontiersin.org/articles/10.3389/fpsyg.2015.02009/full?utm_source=Email_to_authors_&utm_medium=Email&utm_content=T1_11.5e1_author&utm_campaign=Email_publication&field=&journalName=Frontiers_in_Psychology&id=171615.

Gould, D. (2010). Early sport specialization: A psychological perspective. *Journal of Physical Education, Recreation & Dance*, *81*(8), 33–37.

Gould, D., Dieffenbach, K., & Moffett, A. (2002). Psychological characteristics and their development in Olympic champions. *Journal of Applied Sport Psychology*, *14*(3), 172–204.

MacNamara, Á., Button, C., & Collins, D. (2010a). The role of psychological characteristics in facilitating the pathway to elite performance part 1: Identifying mental skills and behaviors. *The Sport Psychologist*, *24*, 52–73.

MacNamara, Á., Button, C., & Collins, D. (2010b). The role of psychological characteristics in facilitating the pathway to elite performance part 2: Examining environmental and stage-related differences in skills and behaviors. *The Sport Psychologist*, *24*, 74–96.

Pearson, D. T., Naughton, G. A., & Torode, M. (2006). Predictability of physiological testing and the role of maturation in talent identification for adolescent team sports. *Journal of Science and Medicine in Sport*, *9*(4), 277–287.

Simonton, D. K. (1999). Talent and its development: An emergenic and epigenetic model. *Psychological Review*, *106*(3), 435.

SECTION V

A guide to coaching different populations

11

LEARNING TO PROBLEMATISE 'THE WAY THINGS ARE' WHEN COACHING FEMALE ATHLETES

'Gender effective coaching' in sport

Luke Jones, Joseph Mills and Zoe Avner

Introduction

On 23 January 2018 former Manchester United, Everton and England player Philip Neville was appointed as the England Women's national football team Head Coach. The appointment was greeted with mixed reactions. Although a respected figure within the game, and seen as a likable, perhaps even gentle, figure, Neville's appointment was widely questioned amongst the football coaching community in England. This questioning was primarily as a result of his relative coaching inexperience and lack of specific experience coaching female players. Neville's appointment has once more magnified the discussion surrounding the qualities required to best coach female athletes.

So what does it take to coach 'gender-effectively'? In this chapter, we add our theoretically-informed thoughts as coaching scholars to this important conversation and explore the taken for granted understandings about 'gender effective coaching', particularly in relation to female athletes. In doing so, we encourage the development of coaching frameworks and approaches that challenge some of the binary, limiting understandings of gender and their related coaching and sporting practices. We frame entrenched contemporary coaching truths about female athletes, and their coaches' continued uncritical acceptance of them, as particularly problematic and constraining for both female athletes and their coaches. And, given our stance as socio-cultural coaching researchers (Avner, Jones & Denison, 2014) this is something that we would like to see problematised and re-imagined (Denison, Jones & Mills, 2019).

The purpose of this chapter is to use our position as socio-cultural coaching theorists to support those responsible for the development and stewardship of female athletes of all ages by introducing the key concept of problematisation, as the first step towards more ethical practice. We will do this by explaining how Anton, our exemplar coach, chose to adopt the key skill/concept of problematisation because of his desire to coach in a more 'gender effective manner'. To achieve our aim, we walk alongside Anton and consider how the dominant attitudes and 'best practices' applied in the coaching of women have emerged and how these practices may limit 'gender-effective coaching'. We reveal how Anton's nagging doubts helped him identify a confusing problem: confusing because Anton's immersion in entrenched contemporary coaching truths made him label his problem as frustrating but inevitable. We go on to explain how Anton's reflection and engagement with social theory and specifically French philosopher Michel Foucault's ideas surrounding truth, knowledge and power, allowed him to identify his 'problem' as socially constructed and therefore 'not true' and as a result; free to change.

Anton's story

Anton is a PhD student studying the sociology of sports coaching and a former varsity men's soccer player. Throughout his PhD, Anton has been exposed to various socio-cultural critiques of sport as a privileged site for both the reproduction and the destabilisation of problematic gender norms and power relations. He is also now an Assistant Coach in a varsity programme in a major North American University Women's soccer programme – 'The Falcons'.

We join Anton and the Falcons during their post-season in an important play-off game against their big rivals the Bears. The Falcons are leading by a goal with ten minutes to go when Courtney, a third year forward, gives away the ball on the half way line by trying a trick she repeatedly tries in practice (with limited success) rather than choosing to conservatively keep possession. The Bears equalise as a result and then, shortly after, riding the wave of positive momentum the Bears score again just before full time and clinch progress to next week's National finals in San Diego. After the game, Anton observes the girls in the changing room and they are sat in their usual cliques – very quiet – some older ones comforting some of the younger players who were quietly crying. He continues to observe as Mike (Head Coach) enters the room, clearly fuming. However, Mike says very little – just telling the players in a low voice to get changed and get back on the coach as soon as they can. Anton remembers thinking that Mike very rarely says anything related to the game during these moments.

On the long coach ride home Mike does not want to talk so Anton sits alone and flips through his phone looking at the game's associated social media posts. When he has had enough of looking at the negative reports he sits back into his seat and stares out the window and reflects upon the game and the aftermath. As the snow-covered prairies zoom past outside Anton continues to think about the day's events.

> When I played the men's game there would be water bottles flying and some kind of immediate letting off of steam. I know that 'old school' approach doesn't really make sense anymore and let's be honest it never really did – coaching has moved on – but I do think Mike always misses a real

opportunity to challenge and push players so that they may learn and grow from these experiences. Maybe there is some middle ground to be found. Why does Mike always do this? I really don't see how saying nothing is helpful to Courtney's development as a player or the team's for that matter. These are elite athletes; we don't need to walk on eggshells around them – let's use these intense moments as opportunities to grow as a team ...

Later that evening the Falcons' coach pulls up to their sports training village and the players wearily disembark in a dejected fashion. Anton watches as Mike stands away from the players as they collect their kit bags from under the vehicle and trudge off to their cars. The last image that Anton has of this day is the solitary and hunched figure of Courtney hanging back, separate from a larger group of players as they disperse into the night.

On Monday morning, with yesterday's defeat on his mind, Anton walks towards the University for his morning class on the socio-cultural dimensions of sport coaching. He has really enjoyed this class which has pushed him to critically reflect on and to question sanctioned, taken for granted 'best coaching practices' and their unintended problematic effects on athletes. For Anton this a new way of thinking about effective coaching and his own coaching practice that he is really excited about. Today's topic of discussion is gender in sport. As the instructor initiates a class discussion on sport as an important site for the reproduction gendered norms and power relations, she draws on Michel Foucault's theoretical tool-kit to highlight the important roles coaches can and should play in problematising gendered sporting practices, Anton is suddenly brought back to yesterday's game and Mike's decision to stay silent.

I think this is all starting to make sense to me – that is, Mike's choosing to remain silent instead of providing Courtney and the other players with valuable immediate feedback. Mike probably thinks that he is doing the right thing by not providing feedback because he is operating under the assumption that female players can't handle it – that they are somewhat too weak/fragile and that they need to be treated differently than male athletes. Wow, this class on Foucault and gendered power relations in sport is really bringing it home. Perhaps this old idea about the female psyche and what motivates female players is holding us back as a coaching staff and as a team. I wonder what I could do differently as a member of the coaching team.

As Anton walks home and gets ready for the night's training session, he is still thinking about how he, as a coach, can disrupt some of these gendered assumptions and norms and what type of feedback would be most effective for Courtney and the team to learn and develop from experiences similar to Sunday's defeat.

Well, based on this past Sunday and multiple other instances, it seems to me that Courtney really struggles with identifying key moments and zones in the field and choosing when to take risks and when to be more conservative with the ball. I think that we, as coaches, need to help her to identify and recognise where and when risk-taking is acceptable and encouraged and when it is not. However, I also really don't want to stifle that risk taking attitude she has because that is what sets her apart as a player, the ability to spark big plays. The last thing we want is a bunch of robot players on the field who can't think for themselves and are afraid of taking risks and losing the ball because they will get yelled at.

As Anton pulls into the training ground's parking lot, he decides he will speak to Mike tonight about how they, as coaches, can communicate/provide feedback to players more effectively and in ways that challenge some of these problematic gendered constructs about the female athlete that they discussed in class. Depending on how Mike reacts, he decides he will also offer to run a practice session to help Courtney and other players make better decisions on the field by asking them to react and problem-solve based on different 'game-like' scenarios.

There is no point in just telling them what we think, they should or should not do. Courtney and the other players need to figure it out and problem solve together. After all, they are the ones on the field, not us!

Making sense of Anton's story

Informed discussion about how to coach any population needs to recognise that the experiences of athletes do not occur in a vacuum, but rather that they occur within the broader historical-socio-cultural contexts of society – unless taking an egg from its omelette is an easy thing to do. These are contexts that have been shaped over time by dominant discourses (ways of knowing) and power relations (ways of doing) (Markula & Pringle, 2006). How are we to make sense of Anton's story against this backdrop? Before we consider how and why Anton arrived at his 'problem' and how this set him up to address a coaching quandary, we need to first contextualise his coaching experiences. Therefore, in the section that follows, we briefly establish the contemporary global context of female sport and move on to review the existing 'best practices' for how to coach females.

The context of female sport

Anton's story is set in contemporary times, but female sport has changed significantly over the last fifty years. In 1975 Patsy Neal and Thomas Tutko lamented that women were being denied opportunities to compete in sport and were being 'deprived by a cultural lag and a society with double standards' (Neal & Tutko, 1975, p. 52). Forty years later, primarily as a result of Title IX of the USA's 1972 Education Act, the single most dramatic change in the world of sport had been the increased participation of girls and women (Cooky, Messner & Hextrum, 2013). However, as Cooky et al. (2013, p. 203) claimed, 'despite the tremendous increased participation of girls and women in sport at the high school, collegiate and professional level sport continues to be by, for and about men'. Increased participation after all, does not mean equity, it just means more women are playing sport. Therefore, while opportunities for women to partici-pate and be coached have increased over recent times, there remains a need to develop more effective and ethical frameworks and approaches to coaching women in sport (LaVoi, 2016). Established and contemporary research that has focused on the social context of women's sport has explored how the 'different nature of women' (derived from historical-socio-culturally constructed norms and sustained by bio-medical readings of the female body) continues to be reinforced in sports settings (Cooky et al., 2013; Hargreaves, 1994). These social constructions have led to the marginalisation of individuals of all genders that do not conform to the expected masculine and heterosexual norms (Messner, 1992) and the continued sexualisation of the contemporary female athlete (Bernstein, 2002; Cox & Thompson, 2000) for consumption via multiple media streams (Kane, LaVoi & Fink, 2013) and trivialisation of her accomplishments. How-ever, while sports historians Osborne and Skillen (2010, p. 192) have noted 'females have not yet achieved equality with their male counterparts in the realm of sport', it is also important to acknowledge that the site of sport is also where historical norms have, at times, somewhat successfully, been challenged. Sport is therefore also a location where binary assumptions regarding gender continue to be contested and, in the contemporary case of South African middle distance athlete Caster Semenya, completely destabilised (Buzuvis, 2010).

Best practice in the coaching of female athletes

It is clear from Anton's reflections about Mike's choices of 'best practices', that he is conscious of certain assumptions and associated 'best practices' that under-pin the female sports coaching context. However, what exactly are Mike's 'best practice' assumptions and where do they come from? So far, we have established that the context of female sport within which Anton operates are governed by historically socio-culturally constructed norms. In this section, before we can move on to talk about Anton's process of problematisation, we must briefly 'map out' the socially constructed 'truths' that have come to dominate the coaching of females (the 'truths' that Mike is relying upon) and where they come from. It is clear from Anton's story that Mike has a well-established understanding regarding what he perceives his female players to be capable of. So where do Mike's assumptions about the female athlete come from?

It is easy to find texts that identify female specific physiological (Ireland & Ott, 2004), biomechanical (Herman et al., 2008) and psychological (Duda & Marks, 2014) characteristics that are assumed to ensure the healthy and successful development of the female athlete as separate and different from men's. Numerous mainstream resources exist about how to best develop, condition and instruct the female athlete's body in competitive sport, including in soccer (Stokell, 2002). It is generally accepted amongst sport scientists that female athletes are faced with unique situations based upon their physiology (Ireland & Ott, 2004). Clearly the cumulative effect of the large body of sports research has significant implications for coaching women – namely that it reinforces and solidifies even, the general belief that female bodies cannot be exposed to and are simply not capable of completing the same training practices as male bodies.

It is not only the physical make up of women that has been measured and categorised by sport scientists and therefore 'known' by everyone else; indeed, the psychological characteristics of females have also been identified as different to those of their male counterparts. Newton, Duda and Yin (2000) found that fostering a 'task-involving' team climate was more likely to be productive than fostering that of an 'ego-involving' climate when attempting to positively influence the motivation of female athletes. This common sense understanding perhaps explains why so many coaches work and adopt practices based upon the assumption that females are more motivated by the social and relational aspects of sport versus males who are more performance and competition driven. For example, Avner, Denison and Markula's (2017) research has recently identified a clear difference in how coaches provide feedback and instruction to female athletes – that coaches are less likely to shout across a room at female athletes, rather preferring to take them aside and provide individual feedback. This finding is important as it highlights just one example of exactly how established gender norms influence coaches' decisions about developing effective relationships with their athletes – in this case that the female psyche is more fragile and needs protecting in the team coaching setting. Clearly, the choices made by Head Coach Mike in Anton's story are a strong example of how this 'truth' about the female athlete has implications for coaching practice.

Since sport scientists advise that the moving female body and mind work differently to those of a male, it is likely that coaches (like Mike) will come to assume that females need to be 'treated differently', less harshly, with extra care or special gloves. Often the findings from sport science legitimise the prescription of alternative management in the instruction and development of the female sportsperson (read 'different to male'). As sport scientists Ireland and Ott (2004, p. 281) pointed out, there are fundamental 'differences between the sexes which must be considered when caring for the female athlete'. This sustains the 'truth' that while male athletes should be 'trained', female athletes should be 'cared' for.

Where does this leave us? Well, sports coaching researchers who are familiar with the concept of the social construction of knowledge may well already engage in problematising certain entrenched coaching practices and attitudes. However, coaches who are less likely to be exposed to different perspectives or the limitations of science might not know how to question many of the things that they do. And, because of the dominance that sport science has as a 'privileged knowledge' in coach education programs, these coaches are much more likely to interpret any sport science research finding as a cast iron truth (Avner et al., 2017b; Denison, Mills & Jones, 2013). As Anton's story has shown, from our socio-cultural perspective, we suggest that there are significant consequences of solely relying upon what the above sport science knowledge suggests about coaching females. Reliance on this knowledge has numerous effects. According to the logic instilled by sports physiology and medicine, female bodies are less able to withstand the physiological demands of certain bodily practices. Therefore, that the female athlete's psyche, character and mentality needs nurturing rather than challenging appears to follow as an unquestioned correlated 'truth'. A problematic, binary understanding of what it means to be a female athlete is legitimised, and this legitimised logic guides and governs the practices and attitudes that make up the fabric of the contemporary coaching of females. Put another way, we see this arrangement as having detrimental consequences for female athletes because, in sports contexts, coaches seem to uncritically internalise sports science knowledge (Avner et al., 2017b). For example, coaches like Head Coach Mike tend to rely on firmly established truths about what supposedly 'naturally' drives and motivates athletes of different genders.

As we have been keen to point out in this section this arrangement then translates into assumed 'best coaching practices' perpetuating and rarely challenging the limiting status quo. It is of course important to acknowledge that we do not dismiss the numerous advantages that sports science brings to the preparation, development and instruction of female athletes. However, we do suggest that the practicing coach reconsiders how automatically adhering to existing assumptions about the female body in sport might be hampering their coaching and in turn, their athletes' development. In the next section, we move on to discuss how Anton developed this broader awareness and because of his own nagging doubts was able to identify a 'problem', and because of his exposure to alternative thinking, was able to give this 'problem' a name and see how he might be able to do things differently in the future.

Learning from Anton's problematisation

To develop as flexible and open-minded coaches, first, individuals need to be willing to problematise the effects of entrenched practices and attitudes found within their coaching context (Denison & Avner, 2011). In the past we have created a Foucauldian-inspired coach education resource specifically designed to help coaches to develop problematisation as a key skill (Jones, Denison & Gearity, 2016). More recently, we have suggested that more Foucauldian-inspired coaching researchers walk alongside coaches and 'actively work with coaches to provide new types of knowledges with different coaching tool kits' (Avner et al., 2017a, p. 26). Anton's story has been intentionally choreographed to show how through a process of reflection backed up with exposure to Foucauldian-inspired critical thinking in his graduate class, he identified and then challenged the dominant understandings underpinning how to 'manage' the athletic female in his immediate sporting context. In this instance, Anton, acting as a reflective coach, challenged existing assumptions based on a gendered and narrow perception of how female athletes 'should be treated', which as a result were preventing the team, and Courtney, from learning and developing. In keeping with the idea that ethical practices will not come from substituting one dominant model of truth for another, in our example, we can see that, thankfully, Anton did not rely upon returning to the promotion of coaching practices that he had experienced as a male soccer player. Rather, Anton used critical reflection to identify and problematise a problem and to catalyse a thought process that can lead to new, more effective and ethical coaching feedback practices. Anton's hope was that his reflective process might allow for both individual and team growth, whilst avoiding reliance upon the prevailing and problematic traditional gender norms and problematic dominant disciplinary training and coaching practices relied upon by his Head Coach Mike.

Foucault and problematisation

The central aim of Michel Foucault's work was to understand how humans acquired knowledge about themselves and how certain human practices have come to be accepted and naturalised. He also sought to understand the various effects of these knowledges and practices – he wanted to know, not only why we do what we do, but also what what we do does (Foucault, 1988). Foucault's aim was to show how discourses and relations of power work together to both produce and constrain people's thoughts and actions by providing a grid of intelligibility for what is normal, desirable, positive and true. In so doing, he aimed to highlight the socially constructed and political nature of knowledge and truth, and thus, open up a space for questioning and thinking and doing differently (Foucault, 1978, 1979). One of the ways that Foucault achieved this aim was by articulating how knowledge and power worked together to privilege only certain ways of being (Markula & Pringle, 2006). For Foucault, power was relational, as in power was not a possession that someone or something had over another, rather power was a strategy that was always performed and so was always producing meaning in whatever context it was practised. Foucault identified how modern power made people believe that certain knowledges and their associated practices were 'true' and therefore undoubtedly effective. In exposing this artificial and constructed logic, Foucault (1979) suggested that their associated practices may, at times, have problematic effects.

So, how do Anton's actions and experiences line up with Foucault's project? Once various beliefs, values and characteristics are established in society as 'true' (not least in the realm of sports coaching) it can seem impossible to shift or change them: why would one change what is 'true'? However, as Foucauldians we advocate that it remains essential to challenge these 'truths' if we 'sense' problems, as Anton did. If these problems remain undisturbed, coaches and their athletes will continue to be undermined without anyone being aware of what the real issue is. In line with this broader ethos, we recommend social theory as a tool-kit that helps coaches see *all* their knowledges and practices as socially constructed and flexible, rather than true and therefore fixed.

Anton's observations of his Head Coach Mike are presented as an example to outline how knowledge and power have combined to establish 'unquestioned truths' about the competencies and capabilities associated with female athletes. We have also endeavoured to show how these 'truths' legitimise specific approaches to coaching females – with restrictive consequences. Relations of power and their effects are impossible to identify if one doesn't have a theoretical tool-kit that can expose them. As a result, we suggest that coaches need as deep an understanding of Foucault's theoretical tool-kit as possible so that they can broaden their awareness, or in simple terms; 'see-more, think-broader and do-better'. Using theory to problematise, or at the very least opening one's mind to the alternative logic promoted in this chapter will allow coaches to think and practice differently. For without theory pointing the way, it is difficult to understand precisely what coaches should be critical about.

With this in mind, we strongly believe that, like Anton, encouraging coaches towards using socio-culturally informed ideas/strategies is essential if we are to help them in their stewardship of athletes of all demographics – including those of all genders. Therefore, in this chapter we have used a socio-cultural lens to consider Anton as a positive exemplar of a reflective coach who has thought about and problematised the implications of the practices common to their coaching space. It has not been our intention to set out a definitive checklist or model for 'best practice' in women's coaching. Indeed, as Foucauldian scholars we would warn against this 'game of truth' (Markula & Pringle, 2006). Rather, we wanted to use this opportunity to promote the applied way of thinking about 'gender-effective' coaching that Anton employed as one that we believe can answer the call for more ethical and productive outcomes in the women's sports coaching/physical activity setting (Davis & Weaving, 2010). In doing so it has also been our intention to move coaches from their 'absolutes' to 'more flexible and fluid' notions of what is possible, true or effective in relation to coaching athletes of different genders in all sports contexts.

We would like to conclude by highlighting the important notion – namely that no dominant knowledge surrounding how to coach people of any gender should claim ultimate authority or be considered as 'set in stone'. Rather, that any coaching knowledge should be considered as fluid, and as such must be open to change (Denison & Avner, 2011). We are of the firm belief that any alternative, marginalised, or re-imagined idea about how to coach 'gender-effectively' should be welcomed and embraced IF it has been arrived at through a careful period of theoretically-informed reflection. After all, we have spent a great deal of time and effort encouraging coaches like Anton to 'think with Foucault' (Denison & Avner, 2011; Denison & Mills, 2014; Denison et al., 2013; Mills & Denison, 2013).

Implications for practice

1) A 'gender effective coach' should keep an eye out for any unwanted and limiting consequences of normalised taken for granted practices and approaches to coaching both men women within their immediate coaching context.
2) When designing their practices and when making decisions about how to relate to their athletes, coaches must be prepared to question and problematise 'best practices' that are informed by existing cultural, physiological and psychological assumptions surrounding gender.
3) A 'gender effective coach' understands the necessity not to rely on but rather to regularly question these existing practices and assumptions.
4) A 'gender effective coach' must constantly reflect upon the choices and practices they choose to adopt in their day-to-day interactions with athletes.
5) A 'gender effective coach' should always be willing to consider the merits of alternative practices that are not underpinned by normalised assumptions surrounding the male and female body and mind.

References

Avner, Z., Denison, J., & Markula, P. (2017a). 'Good athletes have fun': A Foucauldian reading of university coaches' uses of fun. *Sports Coaching Review*, doi:10.1080/21640629.2017.1400757.
Avner, Z., Jones, L., & Denison, J. (2014). Poststructuralism. In L. Nelson, R. Groom, & P. Potrac (Eds.), *Research methods in sports coaching* (pp. 42–52). London: Routledge.
Avner, Z., Markula, P., & Denison, J. (2017b). Understanding effective coaching: A Foucauldian reading of current coach education frameworks. *International Sports Coaching Journal*, 4, 101–109.
Bernstein, A. (2002). Is it time for a victory lap? Changes in media coverage of women in sport. *International Review for the Sociology of Sport*, 37, 415–428.
Buzuvis, E. (2010). Caster Semenya and the myth of a level playing field. *The Modern American*, 6, 36–42.
Cooky, C., Messner, M., & Hextrum, R. (2013). Women play sport, but not on TV. *Communication and Sport*, 1, 203–230.
Cox, B., & Thompson, S. (2000). Multiple bodies: Sportswomen, soccer and sexuality. *International Review for the Sociology of Sport*, 35, 5–20.
Davis, P., & Weaving, C. (2010). *Philosophical perspectives on gender in sport and physical activity*. London: Routledge.

Denison, J., & Avner, Z. (2011). Positive coaching: Ethical practices for athlete development. *Quest*, *63*, 209–227.

Denison, J., Jones, L., & Mills, J. (2019). Becoming a good enough coach. *Sports Coaching Review*, *8*(1), 1–6.

Denison, J., & Mills, J. (2014). Planning for distance running: Coaching with Foucault. *Sports Coaching Review*, *3*, 1–17.

Denison, J., Mills, J., & Jones, L. (2013). Effective coaching as a modernist formation: A Foucauldian critique. In P. Potrac, W. Gilbert, & J. Denison (Eds.), *Routledge handbook of sports coaching* (pp. 388–399). London: Routledge.

Duda, J., & Marks, S. (2014). Psychology of the female athlete. In M. Mountjoy, J. Duda, & S. Marks (Eds.), *Handbook of sports medicine and science: The female athlete* (pp. 20–29). Hoboken, New Jersey: John Wiley & Sons.

Foucault, M. (1978). *The history of sexuality, vol. 1: An introduction*. New York: Vintage Books.

Foucault, M. (1979). *Discipline & punish: The birth of the prison*. New York: Vintage Books.

Foucault, M. (1988). Technologies of the self. In L. H. Martin, H. Gutman, & P. H. Hutton (Eds.), *Technologies of the self: A seminar with michel foucault* (pp. 16–49). Amherst: University of Massachusetts Press.

Hargreaves, J. (1994). *Sporting females: Critical issues in the history and sociology of women's sports*. London: Routledge.

Herman, D. C., Weinhold, P. S., Guskiewicz, K. M., Garrett, W. E., Yu., B., & Padua., D. A. (2008). The effects of strength training on the lower extremity biomechanics of female recreational athletes during a stop-jump task. *American Journal of Sports Medicine*, *36*(4), 733–740.

Ireland, M., & Ott, S. (2004). Special concerns of the female athlete. *Clinics in Sports Medicine*, *23*, 281–298.

Jones, L., Denison, J., & Gearity, B. (2016). Re-thinking coach education with robin usher: An 'usherian' approach to innovative coaching. In L. Nelson., R. Groom., & P. Potrac (Eds.), *Learning in Sports Coaching: Theory and application* (pp. 161–173). London: Routledge.

Kane, M., LaVoi, N., & Fink, J. (2013). Exploring female elite athletes' interpretations of sports media images. *Communication and Sport*, *1*, 269–298.

LaVoi, N. (2016). *Women in Sports Coaching*. London: Routledge.

Markula, P., & Pringle, R. (2006). *Foucault, sport, and exercise: Power, knowledge, and transforming the self*. London: Routledge.

Messner, M. (1992). *Power at Play: Sports and the problem of masculinity*. Boston: Beacon Press.

Mills, J., & Denison, J. (2013). Coach Foucault: Problematizing endurance running coaches' practices. *Sports Coaching Review*, *2*, 136–150.

Neal, P., & Tutko, T. (1975). *Coaching girls and women: Psychological perspectives*. Boston: Allyn and Bacon.

Newton, M., Duda, J., & Yin, Z. (2000). Examination of psychometric properties of the perceived motivational climate questionnaire – 2 in a sample of female athletes. *Journal of Sports Sciences*, *18*, 275–290.

Osborne, C., & Skillen, F. (2010). The state of play: Women in British sport history. *Sport in History*, *30*, 189–195.

Stokell, I. (2002). *Coaching women's soccer*. New York: McGraw Hill.

12

COACHING IN DISABILITY SPORT

From practice to theory

Robert Townsend, Christopher Cushion and Derek Morgan

Introduction

Understanding the complexity of coaching in disability sport remains a pressing concern. While interest in disability sport continues to grow there is a relative lack of insight into coaching in this context, particularly research which illustrates a 'grounded' perspective on practice. As a result, coaching in disability sport is critically under-theorised, and we know comparatively little of the nature of coaching in different disability sport contexts (Townsend, Smith & Cushion, 2016). There have been longstanding calls to understand coaches' learning and development in disability sport (DePauw, 1986), and as a result there is a small, but growing, body of literature which has begun to explore the unique considerations of coaching in disability sport. Such considerations include the informal and unstructured nature of coach learning (e.g. Duarte & Culver, 2014; McMaster, Culver & Werthner, 2012; Taylor, Werthner & Culver, 2014; Taylor, Werthner, Culver & Callary, 2015), the lack of disability-specific coach education (e.g. Cregan, Bloom & Reid, 2007; Douglas & Hardin, 2014; Douglas, Vidic, Smith & Stran, 2016) and the complex and multifaceted role of coaches in disability contexts (e.g. DePauw & Gavron, 1991; Tawse, Bloom, Sabiston & Reid, 2012), all of which invite and encourage comparisons with the narrative presented below. More recent research, however, has challenged the lack of critical insight in disability coaching research (e.g. Townsend et al., 2016), arguing that the research is characterised by a normative focus that downplays the inter-connections between disability and cultural contexts such as sport. The lack of consideration of disability is an important theoretical 'gap', as Smith and Bundon (2016) argue, having a grasp on how disability is explained and understood is vital for individuals working with disabled people in any context, especially in coaching where practice is fundamentally shaped by our working understanding of disability (cf. DePauw, 1997). It is the purpose of this chapter, then, to encourage practitioners and researchers to examine their understandings of disability in the first instance, as a basis for developing coaching practice. What follows are reflections from Derek Morgan, Head Coach of the England Learning Disability Cricket squad, but, first, some context about the team.

Practitioner commentary

Coaching context

Involvement in the England Learning Disability squad means that players are classed as having a 'moderate' learning disability. An intellectual disability is characterised by significant limitations both in intellectual functioning and in adaptive behaviour as expressed in conceptual, social and practical adaptive skills (Buntinx & Schalock, 2010). In order to be profiled to play international disability cricket, the players have to provide evidence of a learning disability onset pre-18 years of age. This is usually evidenced in the form of a statement of special educational needs. Furthermore, the players have to present with an IQ of 75 or less and undergo an 'adaptive behaviour assessment' by an educational psychologist, in which they should show significant limitations in social functioning. The profiling of players to play international learning disability cricket is governed by criteria proposed by The International Association of Sport for para-athletes with an intellectual disability (INAS). This 'classification' system ensures that impairment is present and that it functions as a limitation on sporting performance. Of the fifteen athletes involved in the national squad, a number of players have co-occurring autism spectrum disorders. In addition, many of the players present further complex needs such as mental health issues (e.g. depression and anxiety), obsessive compulsive disorders and other non-associated conditions. The players are not full-time athletes. Training is limited to weekend camps, which typically run across two days, once a month, throughout the winter. The team are recent 'Tri-Series' champions, remaining unbeaten in international fixtures against Australia and South Africa in 2017.

At the risk of sounding a little clichéd, reflecting on the past seven years with this squad I feel that the initial constraint that I had on taking this role was my perception of disability coaching – that is, negative preconceptions of the environment and the people who inhabit it. Throughout my time with the team, my personal learning journey has been very much framed by a process of 'trial and error'. Indeed, in my journey through coach education, I have had no formal training in disability sport, with the exception of *ad hoc* workshops related to adapting and modifying practice. Throughout numerous discussions that I have had in recent years I have repeatedly arrived at a similar conclusion, which is that I have gained and taken from the experience far more than any other coaching environment. I am indebted to the players and support staff that I have shared these experiences with. Throughout this experience I have been exposed to a rich source of feedback, both formally and informally, intended and at times unintended, this has contributed dramatically to raising my self-awareness as a coach and has challenged me to reflect in depth on my practice.

I would consider that the most valuable experience as a result of coaching in disability sport has been the exploration of my personal values and recognition of how I previously attempted to shape coaching environments. At the outset, I had my own personal view of what playing international sport and representing your country meant and the lengths a player should strive for to justify a place within a performance programme. Unsurprisingly this often-created friction and frustration when attempting to apply these expectations and methods to coaching in disability sport. A major turning point came when I finally took the opportunity to consider from a player's perspective what it meant to be part of a national squad and actually what 'their' motives are for engaging in this programme. Fundamentally I have broadened my view of 'success' to now reflect a more holistic understanding whereby we celebrate the previously insignificant moments of, for instance, someone raising the challenge within a task, someone having the confidence to speak in a group setting, someone passing a driving test or gaining an academic qualification – these are all moments that we recognise and celebrate in equal measure alongside winning on the pitch. Furthermore, a key component of coaching in disability sport is recognising the unique relationship between the players, parents and coaching staff. Many players arrive into our environment highly dependent on family and close friends for not only social and emotional support but also more practically transport, travel, communication and planning arrangements to attend training and fixtures. Therefore, we try to maintain a clear dialogue between the players, the parents and the coaches. This is both an enabler and a constraint of the environment and requires the careful management of the relationship as a management group with their parents and family support unit.

At the outset, the immediate challenge I encountered with this squad was the need to inspire the players to be motivated to challenge themselves, to expose themselves to environments and experiences that are outside of their 'norm' and to be reassured that as coaches we will not be judgmental of the players perceived 'failures'. A key part of the training environment is a raised expectation of the players, combined with an environment of challenge which encourages and indeed expects failure, alongside a support system required for the players. We are not afraid to challenge players with tasks that they will find difficult or even impossible to execute initially as we are confident that we can provide a supportive environment and have applied significant resource to developing players' resilience to such challenges. In this sense, I am fortunate to work with a multi-disciplinary coaching and support staff, providing players with personal development and lifestyle, nutrition and hydration, physiotherapy and strength and conditioning support. Whilst conventional advice would recommend avoiding situations or specific drills that cause anxiety and frustration we have confidence that remaining positive with the player, especially when things aren't going well for them in these situations, has significant long-term value. If we consistently concentrate on the things they are doing well and praise the attempt this contributes to raising their self-esteem and confidence.

The nature of the players' impairments can and does impact on the coaching process. Importantly, the players' ability to communicate effectively, regulate emotions, confirm understanding, share feedback and to plan and evaluate their performances are often significantly impaired. Often, the players we work with have low self-esteem and low self-efficacy. However, whilst the players – by definition – have a 'learning disability' they are not learning incapable and unlocking their passion for and belief in their ability to learn is a considerable challenge in coaching, but potentially the most significant point in shaping the coaching environment. In practical terms, growing and developing players' ability to communicate, reflect accurately on their performance and plan ahead are priorities that are addressed through communicating with players on numerous platforms. These include informal conversation, formal 1–1's with coaches and support staff, written presentations or use of social media. This enables the coaching staff to increase contact time with the players and reinforce the key messages we try to embed. Developing the players' ability and willingness to communicate for themselves and accepting the responsibility to do so cannot be undervalued and is a primary objective of integrating players into our environment and contributes heavily to their desire to learn and progress.

The opportunity to train regularly is something that is essential to support sustained development in any sporting sphere, but from my experience it is magnified in an environment where players can face challenges associated with memory and information retention. Therefore, in practice, the opportunity to experience high volumes of repetition often are essential to skill acquisition, therefore this plays a primary role in delivery at training camps. It is essential to remember that athletes with intellectual impairments can and do learn the skills and techniques required; however, experience tells us it can take longer than anticipated. Consequently, the rate at which progress can be achieved will often not reflect mainstream environments. To create an optimal learning environment, in my experience high volumes of repetition, based on principles of play as opposed to technical detail, and wherever possible embedded into a game context, offers us and the players the most desirable practice environment. At a practical level, instructions are simplified and direct with key terms referred to repeatedly to reinforce their relevance to the practice. Connecting practice to the 'game' is hugely relevant to this environment, providing players with a frame of reference where they can link skills and practice to competitive game situations.

As coaches, we challenge ourselves to be patient, regularly returning to practices players can execute and then rebuilding challenges back into the task with emphasis on recognising the attempt and any progress achieved. This requires an openness and flexibility to practice, as, for players, concentration for long periods of time can be difficult. So too, demonstration often plays a valuable role to provide players with a model to work from. Therefore, we work hard as a coaching team to create a training environment with clear structure to break the day into digestible sections. This allows players to plan and prepare for each session but that also allows us to reframe challenges and practices, assess for learning and allows the players an opportunity to rest and recharge mentally for the next session. Traditionally coaches will collect feedback at the end of their session from their athletes, this is no less important for an athlete with a learning disability, as it will give them a chance to share any frustration or difficulties they may be having. To maximise the value of short, focused sessions, in my experience it is important that the briefing is direct, clear and consistent, and it is vital to keep this briefing to a duration that allows players to retain information. We are aware, however, that they may not speak out in a whole group session, so as coaches we seek to gather feedback throughout the session and less formally i.e. whilst collecting equipment, cool down or stretching.

In summary, the challenges that we face working in a disability sport environment are not removed from those experienced by many coaches in many other environments. My personal approach is to seek to create an environment centred around learning and personal growth. We look to recognise the social role the squad plays in the players lives and the contribution the skills developed in our environment make to their wider lives. We strive to facilitate players' learning rather than imposing it and the environment is founded on mutual respect where the expectation is to continually challenge one another and where players set and maintain their own personal and collective standards. If we can consistently concentrate on delivering this rather than concentrating on performance, then we are confident that the performance will follow.

Commentary

Derek's narrative is indicative of many of the constraints and complexities of coaching in disability sport and serves as a useful illustration for researchers to connect with. Coaching in disability sport involves the application and understanding of cultural frameworks regarding the nature of disability. Though not always explicit in coaching discourse and practice, these 'models' of disability represent cultural resources and frameworks that coaches draw upon in their practice and help to capture and explain how coaches understand the athletes they work with (Townsend et al., 2016). Thus, while the use of the models of disability is not intended to provide a definitive theorisation of disability, they help place disability into its microcontext (Thomas, 2007) and their use enables coaches to reflect on their beliefs, attitudes and practices towards disabled people.

Indeed, as we can see from Derek's narrative, the complexity of disability sport can be captured and understood through the lens of disability studies. First and foremost, what is evident from the narrative is the inferential process of 'trial and error' which has framed Derek's learning. This is a persistent issue in disability sport, where coaching practice is based predominantly on informal and experiential modes of learning (Cregan et al., 2007; McMaster et al., 2012; Taylor et al., 2014, 2015) framed by a process of socialisation (cf. Cushion,

Armour & Jones, 2003). In disability sport, problems with experiential learning through socialisation is that coaching concepts can become taken-for-granted and viewed as 'right' or best practice (Townsend, Cushion & Smith, 2018), and reinforced by a self-referenced 'what works' approach (cf. Stodter & Cushion, 2017). Importantly, critical reflection – a key practice that Derek alluded to – is not always possible, as assumptions about disabled athletes can become trapped in a model of uncritical reproduction.

Whilst coach education is a crucial feature of coach development, coaches are generally not trained in the specific circumstances of many disability contexts (Bush & Silk, 2012; Tawse et al., 2012). More often than not, disability coach education provision tends to occupy a separate and distinct 'space' from 'mainstream' coach education (Bush & Silk, 2012) reflecting the 'highly fragmented' nature of disability sport (Thomas & Guett, 2014, p. 390). This means that the ongoing professionalisation of the disability coaching pathway is inhibited as coaches face a lack of structured, disability-specific coach education opportunities (McMaster et al., 2012; Taylor et al., 2014). This means that coaching knowledge and practices are often derived from informal and non-formal sources and coaches are left to self-medicate by taking knowledge generated outside of disability contexts and grounding their understanding in material and experiential conditions in disability sport, as evidenced by Derek's learning journey. Furthermore, research investigating disability coach education has shown how the process of coach development in disability sport often focuses overly on impairment, to such an extent that coach education positions athletes as 'problems' for coaches and coaching to overcome. Such a perspective is reinforced when coach education reduces disability to 'adaptations' or 'modifications' designed to increase coaches' 'confidence' to work with disabled people (Townsend et al., 2018), thus perpetuating exclusion in coaching despite inclusive lexicon.

The medical model has historically been dominant in understanding disability and positioning research (Smith & Perrier, 2014). The central focus of the medical model frames impairment as the *cause* of disability (Swain, French & Cameron, 2003) and therefore the only limiting factor in coaching. From a medical model perspective, the disabled athlete is an object to be 'educated … observed, tested, measured, treated, psychologised … materialised through a multitude of disciplinary practices and institutional discourses' (Goodley, 2011, p. 114). Medical model discourses in performance sport promote a dominant consciousness where all problems are instrumental or technical problems to be solved and that coaching is fundamentally about improving sporting performance against the limitations athletes with a disability have. These practices are often so accepted that they influence, to greater or lesser extents, coaching frameworks that coaches draw upon. Indeed, Derek highlights how his initial 'high performance coaching' expectations influenced his practice, describing moments of tension before recognising and adopting a more athlete-centred approach. However, rather than positioning the athletes as a 'problem' – as in the medical model – social model discourses too are evident in the way that Derek reflected on the coaching environment and his personal assumptions and values related to coaching disabled athletes. In contrast to the medical model, social model discourses reconstruct disability as *entirely* socially constructed (Thomas, 2012). The social model turns a critical gaze towards society and is based on the premise that disability is the product of collective structural barriers that create exclusions and restrictions for people with impairments (Thomas, 2012). The social model provides a conceptual scaffold on which individual attitudes, beliefs and practices can be closely scrutinised and reflected upon. This, as Derek suggests, in his coaching practice, resulted in broadening a narrow view of 'performance' coaching in disability sport – as highlighted above – to encompass a view of 'success' characterised by recognising personal achievement, player independence and learning, and taking time to understand the players' wider social contexts. Such a perspective is liberating, in that the players' disabilities are located in the structures of coaching and outside of the individual (Smith & Perrier, 2014).

It is clear that the medical–social model binary can influence coaching environments, and it too has structured much debate within critical disability studies (cf. Goodley, 2011; Thomas, 2007). Thomas (1999, 2004a, 2004b, 2007), however, sought to rework this binary toward a more *relational* perspective that understands disability as a product of social relationships (Smith & Bundon, 2016; Smith & Perrier, 2014) while at the same time highlighting the very real lived, experienced effects of impairment in social life. This model focuses on the various social mechanisms by which people with impairments can be disabled within sporting contexts. The focus of the social relational model therefore is on the social construction of disability in different contexts and its use helps to analyse the production of knowledge about disability where social relations comprise the 'sedimented past and projected future of a stream of interaction' (Crossley, 2011, p. 35). Using a social relational model in coaching is useful as it highlights the unique construction of knowledge between coaches, athletes and the contexts in which they are situated. The model enables researchers to analyse the understandings of disability at individual, social and cultural levels (Martin, 2013) of coaching and coach education. Recognition and acceptance of the effects of impairment, as described in the social relational model, is an important factor for coaches to consider. Impairment can and does limit engagement in sport. Indeed, the psycho-emotional factors associated with disability that Derek identified such as low self-esteem, low motivation and low self-efficacy can be understood as a product of what Fitzgerald (2005) termed the paradigm of normativity within sport, where disabled people are defined insofar as they deviate from ableist 'norms' of sporting ability (Cassidy, Jones & Potrac, 2009). However, as Derek's narrative suggests, impairment effects can only be 'disabling' in social formations which do not account for them – by recognising the disablism embedded in such normative expectations, he attempts to create an affirmative environment whereby athletes are celebrated for their ability to show progression and development. Furthermore, by attempting to shape a coaching environment that has high levels of contact with the players and their support systems (e.g. families), he creates coaching sessions designed to facilitate player learning, independence and autonomy (Fitzgerald, 2005), and provide opportunities for feedback, the effects of impairment are considered, but are not the central focus of coaching. Using a social relational model here highlights how Derek attempts to give greater appreciation, recognition and power to the athletes in the construction of their sporting experiences (Richard, Joncheray & Dugas, 2015).

The social relational model is useful in highlighting the *relational* nature of both coaching and disability and is a helpful reflective tool for coaches to scrutinise their behaviour and practices. Nevertheless, the attempt to conceptualise coaching against a social relational framework is not always easy for coaches, particularly when considering the structural and cultural pressures that Derek faces, where able-bodied 'performance' ideas can be transposed into disability spaces, causing a tension where medical model ideas can become established in coaching environments. For instance, a key feature of Derek's narrative focuses on coaches' personal characteristics; patience, flexibility and a willingness to learn feature prominently. As a result, experience and reflection has enabled Derek and his coaches to create an environment designed to challenge the players beyond their perceived capabilities, creating a coaching environment built on principles directly related to the coaches' working understandings of disability. While challenge can be progressive within a supportive environment, it must be tempered with a regard for the individual athlete and their impairment effects. This coaching process as described by Derek, though not overt and formal, shows how permeable coaching is to broader social and cultural understandings of 'disability', highlighting the unique considerations of coaching in disability sport, and underlining the fundamental use of the models in framing coach learning and constructing coaching practice.

This chapter has illustrated some of the complexity of coaching in disability sport, highlighting the practical issues faced, while attempting to map coaching practice against theoretical models of disability. In so doing, we have examined the tensions, opportunities and questions within disability sport coaching. First and foremost, the dominance of disability discourses in producing and sustaining many conceptions of coaching requires exposure, challenge and reflection as they can often become embedded in coaching consciousness. We hope that this chapter can stimulate reflective thinking and dialogue on coaching in disability sport, and act as a resource for coaches to connect their experiences to. At a practical level, the lack of disability-specific coach education and development is an area for both concern and possibility, and further developments are required to bring the process of socialisation into coaching under critical control (Eraut, 1994). Furthermore, while it has been suggested that sport provides a context that can challenge and influence the social understanding of disability (DePauw, 1986), coaching rhetoric is often structured by binary understandings or tensions between 'coaching the athlete' and 'coaching the disability'. As such, further research is required to understand the production of disability in different coaching environments, to build an understanding of the working principles that coaches utilise in practice. Finally, research that connects theory to practice is invaluable in developing a much-needed transformative agenda in disability sport coaching.

Implications for practice

The following reflective points provide some guidance for coaches wishing to engage in disability sport though, as with all coaching approaches, this should not be read as a prescriptive 'how to' guide, but mediated by the sporting context, level of performance and individual coaches and athletes:

1) Work *with* athletes, not *on* them.
2) Recognise and accept impairment and adapt practice accordingly.
3) Create coaching sessions that challenge and support in equal measure.
4) Draw on multiple, integrated sources of knowledge to understand the athletes.
5) Continually reflect on your beliefs and assumptions about coaching disabled athletes.

References

Buntinx, W. E., & Schalock, R. L. (2010). Models of disability, quality of life, and individualized supports: implications for professional practice in intellectual disability. *Journal of Policy and Practice in Intellectual Disabilities, 7*(4), 283–294.

Bush, A. J., & Silk, M. L. (2012). Politics, power and the podium: Coaching for Paralympic performance. *Reflective Practice: International and Multidisciplinary Perspectives, 13*, 471–482.

Cassidy, T., Jones, R., & Potrac, P. (2009). *Understanding sports coaching: The social, cultural and pedagogical foundations of coaching practice* (2nd ed.). London: Routledge.

Cregan, K., Bloom, G. A., & Reid, G. (2007). Career evolution and knowledge of elite coaches of swimmers with a physical disability. *Research Quarterly for Exercise and Sport, 78*(4), 339–350.

Crossley, N. (2011). *Towards relational sociology.* London: Routledge.

Cushion, C. J., Armour, K. M., & Jones, R. L. (2003). Coach education and continuing professional development: Experience and learning to coach. *Quest, 55*, 215–230.

DePauw, K. P. (1986). Toward progressive inclusion and acceptance: Implications for physical education. *Adapted Physical Activity Quarterly, 3*, 1–6.

DePauw, K. P. (1997). The (in)visibility of disability: Cultural contexts and sporting bodies. *Quest, 49*(4), 416–430.

DePauw, K. P., & Gavron, S. J. (1991). Coaches of athletes with disabilities. *The Physical Educator, 48*, 33–40.

Douglas, S., & Hardin, B. (2014). Case study of an expert intercollegiate wheelchair basketball coach. *Applied Research in Coaching and Athletics Annual, 29*, 193–212.

Douglas, S., Vidic, Z., Smith, M., & Stran, M. (2016). Developing coaching expertise: Life histories of expert collegiate wheelchair and standing basketball coaches. *Palaestra, 30*(1), 31–42.

Duarte, T., & Culver, D. M. (2014). Becoming a coach in developmental adaptive sailing: A lifelong learning approach. *Journal of Applied Sport Psychology, 26*(4), 441–456.

Eraut, M. (1994). *Developing professional knowledge and competence.* London: Falmer Press.

Fitzgerald, H. (2005). 'Still feeling like a spare piece of luggage?': Embodied experiences of (dis)ability in physical education and sport. *Physical Education and Sport Pedagogy, 10*(1), 41–59.

Goodley, D. (2011). *Disability studies: An interdisciplinary introduction.* London: Sage.

Martin, J. J. (2013). Benefits and barriers to physical activity for individuals with disabilities: A social-relational model of disability perspective. *Disability and Rehabilitation, 35*(24), 2030–2037.

McMaster, S., Culver, D., & Werthner, P. (2012). Coaches of athletes with a physical disability: A look at their learning experiences. *Qualitative Research in Sport, Exercise and Health, 4*(2), 226–243.

Richard, R., Joncheray, H., & Dugas, E. (2015). Disabled sportswomen and gender construction in powerchair football. *International Review for the Sociology of Sport, 52*(1), 61–81.

Smith, B., & Bundon, A. (2016). Disability models: Explaining and understanding disability sport. In I. Brittain (Ed.), *Palgrave handbook of Paralympic studies*, 15–34. Basingstoke: Palgrave.

Smith, B. M., & Perrier, M. J. (2014). Disability, sport, and impaired bodies: A critical approach. In R. Schinke & K. R. McGannon (Eds.), *The psychology of sub-culture in sport and physical activity: A critical approach*, 95–106. London: Psychology Press.

Stodter, A., & Cushion, C. J. (2017). What works in coach learning, how, and for whom? A grounded process of soccer coaches' professional learning. *Qualitative Research in Sport, Exercise and Health, 9*(3), 321–338.

Swain, J., French, S., & Cameron, C. (eds.). (2003). *Controversial issues in a disabling society.* Berkshire: Open University Press.

Tawse, H., Bloom, G. A., Sabiston, C. M., & Reid, G. (2012). The role of coaches of wheelchair rugby in the development of athletes with a spinal cord injury. *Qualitative Research in Sport, Exercise and Health, 4*(2), 206–225.

Taylor, S. L., Werthner, P., Culver, D., & Callary, B. (2015). The importance of reflection for coaches in parasport. *Reflective Practice: International and Multidisciplinary Perspectives, 16*(2), 269–284.

Taylor, S. L., Werthner, P., & Culver, D. M. (2014). A case study of a parasport coach and a life of learning. *International Journal of Sport Coaching, 1*(3), 127–138.

Thomas, C. (1999). *Female forms: Experiencing and understanding disability.* Oxfordshire: Open University Press.

Thomas, C. (2004a). Rescuing a social relational understanding of disability. *Scandinavian Journal of Disability Research, 6*(1), 22–36.

Thomas, C. (2004b). Developing the social relational in the social model of disability: A theoretical agenda. In C. Barnes & G. Mercer (Eds.), *Implementing the social model of disability* (pp. 32–47). Leeds: Disability Press.

Thomas, C. (2007). *Sociologies of disability and illness.* London: Palgrave.

Thomas, C. (2012). Theorising disability and chronic illness: Where next for perspectives in medical sociology? Social theory and health annual lecture. *Social Theory & Health*, *10*, 209–228.

Thomas, N., & Guett, M. (2014). Fragmented, complex and cumbersome: a study of disability sport policy and provision in Europe. *International Journal of Sport Policy and Politics*, *6*(3), 389–406.

Townsend, R. C., Cushion, C. J., & Smith, S. (2018). A social relational analysis of an impairment-specific mode of coach education. *Qualitative Research in Sport, Exercise and Health*, *10*(3), 346–361.

Townsend, R. C., Smith, B., & Cushion, C. J. (2016). Disability sports coaching: Towards a critical understanding. *Sports Coaching Review*, *4*(2), 80–98.

13

COACHING CHILDREN

A guide to maximising their enjoyment

Ed Cope and Neil Plimmer

Introduction

It has become increasingly clear that childhood is the foundational stage of lifelong sport and physical activity participation, and that children's experiences leave a legacy of attitudes and behaviours toward sport that can last a lifetime. The likelihood that sporting behaviours are maintained over time is significantly mediated by the quality of the associated experiences created and managed by the coach (Bailey, 2005). Early experiences are important as they set the tone for everything that follows. Simply put: positive experiences encourage further participation, whilst negative experiences nudge towards drop-out (Smith & Smoll, 1996; Wall & Côté, 2007). In itself, this is cause for concern, but its importance is only heightened by findings that inactive children are likely to become inactive adolescents, and inactive adults (Craigie, Lake, Kelly, Adamson & Mathers, 2011). So, the legacy of early sporting experiences is of significant importance.

Children are a unique group of people who have specific development needs that are not shared by adolescents and adults. Therefore, they require a certain type of coaching if they are to experience sport in a manner that is enjoyable and developmental. Consequently, the purpose of this chapter is to identify what it is children find enjoyable about sport, and what coaches can do to ensure maximum levels of enjoyment and development. We do this by presenting key theoretical insight as determined by the practical issues that Neil has encountered through his years as a children's golf coach. We conclude the chapter with recommendations for children's coaches based on our theoretical and practical understanding.

Commentary

Over the course of the last 20 years my approach to coaching children has evolved significantly. In the early point of my coaching career, my coaching was based on two factors. The first was how I experienced coaching as a child, and the second was how I saw others coaching children within a structured sports setting. Looking back, it is obvious to see how the 'way we have always done it' perpetuated in nearly all coaching that I undertook and observed! It was not until some time later when I became a parent and a more reflective coach that I was able to critique my coaching and consider that it was not focussed on the children, but rather heavily focussed on the sport.

As I developed a greater critical reflective capacity in my coaching, it became clear that children's first experience of sport needed to be less about the sport, which for me was golf, and more about what children needed from that experience. It was therefore a case of reframing my view of what 'coaching' was to this group of people. This meant learning more about such things as how children learn, what interests and motivates them to engage and what types of coaching they like and dislike. As I started to invest my time in child development research, as well as my own 'on the job' experiences as a parent, I reflected on the technically led approach I had become accustomed to seeing in my own practice and those of others. From here, I started on a journey of reconceptualising what golf coaching for children needed to look like.

The first step was to consider what the fundamental components of golf were. This was a challenging task, as the technical components such as how to hold a club, how to stand to the ball and how to swing/move 'correctly' were always the first things that have traditionally been coached. This approach resulted in a highly prescriptive coaching approach both in terms of the coaching behaviours I employed and the type of practice activities I was asking children to engage in. Reflecting back, what I was doing here was imposing golf on to children in a manner that fitted with my view of the game within the structures of the club I worked for, and the sport more broadly.

My earlier approaches to coaching children golf was to head straight to the driving range with a bucket of 100 golf balls and spend the time instructing children to hit them into an open field. My role would be to offer advice and tips relative to their technique. For a number of the children I am not denying this was neither appropriate nor fun, but rather the point is that this was my automatic response. I had not even considered other possibilities for how I could structure the learning environment. What I now offer is the opportunity for children to hit lots of different shots, with lots of different clubs, in lots of different ways, in lots of different places. Much like the game will ask of them when they play on the golf course. Whatever age the children are when they begin, I feel it is vital that the activity we present is representative of what they will experience when they play the 'proper' version of the game. Although it may look nothing like the 'proper' version, it will still be asking the same questions, just in a more appropriate way.

This led me to reflecting on the core principles of the game, which are flight, strike and movement, and consider how these need to change as the task and environment changes. For example, in relation to the flight of the ball, I ask what is the ball doing? How high does it go? How far does it go? In what direction does it travel? For the strike of the ball, what does the club need to do to create the desired flight? And for movement, how does the body need to move the club to create the desired flight? The answer to these questions will always be relative to the decision made in relation to the task encountered, but the important point here is that with my support, children get to explore different ways of moving their body and using clubs to hit different shots in relation to tasks that will constantly change. However old and/or experienced the children are, these tasks/challenges will always be representative to the questions they may get asked when playing golf on a course.

As I looked at different sports and activities that children could participate in, I constantly asked myself the question, how can I make children's experience of golf the most positive it can be? And how do I make this fun, engaging and appropriate to each child, every time? It was(and still is!) this 'every child, every time' approach that drives me to critique my coaching to children. I reflect back on how I delivered fun experiences and saw myself as the 'court jester' whose primary responsibility was to entertain children. There is no doubt that this approach can at times be needed, but I started to ask whether the role of the coach was much more than this, and if I was underplaying the potential impact I was able to have on children's learning and longer-term engagement.

In relation to fun, if we are coaches that aim to enthuse and engage children into sport and physical activity (and as coaches become experts and more professional), I often ask myself 'surely we can do better than FUN?'. I want children to walk away from a session saying they had fun, but when setting up sessions and programmes I look for a deeper level of engagement. This led to me thinking about what I want to achieve when coaching children. Reflecting back, I think this used to resemble what you could typically expect to see at a children's birthday party. For example, it was high tempo, there was lots of noise, smiling faces, laughing and 'silliness', an energetic party host (me), and parents who drop off their children to go and do something else. Comparing this to now, I would like to think my sessions are more closely aligned to what you would see when children play with something like Lego; a quiet hub of activity, children showing lots of concentration and a coach who is more considerate of how best to support each individuals learning and development.

As coaches, we are the architects of the sport that is offered to children and therefore in part responsible for maximising their enjoyment when in our company and care. Children spend much of their waking hours in two places; at home and school, so when we are looking to engage with children we need to take the sport to them.

When I went into the school environment for the first time, to deliver golf coaching sessions, it now seems obvious that I was trying to impose the sport on the children. In schools my coaching needed to align more with what they normally experience in this setting while still being representative of the sport they would experience if they were to play on a golf course. This has influenced my understanding of how children learn and develop their golf, and the need to look at each stage of their development in that particular environment. We can then offer opportunities for children to move from school to golf clubs as I have found we need to make sure that the experience they have in the club matches (and/or is similar) to what they experienced in school. For years, what I offered in schools and what was offered back at the club were very different and this meant that children would often drop out. Now we are not only aware that each experience for each child is unique, but, when they move from school to club we have to be sensitive to the fact that the child 'bought' into golf from their experience of it in school. Therefore we need to manage their golf club experience by setting up similar activities and using similar equipment.

Early positive sporting experiences

What Neil's reflections have attempted to highlight is how the starting point when coaching children should be the child, and not the sport. This (re)conceptualisation when coaching this population group is important when considering the nature of the activities delivered. Children are typically introduced into organised sporting activities between about 4 to 8 years of age, although some may start at an even earlier age. Early experiences of sport are typically characterised by a 'sampling' of a variety of different types of activities (Côté & Hay, 2002). These early stages of engagement are associated with the development of fundamental movement skills and informal play activities (e.g. modified games). The extent to which these early experiences of sport require guided support is a matter of debate among sport scientists (Côté & Fraser-Thomas, 2007; MacNamara, Collins & Giblin, 2015), however, if positioned in a manner Neil alluded to, it does seem to be the case that coaching can accelerate skill development.

Coaches are the architects of the learning environment and can control this and, therefore, they have the ultimate responsibility for creating an environment that fosters healthy and holistic development (Cushion, 2013). Central to the design of a supportive learning environment is the way coaches interact with young children and how they explicitly attempt to deliver on the agreed learning outcomes. Neil discussed how he attempts to move beyond what he referred to as the 'court jester' to thinking more carefully about how he is supporting and impacting the learning and development of children. Coaches are role models for young children, and their behaviours can either foster healthy development or contribute to attrition from sport at an early age (Côté & Gilbert, 2009). Coaches need to deliver activities that are enjoyable, challenging and promote perceptions of competence and belonging (Mageau & Vallerand, 2003; Wall & Côté, 2007). In support of the approach Neil attempts to adopt, evidence suggests that these outcomes are most-likely to be achieved through an emphasis on: (a) deliberate play activities (Côté & Fraser-Thomas, 2007) that are fun and enjoyable (Wall & Côté, 2007) to promote player engagement (frequent time on task) and subsequently develop fundamental motor and manipulative skills; and (b) coach feedback focused on self- referencing rather than normative comparisons (Fraser-Thomas & Côté, 2006) to promote internal motivation (Mageau & Vallerand, 2003). The lack of fun, in particular, has been reported as a frequently cited reason for attrition from sport (Gould, Feltz, Horn & Weiss, 1982) and something we discuss in greater detail later in this chapter. However, as noted by Neil, the outcomes of coaching children extend beyond ensuring children are having a good time.

The foundational principle of Developmentally Appropriate Sport is that children are not mini-adults (Bailey, 2000), which can be expressed by these three core findings from decades of research into child development:

1) Children are not mini-adults;
2) Children are not mini-adults;
3) Children are not mini-adults.

Point '1' relates to the unarguable fact that children's minds and bodies work differently from adults. They process information, pay attention, move and exercise in distinctive ways (Bjorklund, 1997). Many sports scientific principles that underpin conceptions of good practice simply do not apply to children. For example, it has long been taught that benefits of exercise come from sustained activity above a certain threshold. But the most cursory observation of young children's physical activity reveals that it is stop-start, and of varying levels of intensity (Bailey et al., 1995).

Point '2' refers to movement development. With a few exceptions, adults engage in a small number of physical activities that require quite specialised motor skills (Bailey, 2000). These skills predominantly relate to games with names (e.g. golf). Children are still laying down the foundations of their movement competence. Much of the period prior to adolescence is taken up with the development of fundamental movement skills – running, jumping, twisting turning, holding, balancing. These skills are necessary for subsequent sporting activity. They are best developed in a playful atmosphere that is intrinsically motivating (in which children do them for the love of the movements themselves, rather than for a reward; Côté & Hay, 2002) rather than placing too much emphasis on technical mastery, which as Neil alluded to, formed much of his early coaching practice. Also, importantly, these basic movements are best developed through engagement in a wide range of activities that are adapted to reflect the distinctive needs of young people (Bailey, 2000).

Finally, point '3' emphasises that adults play sport for many different reasons including weight loss, elite competition, socialising and reproduction but most children play sport for just two primary reasons; fun (Dismore & Bailey, 2011) and friendship (McDonough & Crocker, 2005). Children join and leave sports clubs for several different reasons, but the influence of other children and coaches affects both decisions (Rottensteiner, Laakso, Pihlaja & Konttinen, 2013). Specifically, the perceptions children develop of these relationships are essential to participation motivation (Partridge, Brustad & Babkes Stellino, 2008), and the relationships children form with their coaches and other children can contribute to the development of both desirable (participation) and undesirable (withdrawal) outcomes.

What do children enjoy about sport?

Hopefully we have already made clear the importance of children having enjoyable sporting experiences. This section addresses literature that has discussed what it is about participation in sport that children find enjoyable. A review of literature in 2013 by Cope, Bailey and Pearce identified children's motivations for taking part in and remaining involved in sport. They found that children experienced enjoyment when:

- The sporting environment enabled them to play with friends (Cope, Harvey & Kirk, 2015; Everley & Macfadyen, 2015; Weiss & Smith, 2002).
- They have positive interactions with socially significant others (i.e. parents, coaches and peers) through the form of support and encouragement (Hagger, Cale, Almond & Krüger, 1997; Stern, Bradley, Prince & Stroh, 1990).
- They have opportunities to develop their competence via the learning of sport specific skills (McCarthy & Jones, 2007).
- They receive social recognition of competence by coaches and parents.
- They are encouraged and experience excitement from undertaking the activity and being challenged (Dismore & Bailey, 2011; McCarthy & Jones, 2007).
- They were provided with the opportunity to experience the feeling of playing the sport (Dismore & Bailey, 2011; MacPhail, Gorely & Kirk, 2003; McCarthy & Jones, 2007; Wankel & Kreisel, 1985).

In opposition to this, factors that lead to non-enjoyment included being punished for making mistakes and being offered low levels of support from coaches and parents (MacPhail, Gorely & Kirk, 2003; McCarthy & Jones, 2007; Wankel & Kreisel, 1985), the promotion of rivalry by coaches with peers, excessive and intensive training, the feeling of needing to please significant others (i.e. parents and coaches), too great an emphasis on winning and being set unreasonable expectations by coaches and parents (MacPhail, Gorely & Kirk, 2003; McCarthy & Jones, 2007; Wankel & Kreisel, 1985).

While Neil did not discuss this issue, coaches also need to have an awareness of adapting their coaching of children depending on their gender (see Chapter 11). Evidence suggests that, generally speaking, boys have more positive attitudes than girls towards sport, and that girls' attitude declines at a faster rate. Most specifically, it has been widely reported, regardless of context, boys enjoy PE more and are less tolerant of missing this subject at school than girls, have higher perceived levels of competence, spend more time participating in sport and physical activity than girls (Brooke, Atkin, Corder, Ekelund & van Sluijs, 2016; Carroll & Loumidis, 2001; Fredricks & Eccles, 2002; Shropshire, Carroll & Yim, 1997) and engage in higher levels of intensity (Fairclough, Ridgers & Welk, 2012). Girls, on the other hand, seem to enjoy activities of a more informal and less traditional nature than boys, such as walking, cycling and swimming in school time with friends, and activities that incorporate music and dramatic approaches, and skipping and chasing games out of school time (Brooke, Corder, Griffin, Ekelund & van Sluijs, 2013; Mulvihill, Rivers & Aggleton, 2000). Providing girls with the opportunity to play with their friends seems a critical factor in their enjoyment and subsequent engagement in sport and physical activity (Cope, Bailey & Pearce, 2013), although other research has found that as long as girls found the activities they participated in to be enjoyable, playing with friends was not always critical (Brockman, Fox & Jago, 2011). Although it does seem that a combination of finding activities enjoyable and being with friends leads to maximum levels of participation in activities (Brockman et al., 2011). In addition, compared to most boys, girls tend to be less interested in competition (Mulvihill et al., 2000). Where sport follows a more traditional structure that places an almost predominant emphasis on team sports, or traditional sports, the research drawn upon here suggests it is likely these will not align well with many girls' interests. As such, for boys and girls to enjoy, and consider them-selves competent in, sport the activities they are being asked to engage in must align with what they want to do (Brooke et al., 2013).

Alternatively, boys often have a resistance towards sports stereotypically associated with girls (i.e. netball), or activities that involve rhythmic movement or dance, saying that they feel 'silly' and self-conscious when taking part in these (Mulvihill et al., 2000). Instead, many boys prefer to participate in more traditional sports such as football (Brooke et al., 2013) that they can participate in close to home (i.e. their garden or on the street outside their home) (Mulvihill et al., 2000).

How should sport be structured for children?

In the previous section we provided an overview of what children enjoy about sport and how this varies by age and gender. The purpose of this section is to focus on what coaches need to think about when structuring their coaching ses-sions to ensure children experience maximum levels of enjoyment. First, we dis-cuss what it is about adult-led, structured forms of sport that children perceive as enjoyable, before considering more unstructured, child-initiated activities that children value and gain enjoyment from.

Neil discussed how in the early stages of his coaching career he would auto-matically head for the driving range and ask children to hit ball after ball and provide technical instructions on what the children should or should not be doing. How adult-led, structured sport is positioned to children impacts the way they experience this. The concepts of mastery and performance-orientated learn-ing environments have been widely discussed in the sport psychology literature in relation to enjoyment and perceptions of competence when participating in sport. A mastery-oriented environment is one that focuses on individual improvement and learning, with a belief that effort and cooperation leads to suc-cess (Smith, Balaguer & Duda, 2006), whereas a performance-oriented environ-ment places emphasis on outcomes measures (i.e. winning, test scores etc.), and comparing performance to others or the 'correct' way to perform (Smith et al.,

2006). Most children seem to be implicitly mastery-oriented and derive more enjoyment from the hedonic pleasure sport brings (Dismore & Bailey, 2011; Wankel & Kreisel, 1985), and are less concerned with winning or competing against peers, particularly for girls (MacPhail, Gorely & Kirk, 2003; Stern et al., 1990). This was highlighted in one study where children reported a greater level of enjoyment when exposed to a mastery-oriented environment (Theeboom, De Knop & Weiss, 1995). Furthermore, children identified as having a mastery-orientation were reported as having more advanced skills than their perform-ance-orientated peers (Theeboom et al., 1995). When children are exposed to a consistently high mastery-/low performance-oriented environment there is some evidence to suggest they decrease their performance goals and maintain a high level of mastery-orientation toward sport (Carr, 2006; Theeboom et al., 1995). Alternatively, when children are subjected to a high performance-/low mastery-oriented environment, there is a tendency to increase performance goals and decrease their mastery-orientation toward sport (Carr, 2006).

If children are consistently subjected to a performance-oriented environment, they tend to measure their competence against the perceptions of external sources (i.e. parents, coaches and teachers), whereas if they are consistently subjected to a mastery-oriented environment, children are more likely to base their perceptions of competence against the amount of effort they put into completing a task (Horn & Hasbrook, 1987). Children who consider the learning environment to be more performance-oriented have been reported to have a more negative attitude toward the session, determine ability as the cause of success, and had greater feelings of boredom in contrast to children who perceived the learning environment as master-oriented, who had greater levels of satisfaction and determined success to be a combination of effort and ability (Hagger et al., 1997).

Sharing many of the characteristics of a mastery-oriented environment are game-based approaches (GBA). While much of the research conducted in this area has been with adolescent people or older (mainly in a secondary school context) there is some evidence with younger children that suggests they find this approach as being more enjoyable than 'skill' or 'drill' based approaches that prioritise the learn-ing of technical skills in a highly instructive environment. For example, it has been found that children have reported high levels of enjoyment when participating in activities that closely resemble real game activity (i.e. Kwik Cricket) rather than 'skill' or 'drill' based practice tasks (Cope et al., 2015; MacPhail, Gorely, Kirk & Kinchin, 2008), which is partly attributable to the greater opportunities for social interaction and learning, as well as finding these activities more enjoyable.

Child-led, unstructured play in sporting contexts

While adult-led, structured sport is important for children's development, and con-sidered as enjoyable if delivered in the ways discussed in the previous section, child-led, unstructured play within the context of sport appears fundamental to children's sporting, as well as broader life development. Neil wrote about trying to frame his coaching sessions in a similar way to how children engage with Lego. Opportunities to be creative, an engagement in higher levels of social interaction and conquering fears and building resilience for future challenges have all been suggested as outcomes of play (Brockman et al., 2011). Moreover, when sport has been presented to children so that it shares characteristics associated with play, it is perceived by children as being more enjoyable and prevents boredom (Brockman et al., 2011), and children have been observed engaging with activities for longer and have appeared to be more engaged (Brockman et al., 2011). An explanation for this is that because children have much greater freedom and choice when engaged in unstructured play within sport and so choose to do activities they want to do, rather than those imposed on them by adults, and which do not necessarily align with their intrinsic motivations (Brooke et al., 2013).

Recommendations

Through both the practical and theoretical insights, we hope this chapter has provided you with an understanding of some principles for what constitutes developmentally appropriate coaching for children. From our perspective, they key learning we wish to suggest for coaches working with children, are:

1) Avoid uncritically accepting coaching approaches based on how things have always been. We are not saying these are wrong, but they should be challenged and questioned based on whether these are the most appropriate.
2) Consider what children find motivating and enjoyable about playing sport and being coached, and then ensure your coaching practices are reflective of this.
3) Think about coaching activities that children find most appealing, and that provides them plenty of opportunities to practice in many different types of learning environments.
4) Support children in their learning, but reflect on when to offer guidance and when to let children practice without support. We are not saying one approach is better than another, it should change depending on what is being learned and when, but coaches should be reflecting on this at all times.

References

Bailey, R. P. (2000). *Teaching physical education*. London: Kogan Page.

Bailey, R. (2005). Evaluating the relationship between physical education, sport and social inclusion. *Educational Review, 57*(1), 71–90.

Bailey, R. C., Olson, J., Pepper, S. L., Porszasz, J., Barstow, T. J., & Cooper, D. M. (1995). The level and tempo of children's physical activities: an observational study. *Medicine and Science in Sports and Exercise, 27*(7), 1033–1041.

Bjorklund, D. F. (1997). The role of immaturity in human development. *Psychological Bulletin, 122*, 153–169.

Brockman, R., Fox, K. R., & Jago, R. (2011). What is the meaning and nature of active play for today's children in the UK? *International Journal of Behavioral Nutrition and Physical Activity, 8*(1), 1.

Brooke, H. L., Atkin, A. J., Corder, K., Ekelund, U., & van Sluijs, E. M. (2016). Changes in time-segment specific physical activity between ages 10 and 14 years: A longitudinal observational study. *Journal of Science and Medicine in Sport, 19*(1), 29–34.

Brooke, H. L., Corder, K., Griffin, S. J., Ekelund, U., & van Sluijs, E. M. (2013). More of the same or a change of scenery: an observational study of variety and frequency of physical activity in British children. *BMC Public Health, 13*(1), 1.

Carr, S. (2006). An examination of multiple goals in children's physical education: Motivational effects of goal profiles and the role of perceived climate in multiple goal development. *Journal of Sports Sciences, 24*(3), 281–297.

Carroll, B., & Loumidis, J. (2001). Children's perceived competence and enjoyment in physical education and physical activity outside school. *European Physical Education Review, 7*(1), 24–43.

Cope, E., Harvey, S., & Kirk, D. (2015). Reflections on using visual research methods in sports coaching. *Qualitative Research in Sport, Exercise and Health, 7*(1), 88–108.

Cope, E. J., Bailey, R., & Pearce, G. (2013). Why do children take part in, and remain involved in sport? A literature review and discussion of implications for sports coaches. *International Journal of Coaching Science, 7*(1), 55–74.

Côté, J., & Fraser-Thomas, J. (2007). Youth involvement in sport. In P. Crocker (Ed.), *Sport psychology: A Canadian perspective* (pp. 270–298). Toronto: Pearson.

Côté, J., & Gilbert, W. (2009). An integrative definition of coaching effectiveness and expertise. *International Journal of Sports Science and Coaching, 4*(3), 307–323.

Côté, J., & Hay, J. (2002). Children's involvement in Sport: A developmental perspective. In J. M. Silva & D. Stevens (Eds.), *Psychological foundations of sport* (pp. 484–502). Boston, MA: Merrill.

Craigie, A. M., Lake, A. A., Kelly, S. K., Adamson, A. J., & Mathers, J. C. (2011). Tracking of obesity-related behaviours from childhood to adulthood: A systematic review. *Maturitas, 70*(3), 266–284.

Cushion, C. J. (2013). Applying Game Centered Approaches in coaching: a critical analysis of the 'dilemma's of practice' impacting change. *Sports Coaching Review, 2*(1), 61–76.

Dismore, H., & Bailey, R. (2011). Fun and enjoyment in physical education: young people's attitudes. *Research Papers in Education, 26*(4), 499–516.

Everley, S., & Macfadyen, T. (2015). 'I like playing on my trampoline; it makes me feel alive. 'Valuing physical activity: perceptions and meanings for children and implications for primary schools. *Education, 3-13*, 1–25.

Fairclough, S. J., Ridgers, N. D., & Welk, G. (2012). Correlates of children's moderate and vigorous physical activity during weekdays and weekends. *Journal of Physical Activity and Health, 9*(1), 129–137.

Fraser-Thomas, J., & Côté, J. (2006). Youth sports: Implementing findings and moving forward with research. *Athletic Insight Online, 8*(3), 12–27.

Fredricks, J. A., & Eccles, J. S. (2002). Children's competence and value beliefs from childhood through adolescence: growth trajectories in two male-sex-typed domains. *Developmental Psychology, 38*(4), 519.

Gould, D., Feltz, D., Horn, T., & Weiss, M. (1982). Reasons for attrition in competitive youth swimming. *Journal of Sport Behaviour, 5*, 155–165.

Hagger, M., Cale, L., Almond, L., & Krüger, A. (1997). Children's physical activity levels and attitudes towards physical activity. *European Physical Education Review, 3*(2), 144–164.

Horn, T. S., & Hasbrook, C. A. (1987). Psychological characteristics and the criteria children use for self-evaluation. *Journal of Sport Psychology*, *9*(3), 208–221.

MacNamara, A., Collins, D., & Giblin, S. (2015). Just let them play? Deliberate preparation as the most appropriate foundation for lifelong physical activity. *Frontiers in Psychology*, *6*(1548). Online. Available at: www.frontiersin.org/articles/10.3389/fpsyg.2015.01548/full.

MacPhail, A., Gorely, T., & Kirk, D. (2003). Young people's socialisation into sport: A case study of an athletics club. *Sport, Education and Society*, *8*(2), 251–267.

MacPhail, A., Gorely, T., Kirk, D., & Kinchin, G. (2008). Children's experiences of fun and enjoyment during a season of sport education. *Research Quarterly for Exercise and Sport*, *79*(3), 344–355.

Mageau, G. A., & Vallerand, R. J. (2003). The coach–athlete relationship: a motivational model. *Journal of Sports Sciences*, *21*(11), 883–904.

McCarthy, P. J., & Jones, M. V. (2007). A qualitative study of sport enjoyment in the sampling years. *Sport Psychologist*, *21*(4), 400.

McDonough, M. H., & Crocker, P. R. E. (2005). Sport participation motivation in young adolescent girls. *Research Quarterly for Exercise and Sport*, *76*(4), 456–467.

Mulvihill, C., Rivers, K., & Aggleton, P. (2000). A qualitative study investigating the views of primary-age children and parents on physical activity. *Health Education Journal*, *59*(2), 166–179.

Partridge, J. A., Brustad, R. J., & Babkes Stellino, M. (2008). Social influence in sport. In T. S. Horn (Ed.), *Advances in sport psychology* (3rd ed., pp. 269–292). Champaign, IL: Human Kinetics.

Rottensteiner, C., Laakso, L., Pihlaja, T., & Konttinen, N. (2013). Personal reasons for withdrawal from team sports and the influence of significant others among youth athletes. *International Journal of Sports Science & Coaching*, *8*(1), 19–32.

Shropshire, J., Carroll, B., & Yim, S. (1997). Primary school children's attitudes to physical education: gender differences. *European Journal of Physical Education*, *2*(1), 23–38.

Smith, A. L., Balaguer, I., & Duda, J. L. (2006). Goal orientation profile differences on perceived motivational climate, perceived peer relationships, and motivation-related responses of youth athletes. *Journal of Sports Sciences*, *24*(12), 1315–1327.

Smith, R. E., & Smoll, F. L. (1996). The coach as a focus of research and intervention in youth sports. In F. L. Smoll & R. E. Smith (Eds.), *Children and youth in sport: A biopsychosocial perspective* (pp. 125–141). Madison, WI: Brown & Benchmark.

Stern, H. P., Bradley, R. H., Prince, M. T., & Stroh, S. E. (1990). Young children in recreational sports participation motivation. *Clinical Pediatrics*, *29*(2), 89–94.

Theeboom, M., De Knop, P., & Weiss, M. R. (1995). Motivational climate, psychological responses, and motor skill development in children's sport: A field-based intervention study. *Journal of Sport and Exercise Psychology*, *17*, 294–311.

Wall, M., & Côté, J. (2007). Developmental activities that lead to dropout and investment in sport. *Physical Education and Sport Pedagogy*, *12*(1), 77–87.

Wankel, L. M., & Kreisel, P. S. (1985). Factors underlying enjoyment of youth sports: Sport and age group comparisons. *Journal of Sport Psychology*, *7*(1), 51–64.

Weiss, M. R., & Smith, A. L. (2002). Friendship quality in youth sport: Relationship to age, gender, and motivation variables. *Journal of Sport and Exercise Psychology*, *24*(4), 420–437.

INDEX

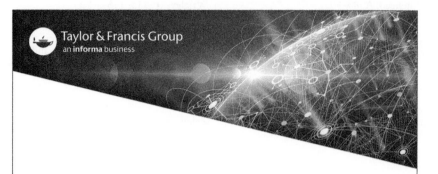